The Immortal Dinner

*A Famous Evening of Genius & Laughter
in Literary London, 1817*

PENELOPE HUGHES-HALLETT

VIKING

To Lucy with love

VIKING

Published by the Penguin Group
Penguin Books Ltd, 27 Wrights Lane, London W8 5TZ, England
Penguin Putnam Inc., 375 Hudson Street, New York, New York 10014, USA
Penguin Books Australia Ltd, Ringwood, Victoria, Australia
Penguin Books Canada Ltd, 10 Alcorn Avenue, Toronto, Ontario, Canada M4V 3B2
Penguin Books India (P) Ltd, 11 Community Centre,
Panchsheel Park, New Delhi – 110 017, India
Penguin Books (NZ) Ltd, Cnr Rosedale and Airborne Roads,
Albany, Auckland, New Zealand
Penguin Books (South Africa) (Pty) Ltd, 5 Watkins Street,
Denver Ext 4, Johannesburg 2094, South Africa

Penguin Books Ltd, Registered Offices: Harmondsworth, Middlesex, England

First published 2000
3

Copyright © Penelope Hughes-Hallett, 2000

The moral right of the author has been asserted

Set in 12/14.75 pt Monotype Bembo
Typeset by Rowland Phototypesetting Ltd,
Bury St Edmunds, Suffolk
Printed in Great Britain by Clays Ltd, St Ives plc

A CIP catalogue record for this book is available from the British Library

ISBN 0-670-87999-1

Contents

Acknowledgements

My first thanks are to Jack Gold who introduced me long ago to Haydon's autobiography by reading to me that writer's account of his Immortal Dinner. The kindness and encouragement of my agent Caroline Dawnay of Peters, Fraser and Dunlop and of Eleo Gordon, my editor at Penguin, have been of the very greatest importance to me. I am grateful to Richard Garnett for so kindly allowing me to see and quote from the letters from Joseph Ritchie to the Reverend Richard Garnett belonging to the estate of the late David Garnett; and to Alan Bell, librarian of the London Library, for so generously transcribing them for me at a particularly busy juncture of his life. I would like to thank Robert Woof of the Wordsworth Trust, with his encyclopaedic knowledge of Haydon and his circle, for advice and for his enabling and generous help with appropriate illustrations. I am fortunate in having an index made by that prince of indexers, Douglas Matthews. I am grateful to Ann Gold for her kindness in undertaking a particularly time-consuming piece of research. Others who have kindly given me advice and help are: Patrick O'Leary; Christina Gee of Keats House, Hampstead; Nicholas Haydon; Andrew Motion; John Jolliffe; Maggie Black; Isabel Rutherford; Sally Franklin; Duncan Wu; Miranda Tennant; John Ehrman; Elizabeth Thomson; Christine Dyer; Venetia Murray; Hugh Owen; Stephen Roe of Sotheby's Rare Books; Caroline Worthington, Keeper of Pictures at the Royal Albert Memorial Museum, Exeter; William Houston and Selwyn Eagle. I should like to thank Norman Ruffell for kindly showing me round his house off Lisson Grove where Haydon's dinner took place. I am, as always, grateful to the staff of the London Library. I also owe thanks to the librarian of the Royal Geographical Society; the Public Record Office; the National Register of Archives; the Foreign and Commonwealth Office; the Banks Archive Project of the British Museum (Natural History) and the Royal Society for information about Joseph Ritchie in the correspondence of Sir Joseph Banks; the librarian of the British Embassy in Paris; the Somerset Record Office; Paul Wood of the Otley Museum, West Yorkshire; R. A. Christophers of the English Language Collections, the British Library; Rosemary Seton, archivist of the School of Oriental and African Studies, University of London; Richard Aspin, Curator of Western Manuscripts, the Wellcome Institute for the History of Medicine; Noo Rah Al-Gailani, librarian, the Wesley Museum, City Road, London; Andrea Gilbert of the Courtauld Institute of Art; Christine Nougaret of the Ministère de la Culture et de la Francophonie, les Archives de France, Paris; Frédéric Lacaille of the Musée de l'Armée, Paris; Cheryl Piggott of the Royal Botanic Gardens, Kew; Stephen Roberts of the Royal Commission on Historical Manuscripts; the Houghton Library, Harvard University, for permission to quote from a letter to Benjamin Robert Haydon from Joseph Ritchie; and the staff of the Theatre Museum. I have been most fortunate in having the help of Claire Péligry of Penguin.

As must every student of Haydon's life and work, I owe a great debt to Professor Willard Bissell Pope's masterly edition of his diaries. Among other works I have consulted, I am particularly grateful for Paul Johnson's *The Birth of the Modern: World Society 1815–1830*, James Hamilton's *Turner: A Life*, Michael White's *Isaac Newton: The Last Sorcerer* and William St Clair's *Lord Elgin and the Marbles*.

I would like to thank my daughter Lucy Hughes-Hallett for her kind encouragement and detailed advice; and my sons

James and Thomas Hughes-Hallett for reading the manuscript and making helpful and perceptive suggestions. Finally, I am grateful to my husband who has for so long endured the intrusive presence of Haydon in the house.

List of Illustrations

Inset Section

1 Benjamin Robert Haydon in Van Dyck costume
2 William Wordsworth in early 1818
3 Lisson Grove in winter
4 Tom Monkhouse, 'dearest coz' of Mary Wordsworth and Sara Hutchinson
5 Earliest surviving portrait of John Keats
6 Lane in Hampstead
7 Leigh Hunt in 1815
8 William Hazlitt in 1824
9 East side of Regent Street
10 Joseph Mallord William Turner in his studio
11 A river scene
12 Charles Lamb as a young man
13 The actress Frances Maria (Fanny) Kelly
14 Interior of a sales room at East India House
15 Haydon's *Christ's Entry into Jerusalem*
16 Detail of *Christ's Entry into Jersualem*
17 Haydon asleep in 1815, by David Wilkie
18 Clare Market in 1815
19 Voltaire in his study
20 Thomas Bruce, seventh Earl of Elgin
21 The Temporary Elgin Room at the British Museum
22 Sarah Siddons and Roger Kemble
23 Edmund Kean as Sir Giles Overreach
24 Apsley House, London
25 William Bewick, Haydon's favourite pupil

Line Drawings in the Text

Illustration Acknowledgements

The author and publishers are grateful to the following for permission to reproduce illustrations:

Inset Section

2, 7, 17, 26, 31, 36, 39, National Portrait Gallery, London; 1, Birmingham Museum and Art Gallery; 3, 18, Bridgeman Art Library; 4, Ann Bryant Art Gallery, East London, South Africa; 5, 6, 13, 23, Trustees of the V & A; 8, The William Words-worth Trust, Grasmere; 9, from Thomas Shepherd and James Elmes, *Metropolitan Improvements*; 10, The Ruskin Gallery, Collection of the Guild of St George, Sheffield Galleries & Museums Trust; 11, The Tate Gallery, London; 12, Friends of Coleridge; 14, Museum of London; 15, 16, St Mary's Seminary, Ohio, USA; 24, 40, Westminster City Archives; 19, e.t.archive; 20, 21, 27, 29, Trustees of the British Museum; 22, 28, 32, Mary Evans Picture Library; 25 from *Life and Letters of William Bewick*, ed. Thomas Landseer; 30 from *The Reminiscences and Recollections of Captain Gronow* ed. John Raymond; 33 from Denham, Clapperton and Oudney: *Narrative of Travels and Discoveries in Northern and Central Africa*; 34, Wellcome Institute Library, London; 35, The Old Operating Theatre, St Thomas's Hospital, London; 37, from Martin: *In the Footprints of Charles Lamb*, 1891; 38, The Highgate Literary and Scientific Institution.

Line Drawings in the Text

Prologue

This is the story of a dinner party. It was given by the painter Benjamin Robert Haydon in his painting room in Lisson Grove on 28 December 1817. The guests included two poets: Wordsworth and Keats; one essayist: Charles Lamb; one explorer: Joseph Ritchie; an uneasy civil servant; and a cast of walkers-on. At least three of those present possessed genius of some kind – and for once that word does not seem excessive. Between them they created an evening of rare brilliance, wit and high-minded discussion. Excitement and tension, conviviality and laughter alternated with noble declamations from both Wordsworth, in the full flow of his power, and Keats, barely twenty-two, on the threshold of his.

The diners' enthusiasms and experiences encompassed many of the burning topics of the day, ranging from the horrors of the operating theatre to the beauties of the new forms of poetry; from the magic of the rainbow seen by the light of the imagination to new advances in scientific discovery; from religion to exploration. Their conversation that evening was so diverse and inspirational as to make their gathering seem a microcosm of the intellectual life of the capital at a time of upheaval and change in a society two years after Waterloo, now adjusting with some difficulty to a state of peace.

At the end of the evening, as soon as his guests had departed into the night, Haydon described his party in one of the twenty-six vellum-bound volumes of his famous diary while every detail was still clear in his mind, even if a little coloured by what he described as his 'excellent port'. Such was the resonance of the occasion that many years later he could look back on it as one of the high points of his life, justifying the name he had given it: the Immortal Dinner.

1. The Host

In December Wordsworth was in town, and as Keats wished to
know him I made up a party to dinner of Charles Lamb,
Wordsworth, Keats and Monkhouse, his friend; and a very
pleasant party we had.
I wrote to Lamb, and told him the address was '22 Lisson Grove,
North, at Rossi's, half way up, right hand corner'. I received his
characteristic reply: 'My dear Haydon, I will come with pleasure
to 22 Lisson Grove, North, at Rossi's, half way up, right hand
side, if I can find it. Yours C. Lamb. 20 Russel[*sic*] Court, Covent
Garden East, half way up, next the corner, left hand side.'

Benjamin Robert Haydon, *Autobiography*[1]

Benjamin Robert Haydon, history painter and host of the
Immortal Dinner, was in no doubt as to his status: genius. In
close partnership with the Almighty, whom he cajoled and
pleaded with on page after page of the twenty-six volumes of
his diaries, he would, he knew, succeed in his aims. These
were clear-cut and precise: to restore the noble and sublime
form of history painting – or High Art, as he preferred to call
it – to its standing in the golden days of Raphael; to refine the
public's taste in the visual arts; and to incite the government
to play its part in this moral and elevated purpose by com-
missioning works of art – preferably his – to decorate public
buildings; and lastly, that he himself, Benjamin Robert
Haydon, should paint the greatest pictures ever seen on the
very grandest scale, and so lead the way towards making his

country supreme in art throughout the civilized world. The inspiring size of his canvases made him tingle with excitement; he loved the challenge of their scale and the heightened emotion generated by their mythic or historically dramatic content. Looking at one of his paintings, he exclaimed, 'What fire, what magic! I bow and am grateful.' And of his *Judgment of Solomon*, 'that wonderful picture', he asked himself: 'Ought I to fear comparison of it with the Duke of Sutherland's Murillo, or any other picture? Certainly not!'[2]

The host of the Immortal Dinner arrived in London from Devonshire in 1804, aged eighteen, to study at the Royal Academy schools, the programme of his future career ready framed in his mind. He never wavered from it through the appalling vicissitudes of his life, which were to include im-prisonment for debt on three separate occasions, the death of several of his children, and ostracism from the Royal Academy. In the realization of part of his dream – the govern-ment's setting of a competition for the decoration of the newly rebuilt House of Lords – his own designs were not even considered, and the humiliation of this blow was no doubt a factor in his eventual suicide. Posterity remembers him more for his friendships and his wonderful diary and autobiography than for his painting. Most of his vast and grandiose canvases are now rolled away and forgotten, while his early chalk drawing of Wordsworth's head recently reappeared on the market, selling for a considerable sum, so endorsing his patrons' disregarded advice to turn from history painting to portraiture. His campaigns against the art establishment tended to escalate into wearying Ancient Mariner-like naggings that his friends came to dread. But he was right after all. The reforms for which he so persistently agitated are today the accepted norm.

Haydon had a large head (an *intellectual* head, he felt) and looked, as Aldous Huxley put it, 'as if Mussolini had been

1. Self-portrait by
Benjamin Robert
Haydon, 1816,
drawn the year
before his dinner.

strangely blended with Cardinal Newman'. In some portraits,
however, the Mussolini element is absent and he appears
gentle and kindly. His fellow artist and friend David Wilkie
drew him in 1815, for example, showing him asleep and
vulnerable, spectacles on his nose, his hairline already receding.
He suffered from very poor eyesight and had even been blind
for a short period after a childhood illness, and when painting
he wore several pairs of strong concave spectacles balanced
one upon another, removing and replacing them as he moved
close up to his canvas or stood back to consider its progress.
Distortions in his work are probably due to this frustrating
routine. As he painted he whispered rapidly and incessantly to
himself.

Because Haydon was so sure of his genius, and because he did possess many of the attributes of that status, including the defining infinite capacity for taking pains, and because his tremendous energy and conviction were so compelling and magnetic, his friends accepted his estimate of himself. And when he was overcome, as later he increasingly was, by bouts of despair, their confidence in him succeeded again and again in restoring his equilibrium, so that he would bounce back triumphantly, his astonishing vanity seemingly undented. That Wordsworth should address a number of sonnets to him – Haydon was well aware of the honour this represented, but did not question its appropriateness – and that Keats at the very outset of his career also wrote a fine sonnet 'Great spirits now on earth are sojourning' partly in his honour, and that Leigh Hunt and several others fêted him in laudatory verse, is a measure of his impact on the literary world of the day.

Two years after his arrival in London the twenty-year-old Haydon was commissioned by Lord Mulgrave, the influential connoisseur and patron of the arts, to paint a picture on the subject of the death of the warrior Dentatus, known as the Roman Achilles, showing him at the moment of his assassins' attack. The young artist was overjoyed: the recognition he felt to be his right had come early. With a fine sense of occasion he knelt down and prayed for blessings on his career:

I poured forth my gratitude for His kind protection during my preparatory studies and for early directing me in the right way, and implored Him in His mercy to continue that protection which had hitherto been granted me. I arose with that peculiar calm which in me always accompanies such expressions of deep gratitude, and looking fearlessly at my unblemished canvas, in a species of spasmodic fury I dashed down the first touch. I stopped, and said: 'Now I have begun; never can that last moment be recalled.'[3]

Every Wednesday, as he worked on this first canvas, he mixed his paints on a piece of pasteboard which he then carried down to Lord Stafford's gallery to compare his colours with those of Stafford's Titians.

Haydon enjoyed working on a commission for a lord because, it has to be said, he was a terrific snob. Unfortunately this did not lead to him to behave with a suitably flexible attitude to his patron's pronouncements. If he felt he knew more about the subject, then he said so, often causing offence to Lord Mulgrave or Sir George Beaumont, the two most important patrons of the arts who were to come his way. John Constable warned him to be more tactful, and events would show the wisdom of this caution; but he was incapable of moderating his behaviour, even though it might endanger those forays into high society he so much enjoyed. He wrote in an ecstasy of bliss about one such visit, later in his life, to Lord Egremont at Petworth, where he was warmly welcomed and shown to a magnificent bedroom:

I really never saw such a character as Lord Egremont. 'Live and let live' seems to be his motto. He has placed me in one of the most magnificent bedrooms I ever saw. It speaks more for what he thinks of my talents than anything that ever happened to me. Over the chimney is a nobleman kneeling. A lady of high rank to the right. Opposite, Queen Mary. On the right of the cabinet, Sir Somebody. The bed curtains are of different coloured velvets let in on white satin.

What a destiny is mine! One year in the Bench,[4] the companion of gamblers and scoundrels – sleeping in wretchedness and dirt, on a flock bed low and filthy, with black worms crawling over my hands – another, in a splendid house, the guest of rank, and fashion and beauty! As I laid my head on my down pillow the first night I was deeply affected, and could hardly sleep.

As to Egremont himself, Haydon found him 'literally like the sun' shining on one and all, so that 'the very flies at Petworth seem to know there is room for their existence, that the windows are theirs'.

At breakfast in walks Lord Egremont; first comes a grandchild, whom he sends away happy. Outside the window moan a dozen black spaniels, who are let in, and to them he distributes cakes and comfits, giving all equal shares. After chatting with one guest, and proposing some scheme of pleasure to others, his leathern gaiters are buttoned on, and away he walks, leaving everybody to take care of themselves. At seventy-four he still shoots daily, comes home wet through and is as active and looks as well as many men of fifty . . . I never saw such a character, or such a man, nor were there ever many.[5]

On leaving Petworth he copied his bread-and-butter letter into his diary, ending: 'In earnestly hoping your lordship may live long, I only add my voice to the voices of thousands, who never utter your lordship's name without a blessing.'[6] But in spite of this effusion Haydon was never invited again. Perhaps he tried to borrow money from his host, or perhaps his exclusion was due to his eccentric behaviour with his bed-clothes. Dinner had been served on the first day of his visit, but no Haydon appeared. Presently he was discovered in his room, his evening coat folded neatly over a chair, his greatcoat buttoned up to his chin, busily engaged in hanging his sheets and blankets on chairs around the room, the window flung wide and a huge fire alight in the grate, as he indulged his mania for fresh air and his suspicions of the possible dampness of strange bedlinen.[7]

For much of his life Haydon was tormented by the fickle behaviour of those of 'rank, fashion and beauty' who crowded his studio on his regular weekly open day and often at other times as well to chatter and exclaim, only to desert him at the first hint of a setback. Charles Lamb left him a note describing an encounter with one such pair:

Dear Raffaele Haydon, Did the maid tell you I came to see your picture, not on Sunday but the day before? I think the face and bearing of the Bucephalus tamer very noble, his flesh too effeminate or painty. The skin of the female's back kneeling is much more carnous. I had small time to pick out praise or blame, for two lord-like Bucks came in, upon whose strictures my presence seemed to impose restraint. I plebeian'd off therefore. Yours in haste (salt fish waiting) C. Lamb.[8]

In keeping with the scale of his other attributes, Haydon's capacity for suffering was immense, and he was bewildered and hurt by the disloyal behaviour of his society acquaintances; but discouragement alternated with moods of elation. 'I have been,' he wrote during a period of success, 'like a man with air balloons under his armpits and ether in his soul. While I was painting, walking or thinking, beaming flashes of energy followed and impressed me.'[9] Once, after contemplating a Raphael cartoon for three hours at a stretch, he felt as if a spirit had dipped him in 'racy nectar'; and sometimes his sensations of epiphany lifted him into a mystic dimension when he experienced Blakeian visions of angels and archangels, 'with their terrific hands', floating in the clouds. His ebullience was infectious: William Hazlitt said that 'he set one upon one's legs better than a glass of champagne'.[10] His laughter was famous. Leigh Hunt, poet, essayist and radical editor, serving a two-year sentence for libelling the Prince Regent, to whom he had referred as 'a fat Adonis of forty', remembered of one of Haydon's visits to him in prison that he called before he was up, demanded breakfast, and made the place echo with his laughter that sounded like the trumpets of Jericho.

When the fat Adonis came to be crowned in the summer

of 1821, Haydon's loyalty to the Hunts did not extend to refusing a ticket for the occasion. The event, which finally took place at the end of July, had been planned down to the last detail by the Prince Regent himself, and postponed for fear of disruption from his wife, as determined to be crowned queen as he was to prevent it. Caroline appeared at the Abbey magnificently dressed for the occasion and attended by her ladies, only to be barred from each entrance and finally having the great door of Westminster Hall slammed in her face. More than 900 invitations had been sent out, and Haydon was delighted to have a seat in Westminster Hall. Pageantry on such a scale was ambrosia to his soul, and in line with the scale of his own pictures, and, besides, he had a great sense of the mystique of the monarchy. He was not to be disappointed. The first priority was to get all the necessary adjuncts to his costume: 'I only got my ticket on Wednesday at two, and dearest Mary and I drove about to get all I wanted. Sir George Beaumont lent me ruffles and frill, another a blue velvet coat, a third a sword; I bought buckles, and the rest I had, and we returned to dinner exhausted.'

Haydon went to bed at ten o'clock in the evening, got up again at midnight, not having slept a wink, and by half past one in the morning he was at Westminster Hall, and other than three ladies he was the first to arrive. When the doors were finally opened at four o'clock he seized an eminently desirable front place in the Chamberlain's box, between the door and the throne. Many of the doorkeepers, he noticed, were tipsy, and quarrels broke out:

The sun began to light up the old gothic windows, the peers to stroll in, and the company to crowd in, of all descriptions; elegant young men tripping along in silken grace with elegant girls trembling in feathers and diamonds, old peers and old peeresses, some in one dress and some in another, many with swords, whose

2. Numbered ticket for George IV's coronation in Westminster Abbey.

awkwardness in managing them showed how unused their sides had been to the graceful encumbrance, and many with coats, velvet and satin, of all ages, all courts, and all times . . . all happy, eager, smiling, and anticipating. Some took seats they had not any right to occupy, and were obliged to leave them after sturdy disputes. Others lost their tickets. The Hall occasionally echoed with the hollow roar of voices at the great door, till at last the galleries were filled.

Haydon was entranced by all he saw, until at last the time came for the entry of the king:

The appearance of a Monarch has something of the air of a rising sun; there are indications which announce his approach, a streak of light, the tipping of a cloud, the singing of a lark, the brilliance of the sky, till the edges get brighter and brighter, and he rises majestic-ally into the heavens. So was the King's advance. A whisper of mystery turns all eyes to the throne! Suddenly two or three run; others fall back; some talk, direct, hurry, stand still, or disappear. Then three or four of high rank appear from behind the Throne; an interval is left; the crowds scarce breathe! Something rustles, and a being buried in satin, feathers and diamonds rolls gracefully into his seat. The room rises with a sort of feathered, silken thunder! Plumes wave, eyes sparkle, glasses are out, mouths smile, and one man becomes the prime object of attraction to thousands! The way in which the King bowed was really monarchic! As he looked towards the peeresses and foreign ambassadors, he looked like some gorgeous bird of the east.

The king then proceeded to his crowning and there was a wait of several hours, during which his unfortunate and dis-carded wife made her vain attempt to gain entry. Young girls strewed flowers on the ground over which the new monarch would walk. And after the banquet was over came what Haydon felt was the finest sight of the day, when the great doors of the Hall were opened for the ritual entry of the King's Champion in full armour, escorted by Wellington and Howard, all three on horseback. A herald read the challenge to any enemy of the new king, the Champion's glove was thrown down, and the hieratic figures moved forward to the throne:

My imagination got so intoxicated that I came out with a great contempt for the plebs, and as I walked by with my sword, I said to myself '*odi profanum* etc'.[11] I got home quite well, and thought sacred subjects insipid things. How soon I should be ruined in luxurious society![12]

Before embarking on a new piece of work Haydon prayed earnestly, on one occasion asking that he might be granted the energy to create a new era in art and to rouse the people and the influential patrons of the arts to a just estimate of the moral value of historical painting. Such compendium and specific prayers recur throughout his diaries, and, if they were satisfactorily answered, the Almighty was rewarded with a blanket letter of thanks on the last day of each year. Although it may be easy to mock his brand of religion, to him it was very real, a necessary sustenance in the daily battle of his life, and he became restless and unhappy if deprived of its observance. Once he missed church because he had promised to take an acquaintance to see Wilkie's picture *The Cut Finger*, but 'he did not come at the time; and as I never wait for anybody I made calls and idled the day. No church. No religious meditation. Very bad.'[13]

A few years after his arrival in London from Devonshire, Haydon embarked on a course of borrowing money, first from his friends, later from moneylenders, which was eventually to wreck his life. The mystery is that people continued to lend him funds when experience must have warned them they would never be repaid, but this is partly explained by the fact that he was regarded by his contemporaries as a very great painter indeed. And this was Haydon's own justification: that he was owed a reasonable living after all he had done for English art. Many of his friends agreed with his assessment, so that in paying Haydon's debts they felt they were making a contribution to the furtherance of the cause. Besides, he was attractive: the magnetism that made him such irresistible company also helped him raise a loan. Later in his life Mary Russell Mitford declared that she had never known anything so rapid, so brilliant or so vigorous as his talk, and many others came similarly under his spell. He borrowed copiously, indiscriminately and ruthlessly, even from his own pupils. Nor were tradesmen safe from his importunities. He coaxed his wine merchant to supply him free, asking if the man thought it right he should be deprived of the wine necessary for his health, whereupon his victim sent him a dozen bottles; his landlord waited indefinitely for the rent; the owner of the eating house he frequented said it would be an honour to supply free dinners until times were better, and the pretty waitresses, hearing he was bankrupt, eyed him, he said, 'with a lustrous regret'. He was frugal and lived simply, working hard most of the time; but if it was a question of paying for the best models, or for the quantities of expensive paints he needed to cover his gigantic canvases, then it was a different matter, and as time went on he became more and more reckless about such expenses. Commissioned to paint a portrait of the Duke of Wellington, who refused to lend his uniforms or equipment, Haydon had replicas made by the duke's own saddler, heavily worked saddle-cloths and so forth, then decided at the last moment that the effect was unpleasing and threw a dark cloth over the whole, only revealing a little corner of the expensive glitter beneath.

Haydon had a great weakness for pretty girls. 'What a delightful moment is that of declaring a passion which has long possessed one to a pure, delicious girl,' he declared in his diary:

In a silent evening, accidentally alone with her, the flutterings of heart, the longing for disclosure, the trembling approaches! She sits – you venture to sit near her! . . . an involuntary sigh; you put your arm on the back of her chair without daring to touch her lovely shoulder – awed, for fear of offending, you dare, agitated and shaken, to touch her soft hand! She withdraws it not! You press with a start of passion the gentle, helpless hand to your full and burning lips! O God! with the look of an Angel she turns up her exquisite mouth, and as you kiss it, your lips cling, with a lingering at every little separation and you suck ecstasy till your brain is steeped in steam. Does not this speak all a man would wish? No cant, no dropping on knees, no speaking to Fathers, or consulting cold blooded, brutal brothers – not even a word to her dear self![14]

Later his romantic dreams seem to have become more domestic:

What a delight it is after a week's successful labour to sit on a Sunday morning at breakfast, with a bright sky that promises a glowing day, with a good appetite and smoking tea, a clean cloth, a sparkling fire, Shakespeare, Homer, Milton, Tasso, Ariosto or Spenser to dip in by turns lying at your side; alternately reading and looking at your Picture, firing with urgings of greatness and anticipations of immortality, or beaming with fancy and searchings of spirit, shaking off the little troubles of life like drops from a Lion, and then to look opposite and see reflected in a lovely face, your own feelings, mingled with love and devotion to yourself.

But lack of funds impinged on the delicious vision: 'There is nothing complete in this World without a woman, a true, shrinking, gentle, devoted woman, but of what use is my thinking so now? I had better not give way to such feelings.'[15]

The catalogue of impressive authors listed above sounds a little like window-dressing, but this was not so, Haydon's passion for great literature being a central factor in his life. It stemmed from his early years in his father's Plymouth book-shop, where he was a reluctant apprentice, and where he took advantage of his situation to immerse himself in whatever books were to hand, an appetite first stimulated by masters at the local grammar school, of which he became head boy. When in later years he was forced on more than one occasion to sell his belongings to satisfy his creditors, his precious books were the objects he held on to with the fiercest determination, taking precedence even over his paints, the tools of his trade. He had a working knowledge of Greek and Latin, wrote fluent French and a little German and Italian, and was perfectly able to hold his own in debate with the other guests at his party, and even with that great intellect of the early nineteenth century, the critic William Hazlitt.

The opening of Waterloo Bridge in 1817 was of especial significance to the fiercely patriotic Haydon, as he looked back on the excitement of hearing the first news of the battle two years earlier, after dining with the liberal editor and critic John Scott in the Edgware Road. On his way home, rather late, he was crossing Portman Square when a Foreign Office messenger rushed up to him, asking which was Lord Harrowby's house, as he was taking him the news that 'the Duke has beat Napoleon, taken one hundred and fifty pieces of cannon, and is marching to Paris'. Haydon was bewildered:

'Is it true?' I asked. 'True!' said he; 'which is Lord Harrowby's?' Forgetting in my joy this was not Grosvenor Square, I said: 'There,' pointing to the same spot in Portman Square as Lord Harrowby's house occupies in Grosvenor Square, which happened to be Mrs Boehm's, where there was actually a rout. In rushed the messenger through servants and all, and I ran back again to Scott's. They were gone to bed but I knocked them up and said: 'The Duke has beat Napoleon, taken one hundred and fifty pieces of cannon, and is marching to Paris.' Scott began to ask questions. I said, 'None of your questions; it's a fact,' and both of us said 'Huzza!'[16]

Haydon went home, but rose the next morning with his brains still whirling with the news. Sammons, his favourite model, six foot three inches tall and corporal of the Life Guards (later to become his general factotum) arrived for a sitting, and Haydon tried to work, but both men were in too much of a state to continue. Sammons rushed off to find out more news

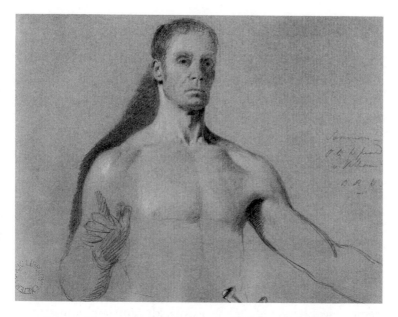

3. Corporal Sammons, 2nd Regiment of Life Guards, Haydon's servant and favourite model, *c.*1820. 'Pity he proved a villain,' Haydon wrote later on the drawing, after dismissing the married Sammons on account of some misdemeanour with a young woman. He was soon reinstated.

from his fellow soldiers, while Haydon, 'in a steam of feeling', went in search of newspapers. He read the *Gazette*, ordered a *Courier* for a month, called at a confectioner's and 'read all the papers until I was faint'. Not all his friends were such fervent patriots. For Leigh Hunt, Napoleon's fall represented the end of hope for a republican France and the probable return of an incompetent and repressive monarchy. Haydon dined with him two days after the news broke, and found him quiet and despondent, 'but knowing it must come by and by and putting on an air of indifference, he said: "Terrible battle this, Haydon." "A glorious one, Hunt." "Oh, yes, certainly," and to it we went.'[17] Hazlitt, for whom Napoleon was the towering hero of the era, felt in despair; his belief, Haydon said, being that 'crimes, want of honour, want of faith, or want of every virtue on earth, were nothing on the part of an individual raised from the middle classes to the throne, if they forwarded the victory of the popular principle whilst he remained there'.[18] After this crash of all the hopes stimulated by Napoleon's escape from Elba, he can have been in no mood to put up with an overexcited, jubilant Haydon, who found him 'prostrated in mind and body: he walked about unwashed, unshaved, hardly sober by day, and always intoxicated by night, literally, without exaggeration, for weeks; until at length wakening as it were from his stupor, he at once left off all stimulating liquors, and never touched them after'.[19] Haydon's own view of Napoleon was of a fiendish tyrant who richly deserved his downfall; and this was also Wordsworth's, for whom he was a satanic figure, 'that audacious charlatan and remorseless desperado'.[20] Wordsworth remained constant to this judgement, but Haydon sometimes had sneaking feelings of admiration for the fallen emperor, for his charisma and for the glamour of his days of absolute power. His feelings for Wellington since the battle of Vimiero 'amounted to the supernatural', although he regretted his hero's apparent lack of warmth and sympathy, linked in his mind no doubt to Wellington's lack of cooperation with the painter about sitting for a portrait.

For a while after Waterloo, Napoleon seemed to have disappeared, and speculation about his whereabouts raged. On 8 July *The Times* published rumours of a large American vessel waiting for a special passenger at Le Havre, but another source of information had it that the emperor had already been arrested. *The Times* meanwhile took this early opportunity of raising the subject of looted works of art:

The French Government will be inconsistent, and therefore weak, if, in condemning the crimes of the Revolution, it wishes to keep the fruit of those crimes, if it does not restore every statue, and every picture, and every medal, and every manuscript which the robbers who now await punishment tore from their unoffending owners.

But by August Napoleon was in Plymouth harbour, a prisoner on board the *Bellerophon*, the veteran of Trafalgar, known in the fleet as the *Billy Ruffian*, 'cheered by thousands' and still hoping to find asylum in England. Haydon longed to witness this extraordinary scene in his home town, but restrained himself in favour of working on his current picture. His sister, Mrs Harriet Haviland, sent him an account from Plymouth on 2 August of having seen the emperor:

On Friday I went out to see Buonaparte, but the guard boats kept us at such a great distance I was rather disappointed, as it was impossible to clearly distinguish his features. He seems a good figure and dignified; and to the disgrace of the Plymouthians be it said, yesterday, as he withdrew, the people rose up in their boats and applauded him. There is so much that is mysterious and prepossessing about him, and now in his great misfortunes so much pity is felt, that it is dangerous, I think, to the loyalty of the people to keep him here long; they all seem fascinated. Napoleon has a large stomach, though not otherwise fat. He walks the deck between five and six.[21]

Sketching the scene was the then unknown Charles Eastlake, Haydon's first pupil. The young artist later worked his drawings up into a canvas entitled *Napoleon on Board the Bellerophon*, which he sold to a group of five Plymouth businessmen who bought it as a speculation and made a fortune from touring it round the country. Eastlake's share of the profits came to £1,000. Part of this he wisely spent on some months in Italy, painting and acquiring a knowledge of classical work, upon which his future success was founded: later in life he became president of the Royal Academy and head of the National Gallery.

To cheer himself up for having missed such a historic sight, Haydon organized a party in his rooms of David Wilkie, John Scott and Corporal Sammons, the latter producing several of the Waterloo wounded to tell their stories. Sammons also brought a letter from a comrade still in Brussels, which Haydon read out. It included a nice little glimpse of Wellington cheering his men: 'I saw many of my comrades fall, before I got the wound, but we got three eagles, and Lord Wellington said that gained the applause of the whole of the British.' Sammons, who had fought all through the Peninsula campaign, to Haydon's amusement 'always seemed astounded that the battle of Waterloo had been gained and he not present' and he now underlined his authority as corporal over the mere privates by explaining military jargon to the assembled company as the moving tales of the battle were told. Haydon was fond of his model but not blind to his faults:

He would have brought a million safe and sound from Portsmouth to the King's Mint, but he popped his hand into King Joseph's coaches at Vittoria and brought away a silver pepper-box. He was an old satyr, very like Socrates in face, faithful to me, his colonel, and his King; but let a pretty girl come in the way and the Lord have mercy on her![22]

David Wilkie was always amused by Sammons, and Hazlitt, Haydon said, held regular discussions with him about Spain and Napoleon, 'but Sammons was proof, and always maintained the Duke was the better man'.[23]

In early May 1815, a month before Waterloo, William Wordsworth and his wife Mary were in London, staying in lodgings off Cavendish Square, and shortly after his arrival the poet met Haydon with Sir George Beaumont and his wife at their North Audley Street house. The Beaumonts and the Wordsworths had been close friends for some years, since Coleridge had introduced the poet to Beaumont, the generous patron of artists and writers, having first told Wordsworth that he had described him to Sir George as 'a great poet by inspirations and in the moments of revelation, but that you were a thinking feeling philosopher habitually – that your poetry was your philosophy under the action of strong winds of feeling – a sea rolling high';[24] and further that Lady Beaumont, given to excesses of sensibility, had declared on reading one of Wordsworth's poems that had he entered the room she would have fallen at his feet. The friendship, begun with such auspicious brio, continued for the rest of their lives. Beaumont, himself a talented amateur landscape painter, had also been a wonderfully kind patron and friend to Haydon, including him in the circle of rising young stars such as John Constable and David Wilkie whom he liked to gather around him.

In such a sympathetic atmosphere both Wordsworth and Haydon could feel relaxed and receptive; there was an immediate rapport between the poet at the height of his acclaim and the young painter beginning to enjoy success, and during the following weeks the two continued to build on their first acquaintance. A warm relationship began to develop between the disparate pair, fuelled partly by their high-minded dedication to their work and conviction of the special nature of their destinies. On 23 May they breakfasted together, spending, Haydon said, two delightful hours. By 13 June he had coaxed his new friend to submit to having a plaster cast made of his face. This was a preliminary for his portrait in Haydon's gigantic work in progress. The picture was to be entitled *Christ's Entry into Jerusalem*, and the artist planned to include portraits of his friends in the crowd pressing round the central figure.

The process of making a plaster mask was not without hazard. In 1810 Haydon had attempted to make a cast of the entire torso of an exceptionally beautiful negro from Boston, 'a perfect antique figure alive'.[25] After making many drawings of this man, whose name was Wilson, and taking casts of various joints, Haydon decided to attempt a cast of his entire torso. This was a difficult and also dangerous procedure. Haydon evolved a strategy of building a wall around Wilson, the plaster then to be poured in encasing him, making for an even effect:

Seven bushels of plaster were mixed at once and poured in till it floated him up to the neck. The moment it set, it pressed so equally upon him that his ribs had no room to expand for his lungs to play and he gasped out, 'I – I – I die.' Terrified at his appearance, for he had actually dropped his head, I seized with the workmen the front part of the mould and by one supernatural effort split it in three large pieces and pulled the man out, who, almost gone, lay on the ground senseless and streaming with perspiration.[26]

Wilson recovered, though the surgeon called in to restore him said he would have died in another few seconds, and the mould was brilliantly successful, but Haydon had learnt his lesson and did not venture on any more such experiments. On a later occasion he was present at an attempt to take a cast of the face of Francis Jeffrey, the powerful editor of the *Edinburgh Review*, in front of an admiring circle including his fellow editor, the cleric Sidney Smith, once described as the most playful, impudent, careless cassocked infidel ever met with:

Breakfast was ready and visitors began to drop in. By this time Jeffrey's coat was off, his chin towelled, the plaster ready, his face greased, and the ladies looking with a mixture of interest and quiz

4. Wilson, the perfect model, who narrowly escaped suffocation at
Haydon's hands during an attempt to obtain a cast of his whole
torso. Benjamin Robert Haydon, 1810.

that was funny. Mrs Jeffrey began to look anxious, for casting a face has something of the air of cutting off a man's head. She did not like to seem too fond and fearful before others (this was true affection); she fidgeted on her seat, moved nearer, and at last made a rush for the sofa with a look as if to say, 'it's no use, I will not be ashamed'. Grasped tight in her hand so that it was hardly visible, I saw the top of a smelling bottle! . . . The plaster was now brought, a spoonful taken up, Jeffrey ordered to keep his mouth closed and his nerves firm, and the visitors to be quiet. Sidney was dying with laughter, and kept trying to make Jeffrey laugh, but it would not do. When his face was completely covered, up rose Sidney Smith, and standing before him with the mock action of an orator, 'There's immortality,' said he. 'God keep me from such modes of obtaining it.' Unfortunately the moulder had nearly blocked up Jeffrey's nostrils and breathing became painful; his nerves gave way and the mould was obliged to be jerked off and broken. So much for this attempt at immortality.[27]

These instances give some idea of the ordeal involved in taking a cast, but in Wordsworth's case there was no mishap, Haydon remarking that he bore it like a philosopher. Haydon had invited John Scott to meet Wordsworth over breakfast, and on his arrival took him in to have a look, so that Scott could say his first glimpse of so great a poet had been on such a curious occasion. Wordsworth, wrapped in his host's dressing gown, was sitting with his hands folded, 'sedate, steady and solemn'. Haydon slowly opened the door, 'and there he sat, innocent and unconscious of our plot against his dignity, unable to see or to speak, with all the mysterious silence of a spirit'.[28] Protruding from his nostrils would have been straws to facilitate his breathing, adding a bizarre touch to the tableau. Wordsworth emerged cheerfully and proceeded to delight the two young men with his 'bursts of inspiration'. Later he and Haydon sauntered together to Hampstead. 'Never did any man so beguile the time,' exclaimed Haydon, adding, 'I don't know any man I should be so inclined to worship as a purified being.'[29] This glimpse of Wordsworth at his best is particularly precious, coming during a winter when he was often depressed and anxious and criticized by his friends for his consequent irritability.

Wordsworth himself also welcomed the new friendship between himself and Haydon. He wrote to the young man from Lowther Castle, Cumbrian seat of his patron Lord Lonsdale, enquiring sympathetically after the progress of *Christ's Entry into Jerusalem*. He renewed a promise to send Haydon a handwritten copy of one of his poems, stipulating something from the artist's pencil in return. Wordsworth fulfilled his part of the bargain on 21 December, sending Haydon three sonnets including 'High is our calling, Friend!', which flatteringly linked the two men as creative artists, concluding, 'Great is the glory, for the strife is hard!' He told Haydon that he had been inspired to write the sonnet by the latter's letter of 27 November 1815, in which Haydon had spoken of 'always remembering with secret delight the friendship with which you honour me, and the interest you take in my success. God grant it ultimately be assured! I will bear want, pain, misery and blindness, but I will never yield one step I have gained on the road I am determined to travel over.'[30] In his diary Haydon wrote of his elation: 'It is impossible to tell how I felt, after the first blaze of joy, feeling as it were lifted up in the great eye of the world, and feeling nothing more could be said of one.'[31] For his part, Wordsworth was soon signing himself to Haydon with, for him, unusual warmth, 'Believe me with great respect and true affection'. Over the years Haydon's feelings about Wordsworth were to undergo violent ups and downs, but for the time being all between them was *couleur de rose*.

In 1816 Haydon was introduced to his future wife, Mary Hyman, by his friend, the Plymouth-born actress Maria Foote.

5. The actress Maria Foote, 1815, by Benjamin Robert Haydon. She was a childhood playmate of Haydon's from his Plymouth days.

Maria and Haydon enjoyed a light-hearted and teasing relationship, and there are a number of references to her and sketches of her in the early parts of his diary. She also sat for him for a formal portrait, insisted she could paint the hair better than he, which amused him, 'and taking the brushes out of my hand, with a delicate apprehension and graceful shrink as she touched the paint, for fear of her black silk, just put on for the first time, flounced four times to the knee, she dabbled a lock over the forehead, and then laughed with a rich thrilling at her own lovely awkwardness'.[32]

Haydon's account of the meeting with his Mary is written in a mysterious and agitated manner: 'One evening, just after the sun had gone down in its gold and crimson glory, as I was lying in my armchair lost in meditation on my day's labour, my past uproar and my future success, dreaming of Rafaelle and the Greeks, the door opened without the least ceremony and like a vision there stood M— F—'[33] This was Maria, who asked him to escort her to a friend's house.

I walked up into a neat, small drawing room, and in an instant the loveliest face that was ever created since God made Eve smiled gently at my approach. On the sofa lay a dying man, and a boy about two years old by his side. What did it all mean? I never spoke a word, and on seeing M— home, returned to the house and stood outside in hopes she would appear at the window.[34]

Haydon was in love as never before. He watched the house for several days, growing more and more enraptured, until 'resistance was relinquished with glorious defiance of restraint! Her conduct to her dying husband, her gentle reproof of my impassioned and unrestrained air, rivetted my being.'[35]

After her husband's death the couple were free to marry, although it took five years before Haydon felt able to afford such a step. Mary lived quietly in Devonshire until 1821, looking after her little boys, returning from time to time to see her lover in London.

One of Mary's visits before their marriage was in June 1817, at the time of the opening of John Rennie's Waterloo Bridge by the Prince Regent on the second anniversary of the battle. Work on the new bridge, originally to be called the Strand Bridge, had begun in October 1811, financed not by the government but by a privately formed company which hoped

6. Mrs Mary Cawse Hyman, 1816, by Benjamin Robert Haydon, whom she married in 1821. For Haydon she was the most beautiful creature in the world and, in spite of an occasional lapse on his part, they were very happy together. Inscribed: 'My lovely Mary when first I saw her.'

to recoup the cost of the investment by charging a substantial toll – a hope not to be realized, in spite of a penny toll being charged for the next sixty years. By the time of the bridge's completion it had cost the then enormous sum of £1,050,000.[36] The Italian sculptor Antonio Canova, who attended its opening, exclaimed that it was the noblest bridge in the world, worth a visit from the remotest corner of the earth.

The prince, accompanied by the Dukes of York and Wellington, arrived to perform the opening ceremony by barge, passing under the central arch and landing on the south side, disembarking to cross the bridge on foot, together with a crowd of other dignitaries, and then returning to their barges on the city side. The river was crowded with sightseers in little boats, cheering the event, among the crowd being Constable, recording the scene,[37] and Haydon with Mary Hyman. 'On that lovely sunny day,' Haydon recalled three years later:

we glided away up the glittering river and passed the evening in sunny shade and sweet conversation, my poor heart opened as if by the touch of a talisman . . . The next day we strolled into a lovely meadow near Kilburn, and affected by the beauty of the day, the sunny warmth of Nature, the warbling birds and sighing leaves as they rustled at the gentle wind, sat down in the sun and disclosed our feelings to each other in the tenderest strain. I had been so long in secluded abstraction, that her presence affected me like enchanting music.[38]

It was during this visit of Mary's that she and Haydon became engaged, and they were married the following year. She was to have five sons and three daughters by Haydon, and their marriage was an exceptionally happy one. He thought the finest sight on earth was to see Mary wake and watch the 'gradual lovely stealings of consciousness over her divine face. I wish no other face to welcome me to heaven, and I should think heaven without it a perpetual twilight.'[39] Even when later in life Haydon was briefly infatuated with the notorious beauty Mrs Norton, his love for Mary was never really troubled. As for Mrs Norton, Haydon admitted to Elizabeth Barrett Browning that his children, out of loyalty to their mother, had smashed a bust of her which stood in Haydon's studio. Mary remained a rock to lean on throughout the exhausting dramas of her husband's life, from quarrels with his important patrons to spells in debtors' prison, leaving wife and children to sink or swim on their own.

But in 1817 Haydon was still alone and missing Mary. He was increasingly worried, too, about his sight, and the periods when he was unable to see to paint were becoming more frequent. Early in the previous year he had written of his sense of elation on recovering from four wretched months with one of his attacks of eye inflammation. That diary entry had been full of sensuous enjoyment: 'My very fingers seemed to revel as they touched their old acquaintances the brushes. The colours of the palette stood up with a buttery firmness, the oil seeming to give them as much pleasure as a cool stream does the cows with tail on end, on a June day.'[40] But now his general health suffered as well, and his famous energy began to desert him. Much of this state of affairs stemmed from his living conditions. His lodgings in Great Marlborough Street were cramped and airless. His paintings had to be propped up at an angle, as they were too big to stand upright in his small room. He worked either standing on a chair or, more dangerously, lying on the floor among the fumes from his paint mixtures. His models emerged from long sessions tired and sick, but the painter himself had to go to sleep in the same fetid atmosphere, and the smell of unwashed sheets and food debris. He felt desperate, and his friends urged him to move; but, as usual, he had no money.

Then a familiar solution struck him: he would apply to 'some rich man'. The first candidate selected did not answer his letter, although Haydon said plaintively, 'I had hoped that perhaps he would be pleased with the opportunity afforded him.'[41] His choice next fell on Jeremiah Harman, then governor of the Bank of England, and here he was successful, amazingly being given the £300 he needed to accomplish the move from Great Marlborough Street. But by December, the cost of establishing himself having proved greater than he had budgeted for, Haydon was once again out of funds, and turned to the eighty-year-old Thomas Coutts, founder of Coutts & Co., with whose wife he had a slight acquaintance. Again he was lucky, the banker generously lending him £400 on no security and without, as he frankly told Haydon, much expectation of reimbursement. His only mild proviso was that Haydon should keep the transaction a secret so as to avoid generating more begging letters from other impecunious artists. Haydon was duly grateful and wrote out one of his compendium prayers into his diary of 12 December 1817:

O God, unable to be punctual in my dealings with men, grant by the time proposed to repay this worthy man, what he has so affectionately advanced me, I may be able, fully able, to repay it, and may honourably and virtuously repay him. Grant he and all my Friends may live to see me flourish, free from debt, living in virtue and in honour.[42]

And while he was at it, he added a plea for the successful progress of his work in hand: 'Spare my eyes, and grant every requisite of body and mind now to go on and compleat my Picture, for Jesus Christ's sake, Amen.'

When the moment came to leave Great Marlborough Street, where he had spent nearly ten years of alternating struggles and successes, Haydon felt melancholy, particularly at saying goodbye to Perkins, his patient landlord, who had endured all his vagaries, even letting him bring a horse into the ground floor of the house to act as a model. He reflected gloomily on the awful nature of change, and how on his arrival he had been healthy, vigorous, and 'with a rosy colour and a luscious head of hair. I am now leaving it with my health shattered, my strength affected, my colour going, and my hair falling off.'[43] He looked back luxuriously on the horrors of his old lodgings, and also some of the glories he had experienced there:

Here I lived, here I painted Macbeth, Dentatus, and Solomon, and three parts of my Christ entering Jerusalem; here I suffered the extremest human misery and highest human success; here I was blind, and starving, and here I was visited by celebrated beauty and rank, by illustrious Foreigners, and Canova and Talma, and here I experienced the most brutal neglect.[44]

Once he was over the inevitable horrors attendant on moving house, Haydon was delighted with his new lodgings at 22 Lisson Grove North, Paddington, belonging to the sculptor and Academician John Charles Rossi. Rossi was a successful sculptor, his chief works including the monuments of military and naval heroes in St Paul's Cathedral. He was also employed by the Prince Regent in the decoration of Buckingham Palace. He was twice married and had eight children by each wife, and, like his new tenant, he was perpetually in financial difficulties. He was an obliging landlord and divided up his house, giving Haydon that part adjoining a large and airy studio, at a rent of £30 a quarter, and insisted that he himself would carry out all necessary alterations. At first Haydon felt disorientated:

All was in the future, a wild abyss, untrod, unknown! There is no pain like the uncertainty of a beginning, nothing that weighs the faculties down so acutely and so oppressively as the disarranged confusion and scattered desolation of furniture, books, and pictures unhung, unsettled, and undusted. For the moment one is suspended.[45]

His mood soon lifted and he went to work with his characteristic energy and speed, and by the next morning he luxuriated in his good fortune: 'I breakfasted for the first time in my life on my *own* tea cups and saucers. I took up my *own* knife. I sat in my *own* chair.'[46] But that night he felt restless, alone in his part of the house with his new servant girl. He heard her gown rustle on the stairs as she went to her room. 'Was it manly,' he asked himself, 'to let a nice girl sleep so near one and at least without making an attempt?' But then another voice prompted him: 'Was it manly to take advantage of the helpless girl, whose Father had expressed his great comfort in having his favourite daughter under my care!'[47] The second voice prevailed on that occasion, but a few days later several lines were rather suspiciously scratched out of his diary.

Not long after Haydon's move, in the early hours of the morning of 5 November, Princess Charlotte died after giving birth to a stillborn son. The nation, whose hopes had been on the princess and on her child as a new light for the future after the long decline of George III and the increasing unpopularity of the Prince Regent, was plunged into mourning sharpened by disappointment. Haydon was shattered:

She was our rallying point, our hope, our sunny land of promise and consolation. She was young and would have brought to the Throne all the better feelings of experience and youth. She would have wanted a new set, with vigorous intellects, in the Art. *I know* she had higher views and sounder feelings than any of her family.[48]

Haydon had once seen her looking at prints in a shop, and on this tenuous connection he took a slight bow from her in her carriage in the park to be personally for him: 'It was not on a Sunday but on a common day, and it was so particularly meant to me that the six or seven Gentlemen standing near me immediately scrutinized me with all their eyes.'[49] While dukes, earls and lords gave Haydon intense pleasure, a bow from a princess meant even more. He was a great royalist at this stage in his life, although as the Regency went on he became more critical and less easily impressed. On her burial day Haydon took himself off to the country, to the top of Hampstead, 'to muse' and to listen to distant church bells ringing 'in mournful harmony' through the sunny mist:

It looked as if her blessed spirit had been received into happiness and had influenced the very air. On a sudden the bells ceased, with a distant sinking like aeolian harps, and I immediately imagined the people all in at prayer, and I saw as it were a steam of incense agitate the air, like the steam from a lime kiln, and ascend up in a straight line till it lost itself in the sky! I thought of all the churches in the whole Empire like a map spread out before me, and I saw thousands of steams ascending like silvery smoke![50]

Commemorative medals and other objects were sold to mark the occasion. Editors were showered with poems about the dead woman's virtues. Keats told his brothers that his sister Fanny had asked for 'a medal of the Princess'; and Dora Wordsworth was also promised one on her parents' return from their London visit. Sir Richard Croft, the *accoucheur* who had attended the disastrous confinement, was accused of negligence and committed suicide.

The luxury of his large new painting room – Haydon disliked the word 'studio', considering it foreign and affected – inspired him to periods of concentrated work throughout the autumn, and by December of 1817, with *Christ's Entry into Jerusalem* well advanced, he began to plan a dinner party at which he could show off both his picture and his new establishment, and at the same time please his young friend John Keats by introducing him to Wordsworth. He settled on Sunday 28 December, three days after Christmas, as the date, and set about writing the invitations. Wordsworth, Keats, Charles Lamb and Mary Wordsworth's cousin Tom Monkhouse were invited; and others were asked to drop in later for tea or supper. These latter included Joseph Ritchie, a young surgeon about to lead an expedition to trace the course of the river Niger from its source to its outlet, and John Landseer, the engraver, whose three sons were pupils of Haydon's, one of them, Edwin, later becoming celebrated as the animal painter. No women were included in this bachelor evening. Invitations were accepted and the stage was now set for what was to become famous to posterity as the Immortal Dinner.

2. Crossing London

I copy out a sonnet by a young poet, Keats, addressed to me, but
beginning with you. I should wish very much to know what you
think of it. He promises a great deal, and said in a letter to me,
when I said I should enclose it to you, 'The idea of your sending it
to Wordsworth puts me out of breath; you know with what
reverence I should send my well-wishes to him.'

Benjamin Robert Haydon to William Wordsworth,
31 December 1816[1]

As Haydon's guests began to make their various ways to Lisson
Grove on the afternoon of 28 December, the weather was
dull but dry and the London streets wrapped in Sunday quiet.
The light was still good, as their host preferred to eat a little
earlier than was fashionable, so that their invitation would
have been for about half past three or even three o'clock.
William Wordsworth and Tom Monkhouse had the shortest
distance to travel. Monkhouse had lately moved to 28 Queen
Anne Street, off Cavendish Square, and had arranged for the
Wordsworths and Sara Hutchinson − Mary Wordsworth's
sister and Coleridge's adored 'Asra' − to stay in lodgings just
off the square at 48 Mortimer Street. The Wordsworths were
in London in order that Wordsworth could spend some time
with Christopher Wordsworth in winding up the affairs of
their late brother Richard, a task which the poet was finding
trying in the extreme. Monkhouse was a popular giver of
literary parties, although he tended to be overawed in the

company of the contemporary literary giants. In general he was a great favourite, especially with his Wordsworth cousins. In December 1817 he was trying to recover from an unhappy love affair, and was pleased to have them at hand to amuse him and divert his attention from his problems. Mary and Sara were inclined to take advantage of his good nature and make use of him as a general messenger, writing peremptory letters to their 'dearest coz' full of small commissions and errands, all of which he was happy to carry out. Wordsworth was also fond of his young cousin by marriage, and Sara told Monkhouse that he was 'quite a child' of Wordsworth's own:

He is determined that nothing shall be wanting, on his part, to persuade people that you really are all that he predicted you would be – We often laugh at him when he is *puffing you* off, as we call it, telling him to beware and not . . . cram you down everybody's throat – and over shoot his mark.[2]

Monkhouse's quality of inviting confidences was one of his most attractive characteristics. He was an especial pet of Mary Wordsworth's, and after the Wordsworths had left London and gone north again towards the end of January, she wrote a touchingly intimate and affectionate letter of thanks to her 'dearest cousin', saying that after he had seen her off on her journey

all your kindnesses to us and the thought of all your own transitory perplexities remained with me and softened my heart in a way which, on such occasions, it used to be melted in the days of my youth and before severe domestic losses had seemed to me to have changed my nature; and it was not until we had passed the noise of the great city that I could rally my spirits.[3]

She signed herself with warmth as 'Most tenderly and most affly yours'. For his part Monkhouse had rather enjoyed the cachet of having the great poet under his wing, and the arranging of parties, shopping expeditions and visits to the opera and theatres for the two women, without whom Wordsworth was always reluctant to leave home, needing the comfort and reassurance of his 'petticoats', as Coleridge impatiently called them.

The winter of 1817 was notable for its cold and dense fogs. It came at the end of a succession of bitterly hard seasons, beginning with the Great Frost of 1813–14 when the Thames froze over and the last of the river fairs took place, with whole oxen roasted on the ice. This was before the demolition of old London Bridge had increased the flow of the Thames, after which ice formed less readily. Delegates travelling to the Congress of Vienna that earlier winter had suffered miserably from the extraordinary cold, men's moustaches freezing as hard as rapiers as they sat imprisoned in their carriages, their windowpanes never thawing out enough to show them the desolate landscape through which they were passing. It is thought that both the fogs and the heavy haze which characterized the early nineteenth-century climate stemmed from the fall-out from a series of disastrous volcanic eruptions. The worst of these came in April 1815 from Mount Tamboro in the East Indies, the effects of which persisted over much of the northern hemisphere, reaching a peak in 1816. The resultant haze of stratospheric dust caused unusual optical effects, which may have been one reason for the characteristic cloud formations in Constable's and Turner's skies, and particularly for the colours in Turner's sunsets. The haze was irritable to the eyes, and particularly dangerous to the vulnerable Haydon, who suffered increasingly from eye troubles; also to Wordsworth, although he had not yet begun to wear the protective green eye-shade to which he resorted from time to time a little later in his life. This fall-out seems also to have been a factor in the ensuing series of exceptionally cold and wet summers resulting in ruined harvests, with a consequent rise in the price of bread, which added to the distress of the immediate post-war years. Average summer temperatures in 1816, for example, fell to 56 degrees Fahrenheit, the lowest since the little ice age of the late seventeenth century. That year had been the worst year of all, and was talked of as 'the year without a summer', with fires burning on London hearths right through what should have been the warmest months. The cold even influenced fashion, compelling a return to more modest high-necked winter wear for women. William Bewick, later to become Haydon's favourite pupil, had arrived in London full of hope and excitement at the thought of seeing the city which had for long been the object of his dreams, with only £20 in his pocket to live on, and in a heavy shower of rain. He thought that the dense smoke and wet made it seem as if he were entering 'an inhabited cloud'.[4] The obnoxious fogs of the time were partly due to the prevalent use of sea coal – poor-quality coal, that is to say, brought by sea from Newcastle. Haydon liked to study the movements of the pall of cloud from the hills near London, looking down upon it and catching glimpses as it drifted over St Paul's, 'announcing civilization and power'. And Charles Lamb, passionate champion of the capital, agreed with Haydon's view: 'I love the very smoke of London because it has been the medium most familiar in my vision.'[5]

Sara Hutchinson wrote in December 1817 from the Words-worths' Mortimer Street lodgings to her niece Dora, left behind at Rydal Mount, their house outside Grasmere, com-plaining of the inconveniences brought by the fog. The Wordsworths and Tom Monkhouse, she said, had just been forced to abandon their coach a mile from home, the fog being so dense that the coachman could not find his way, and she herself could not see the houses on the other side of the street. 'The fog is not only thick but of a yellow colour and makes one as dirty as smoke.'[6]

Haydon disagreed with Sara Hutchinson's complaints about fog and smoke:

So far from the smoke of London being offensive to me, it has always been to my imagination the sublime canopy that shrouds the City of the World. Drifted by the window or hanging in gloomy grandeur over the vastness of our Babylon, the sight of it filled my mind with feelings of energy such as no other spectacle could inspire. 'Be Gode,' said Fuseli to me one day, 'it's like de smoke of de Israelites making bricks.' 'It is grander,' said I, 'for it is the smoke of a people who would have made the Egyptians make bricks for them.' 'Well done, John Bull,' replied Fuseli.[7]

All Haydon's guests would have walked to his party. To such a walker as Wordsworth in particular, the distance from Cavendish Square to Lisson Grove seemed negligible. De Quincey described the poet's legs as certainly not ornamental, but 'serviceable beyond the average standard of human requisition; for I calculate, upon good data, that with these identical legs Wordsworth must have traversed a distance of 175 to 180,000 English miles'.[8] On Sunday 28 December the weather was favourable, and although Monkhouse would have kept a horse and carriage at livery in a neighbouring mews, there was nothing on this occasion to prevent the two men setting out on foot. Wordsworth no doubt wore his brown overcoat, but not the boots he had borrowed from his patron Lord Lonsdale to keep himself warm on the journey south from the Lakes, when he had travelled for reasons of economy on the outside of the mail coach. Under their greatcoats both men wore trousers – knee breeches and stockings were no longer seen except on more formal occasions – high white neckcloths and waisted jackets, and both would have worn their tall hats. The all-powerful influence of the Regency fashion icon, Beau Brummell, who wore only black in the evening, would have

7. *Regent's Park and Marylebone*, 1813, by Richard Horwood. On
the lower part of the left of the map and going off at an angle from
the New Road – later to become the Marylebone Road and
simply called the Road here – is Haydon's Lisson Grove. Nash's
designs for the area were well under way by 1817.

ensured that their clothes were dark, although neither would have been pleased to admit to such an influence, nor is it very likely that Wordsworth himself would have been aware of it.

As they set out together the two men passed the Mortimer Street house of Joseph Nollekens the sculptor, where Dr Johnson had sat for his bust. Nollekens was a miser and said to live in conditions of the greatest squalor, although he died possessed of a large fortune. On the north side of the street stood James Paine's Middlesex Hospital, completed forty years

8. The Middlesex Hospital, built by James Payne towards the end of the eighteenth century. The original building had been 'for the sick and lame of Soho'.

earlier when the outlook at the back was still directly on to fields: most of the great eighteenth-century hospitals had chosen such sites for reasons of health. Less-than-healthy ponds and marshland separated the Middlesex from the Tottenham Court Road to the east. The building of the hospital had been partly financed by Handel and Garrick;

9. Regent's Park: East Gate, a Villa and St Katharine's Hospital,
*c.*1825, by Thomas Shepherd. Nash's original plan included
fifty-six villas dotted about the park, all stuccoed and glittering, but
in the event only eight were built.

the great composer and the actor had each given a series of
gratis performances to help raise the necessary funds. On the
other side of Cavendish Square, on the corner of Queen Anne
Street and Harley Street, Monkhouse had J. M. W. Turner as
a neighbour, working at the time on his *Liber Studiorum* series
of engravings. Here, on the first floor, the painter had built
himself an extensive private gallery to display his paintings.

Leaving Queen Anne Street, the two diners would next
have turned into Langham Place, where five years later John
Nash would build All Souls Church in the curve of the road
to form a satisfying focus for the north end of his bold scheme
for Regent Street, currently known as the New Street. Work
was under way on the construction of this dramatic gash,
cutting a serpentine swathe through the disorganized mess of
Soho to the east, and opening up the wide streets leading to
the grand estates to the west, until it was finally to link the
Regent's Carlton House in St James's Park to Nash's projected

new Regent's Park to the north of Portland Place, in the Marylebone fields. Already completed was the spectacular expanse of Park Crescent, a golden stretch of stuccoed and colonnaded dignity, forming the entrance to the new park. Nash had envisaged the park itself as one huge pleasure garden dotted about with grand villas surrounded by shrubs and groves, and with lakes and larger trees, but his Kubla Khan-like vision was never entirely realized.

The diarist Henry Crabb Robinson, faithful recorder of the London literary life of the day, drove through the new park the following year and found much to admire. He felt that, once the trees had matured, the whole complex of the park and the approach to it would be valued by posterity even more than the victories of Waterloo and Trafalgar, glorious though these were.[9] Ironically, by the time that Regent Street was completed Carlton House had been demolished, although George IV did not live long enough to make the projected move into Buckingham House, by then greatly extended by Nash, and about to become the royal palace.

Nash's Regent Street project was by no means the only building work to be seen in London in 1817, and the noise everywhere was terrific. The French-born American Louis Simond, borrowing a friend's house off Portman Square while he was on a visit to England, complained of a colony of Irish builders' labourers crammed into a neighbouring cul-de-sac and filling every cellar and garret:

a family in each room; very poor, very uncleanly and very turbulent. They give each other battle every Saturday night particularly, when heroes and heroines shew their prowess at fisty-cuffs. We should never have known that there were such wretches as these in London, if we had not happened to reside in Orchard Street, Portman Square, which is one of the finest parts of the town.[10]

Noisy workmen were the least of the worries in a year of escalating danger of civil revolt. Eighteen seventeen had started with the suspension, for the second time, of habeas corpus in the wake of a number of angry demonstrations that had occurred the previous year. These had been provoked by the poverty, hunger and discontent left after the French wars, conditions which were exacerbated by a significant population explosion. Unemployment had risen, and was made worse by the increase in industrial machinery taking the place of a man's work. Machine breaking was made a capital offence. In November 1816 a huge meeting was held in Spa Fields in north London, addressed by the radical Henry 'Orator' Hunt, which turned into a drunken semi-insurrection, as part of the crowd broke into a gunsmith's, stole all his stock of weapons, and marched threateningly on the city. The leaders were tried for high treason, but were later acquitted when it was shown that the spy who had informed on them, Castles, was a bigamist, brothel-minder and agent provocateur. Before Christmas there were demonstrations against the Prince Regent, whose extravagant lifestyle was seen as disgraceful at such a time of general poverty, and there was an attempt on his life, which was the trigger for more government retaliation. Throughout 1817 there was a dangerous atmosphere and evidence of continued violence. There were many instances of arson.

Those of a radical and reforming tendency sympathized with the oppressed and rejoiced in any amelioration of their lot. Keats and his friends were horrified by the repressive measures imposed by authority, particularly resenting the suspension of habeas corpus. Wordsworth, on the other hand, thought that the maintenance of order was the first consideration and that the action was a sensible safeguard against anarchy. He had written to Haydon earlier in 1817 expressing his sense of foreboding:

Faction runs apace – The friends of liberty and good order are alarmed at the corruption of opinion among the lower classes, and the reformers and revolutionists are irritated and provoked that their plans have for the present been defeated. For my own part I am full of fears, not for the present; the immediate danger will, I think, be got over, but there is a malady in the social constitution which it will require the utmost skill to manage, and which if it is not met with firmness and knowledge will end in the dissolution of the body politic.[11]

A week before the Immortal Dinner the radical bookseller William Hone, arrested in September on a charge of publishing blasphemous material likely to injure public morals and bring the Book of Common Prayer into contempt, was brought to trial. He had written and published political parodies on the litany, the creed and the catechism. Hone conducted his own defence over a period of three days in three separate trials with such brilliant success that he was acquitted on all counts.

Wordsworth considered his acquittal to be regrettable and Dorothy Wordsworth thought the jury 'most culpable'. The Wordsworths, so radical in their youth, had now changed from their fervent republicanism then to an emphatically Tory position. Their concern with the suffering of the poor never left them, very much the contrary, but they were convinced that order must at all costs be maintained. Wordsworth, having seen the reality of revolution in France, now feared, and continued to fear for a long time, what he saw as a real threat of revolution. Events in the years following Haydon's dinner did nothing to comfort him. The price of bread continued to rise, followed by more riots. In August 1819 came the disaster of Peterloo, during a peaceful reform meeting of between 60,000 and 100,000 people in St Peter's Fields, Manchester, when, on the order of the magistrates, the local yeomanry violently broke up the meeting in a manner which soon became completely out of hand, resulting in eleven dead and more than 400 wounded. The government chose to congratulate the magistrates, and rushed through more repressive measures, known as the Six Acts, which caused bitter outrage. At this juncture Wordsworth's fear of revolution came very near to realization. A year later came the Cato Street conspiracy, a plot to murder Liverpool's entire cabinet as they dined in Lord Harrowby's house in Grosvenor Square. The conspirators were betrayed by an informer and arrested in a loft in Cato Street, on the Portman estate. Their aim had been to overthrow the government and achieve some measure of democracy. The plan failed, but only by mischance: it could very easily have succeeded. If this had happened during Simond's visit to Portman Square, he would have had a real reason to feel aggrieved.

Eighteen seventeen was the year that the Duke of Wellington, unperturbed by the climate of unrest, bought Apsley House from his brother for £42,000, an enormous sum. His plan was to transform the house, with its famous address of No. 1, London, into a glittering showcase for the display of his collection of trophies, silver, gold and porcelain, including the magnificent dinner service painted with scenes from all his victories. The delicate Adam ceilings in pink and green were too low-key for his purpose of achieving magnificence on an almost imperial scale, and were gilded over. The enormous nude statue of Napoleon by Canova, disliked by both Napoleon and the duke, was installed at the foot of the staircase: a gift from the government in gratitude for his services in the Peninsular campaign, Wellington could not very well dispense with it. In 1817 the Adam brick exterior still remained, although ten years later the house was enlarged for the duke by the Wyatts, refaced in Bath stone, and the Corinthian portico added. Crowds would wait outside as guests for the duke's great dinner parties arrived in their carriages; and he would sometimes invite the public in to admire all the golden splendour.

On reaching the New Road – now the Marylebone Road – Wordsworth and Monkhouse would have made their way north, leaving the newly completed Dorset Square to their right. This had been the site of Thomas Lord's first cricket ground, and building had begun soon after he moved it to St John's Wood, the square being named for the Duke of Dorset, an early enthusiast of the game. The remainder of their walk became increasingly rural, as the two men approached the corner of Lisson Grove and what is now Rossmore Road. The market gardens of Lisson Green, the laundry fields where people could lay out their linen to bleach in the sun, and the dairy farms of St John's Wood were already giving way to the building of new houses, the area being innovative in possessing the first pairs of individually designed semi-attached villas.

On their arrival at 28 Lisson Grove North, Corporal Sammons of the Life Guards, or one of the two guardsmen he had inveigled into helping him with the party, relieved the guests of their coats and hats, and showed them into Haydon's new painting room, where their host awaited them.

As soon as Wordsworth had arrived in London at the beginning of December 1817 Haydon made a drawing of his head as a further preliminary to including the poet's portrait in his *Christ's Entry into Jerusalem*. Haydon was delighted with his sitter, who read aloud from Milton and from his own work: 'He is a most eloquent power. He looked like a spirit of Nature, pure and elementary. His head is like as if it was carved out of a mossy rock, created before the flood! It is grand and broad and persevering. That nose announces a wonder.'[12] As Haydon began to transfer the drawing to canvas, Wordsworth read from *The Excursion* 'in his finest manner' and Haydon mused on the poet's power to achieve 'an intense perception of human feelings regarding the mystery of things by analyzing his own'. It is disconcerting to remember that at that time no one outside Wordsworth's most intimate circle had any idea of the existence of *The Prelude*, nor would they have until after the poet's death thirty-three years later. So Haydon's appreciation of the poet's genius was necessarily founded on his shorter poems and most recently published long work, *The Excursion*, the latter little read or regarded now.

Wordsworth arrived at Lisson Grove in a genial mood, unusual for him that winter. He had been suffering a period of malaise, which had led to a number of complaints about his taciturnity, embarrassing degree of egoism and general prickliness. The previous evening Monkhouse had given a small party in Queen Anne Street, hoping to effect a rapprochement between Wordsworth and Coleridge after a long and damaging estrangement. This had come about after a distorted account reached Coleridge of some criticisms made by Wordsworth of his difficult behaviour during a prolonged visit to the Wordsworths at Grasmere. Various friends had attempted to end the rift, so painful to both parties, and effect a reconciliation, and Monkhouse was the first to succeed in achieving a meeting between the two. Unfortunately Wordsworth had evidently shown himself at his worst during the evening, replying to a timid Coleridge's tentative remarks, according to Crabb Robinson, with 'dry unfeeling contradiction'. He continued to be abrupt and dismissive throughout the evening, driving the diarist to note that 'for the first time in my life I was not pleased with Wordsworth'.[13] Charles and Mary Lamb, also present, agreed that the poet's behaviour had been difficult to excuse.

There were various extenuating reasons for Wordsworth's unease. In addition to his worries over the settling of his late brother's estate, which meant his spending far too long fussing over the minutiae of the provisions of the will, his eyesight seemed to be worsening and he felt himself threatened by blindness. Worst of all, as a result of all these small distractions, he had latterly found himself unable to compose his mind to write, in the absence of the atmosphere of calm essential to him. But perhaps his predominant annoyance on this particular occasion sprang from Coleridge's autobiographical *Biographia Literaria*, which had been published that summer. Wordsworth resented Coleridge's extensive discussion of his work in the book, finding his passages of praise over-effusive and his criticisms intolerable, and fearing that Coleridge's remarks might do him damage with the critics. Catherine Clarkson, wife of the anti-slavery reformer Thomas Clarkson, and friend of both the Wordsworths and Crabb Robinson, wrote to the latter in defence of Wordsworth's behaviour to Coleridge on the reunion: 'A man of the world in W——s place would have been kind before strangers, cold in private. W——s better nature I have no doubt would make him affectionate in private and only cold before strangers because his whole mind could not be expressed before them.'[14] At some point either before or shortly after Haydon's dinner, Wordsworth showed himself once more in his old generous and protective guise towards Coleridge, who was about to embark on another of his famous courses of lectures. He wrote to *The Times*'s critic John Payne Collier recommending the course to his attention: '. . . his thoughts as well as his words flow spontaneously. He talks as a bird sings, as if he could not help it: it is his nature . . . You have long been among his friends; and as far as you can go, you will no doubt prove it on this as on other occasions. We are all anxious on his account.'[15]

Perhaps Mrs Clarkson had been right in her diagnosis, or perhaps Wordsworth was triumphant at having, as he saw it, come best out of his encounter with Coleridge; but for whatever reason, by Sunday afternoon his mood had lightened.

This was crucial to the success of Haydon's party: at forty-seven Wordsworth was more than ten years older than his host, and more than twenty years older than Keats, the youngest guest, who regarded him, at this stage at least, with the deepest veneration; and a gloomy contentious senior would have had a dampening effect on the high spirits of the rest of the company.

Happily on this occasion, all was well; but if it had not been, then Charles Lamb's gentle wit would have provided the best antidote to counteract the atmosphere. Lamb had not yet begun to write his Elia essays, but his and his sister Mary's *Tales from Shakespeare* had already appeared; a play of his had been performed at Drury Lane; and he was celebrated as a writer and theatre critic. None of his literary activities made him much money, however, and at one point he had been driven to contribute jokes to the *Morning Post* at sixpence a joke to augment his small salary.

Lamb was employed for his whole working life as a clerk to the East India Company in Leadenhall Street, so until his retirement it was necessary for him to live within fairly easy reach of his office. By 1817 the East India Company's main business lay with China and the trade in tea, of which it held a near monopoly. This was on a considerable and growing scale – by 1830 the country's revenue from tea imports stood at £30 million a year, the largest single item in the national trading account, and generated a further £3 million in duties levied. Lamb, as a member of the accountants' office, attended sales in the Company's sale rooms, recording the day's business in, among other commodities, indigo and piece-goods, as well as in the vast quantities of tea stored in its City warehouses. The Company's most notable contribution to the face of London was the construction of a road linking the docks to the City (now Commercial Road and East India Dock Road),

10. *East India House* by Herbert Railton. Charles Lamb worked in the East India Company's imposing mansion in Leadenhall Street for thirty-three years, his whole working life.

which terminated in a great granite portico built by Rennie, the Company's engineer, at the entrance to the docks.

Lamb thought of his work as the cruellest drudgery, but by all accounts it sounds as if it had been a somewhat leisurely affair. He was impervious to discipline, answering a complaint from his superior, 'I notice, Mr Lamb, that you come late

every morning,' with 'Yes, but see how early I go!' He told
his colleagues long stories; he was visited endlessly by friends
eager to make use of the Company's writing paper, pens or
pencils, or, better still in those days of expensive postage,
obtain a frank for a letter; and most of all eager to chat and
listen to Lamb's anecdotes and atrocious puns. But in spite of
welcome interruptions and the fact that he used the Company's time for his own writing, his work there undoubtedly
did remain a dull routine, and when he retired he was for a
while ecstatic at his freedom, although he was a little shocked
to find how much he missed the bustle of the office days and
the companionship of his fellow clerks. He was troubled by
an impression of wasted life. Writing to Wordsworth in April
1815, he spoke despondently about the sterility of his work
and its increasing pressures:

I never leave till four, and do not keep a holiday now once in ten
times, where I used to keep all red-letter days, and some five days
besides, which I used to dub Nature's holidays. I have had my day.
I had formerly little to do. So of the little that is left of life, I may
reckon two-thirds as dead, for time that a man may call his own is
his life; and hard work and thinking about it taints even the leisure
hours, – stains Sunday with work-day contemplation.[16]

Lamb belonged to the Wordsworth class of walker, and was
never happier than when crossing great swathes of London by
night or by day, sometimes accompanied by his sister Mary.
Some years earlier he had written to Wordsworth, refusing an
invitation to Dove Cottage, and giving an explanation of his
reasons:

I have passed all my days in London, until I have formed as many
and intense local attachments as any of you mountaineers can have
done with dead Nature. The lighted shops of the Strand and Fleet

Street; the innumerable trades, tradesmen, and customers, coaches, waggons, playhouses; all the bustle and wickedness round about Covent Garden; the very women of the Town; the watchmen, drunken scenes, rattles; life awake, if you awake, at all hours of the night; the impossibility of being dull in Fleet Street; the crowds, the very dirt and mud, the sun shining upon houses and pavements, the print-shops, the old book-stalls, parsons cheapening books, coffee-houses, steams of soups from kitchens, the pantomimes – London itself a pantomime and a masquerade – all these things work themselves into my mind, and feed me, without a power of satiating me. The wonder of these sights impels me into night-walks about her crowded streets, and I often shed tears in the motley Strand from fulness of joy at so much life. All these emotions must be strange to you; so are your rural emotions to me. But consider, what must I have been doing all my life, not to have lent great portions of my heart with usury to such scenes?[17]

Charles and Mary Lamb did in time make one visit to the Lakes, which to their surprise they rather enjoyed, although they were relieved when they found themselves once more in the city. Lamb wrote to his friend, the China expert and traveller Thomas Manning, describing his holiday, and admitting that

In fine, I have satisfied myself that there is such a thing as that which tourists call romantic, which I very much suspected before: they make such a spluttering about it, and toss their splendid epithets around them, till they give as dim a light as at four o'clock next morning the lamps do after an illumination.[18]

Wordsworth disagreed profoundly with Lamb's partisan view of London. In 1802 the Lambs had taken him and Dorothy to see Bartholomew Fair, which struck the poet as an appalling Hieronymous Bosch-like vision:

What a hell
For eyes and ears! what anarchy and din
Barbarian and infernal! . . .
Tents and booths
Meanwhile, as if the whole were one vast Mill,
Are vomiting, receiving, on all sides,
Men, Women, three-years' Children, Babes in arms.[19]

But he did experience one visionary moment in London, at a time of anxiety about Coleridge, with whom he had passed the whole night in useless pleading about the latter's destructive drug habits and way of life, leaving him only as dawn broke. He described this in a letter to Sir George Beaumont:

I had passed through Temple Bar and by St Dunstan's, noticing nothing, and entirely occupied with my own thoughts, when, looking up, I saw before me the avenue of Fleet Street, silent, empty, and pure white, with a sprinkling of new-fallen snow, not a cart or carriage to obstruct the view, no noise, only a few soundless and dusky foot-passengers here and there . . . and beyond, towering above it, was the huge and majestic form of St Paul's, solemnized by a thin veil of falling snow . . . My sorrow was controlled, and my uneasiness of mind – not quieted and relieved altogether – seemed at once to receive the gift of an anchor of security.[20]

Like Haydon and Monkhouse, Lamb, with his sister Mary, had just moved into new lodgings, leaving Inner Temple Lane for 20 Russell Street, Covent Garden, above a brazier's shop. Lamb wrote to Dorothy Wordsworth on 21 November:

Here we are, transplanted from our native soil. I thought we never could have been torn up from the Temple. Indeed it was an ugly wrench, but like a tooth, now 'tis out, and I am easy . . . We are in the individual spot I like best, in all this great city. The theatres, with all their noises, Covent Garden, dearer to me than any gardens of Alcinous, where we are morally sure of the earliest peas and 'sparagus. Bow Street, where the thieves are examined, within a few yards of us. Mary had not been here four-and-twenty hours before she saw a thief. She sits at the window working; and casually throwing out her eyes, she sees a concourse of people coming this way, with constable to conduct the solemnity. These little incidents agreeably diversify a female life.[21]

On leaving his new Russell Street lodgings on 28 December, Lamb would have made his way through Covent Garden market, in 1817 at its most anarchic. By the middle of the eighteenth century the market area had become disreputable and dangerous, with brothels and an extraordinary number of Turkish bath establishments proliferating. It was here that Fanny Hill's lodgings were set. There were gambling dens, and duels were fought in the taverns, while press gangs found the area to be rich in pickings as men tumbled drunkenly out into the streets at the end of the evening. But some twenty years or so before Haydon's dinner, the nature of the market had changed. Traders in every kind of commodity began to set up their stalls, selling wares ranging from crockery to live hedgehogs sold as pets to eat up the armies of beetles from householders' damp basements.[22] The arrival of these new stallholders made the legitimate fruit, vegetable and flower stallholders yet more crowded; and everyone became truculent, noisily refusing to pay their dues to the Bedford estate. Chaos reigned, fights continually broke out, and the noise was unbearable from as early as four in the morning, when traders began to arrive from the market gardens outside the city to set up their stalls, until quite late in the evening. In spite of all attempts to get things under control, there was no real improvement until a large covered market was built for the stallholders and legislation enforcing penalties came into being in the eighteen-thirties.

Nearby were the two great theatres, the Covent Garden Opera House and Drury Lane Theatre, resplendent in their new form, having been burnt down in the disastrous fires of 1808 and 1809 respectively.

Sheridan was the manager of the Theatre Royal Drury Lane at the time of the fire, and was attending an important debate at the House of Commons when it broke out, the flames being clearly visible even at that distance. He refused the offer of an adjournment, saying that he could not allow a catastrophe of whatever dimension to interfere with the business of the country.

Lamb resented that on his one free day from the office, Sunday, also the day of Haydon's dinner, the bustle and excitement of the streets was stilled, bookstalls shut up, and all the strange and exotic side-shows closed down. He was inclined to dislike the new building improvements, so much praised by everyone else, feeling nostalgic for the City's now-vanished ancient streets. He heartily disliked the Prince Regent and complained that as well as imposing the ubiquitous and unpleasantly brash-looking new stucco on the capital, he had ruined the old green parks. He wrote about this to Wordsworth:

The very colour of green is vanished, the whole surface of Hyde Park is dry crumbling sand (Arabia Arenosa), not a vestige or hint of grass ever having grown there, booths and drinking places go all round it for a mile and a half, I am confident – I might say two miles in circuit – the stench of liquors, *bad* tobacco, dirty people and provisions, conquers the air and we are stifled and suffocated in Hyde Park.[23]

The reason given for Lamb's present move to Russell Street, which was rather less convenient for his daily journey to East

India House than his old Temple lodgings had been, was that these had become altogether too decrepit, and this may well have been true; but he probably had an additional motive intimately connected with the central tragedy of his life. At the end of 1795, when Charles was twenty, he suffered a breakdown sufficiently severe to necessitate some weeks in a mental asylum. He made a rapid and full recovery, and such a lapse was never to recur, but the incident left him terrified of what the future might hold. He announced this nightmare episode abruptly to Coleridge, at that time his closest friend:

My life has been somewhat diversified of late. The six weeks that finished last year and began this, your very humble servant spent very agreeably in a madhouse, at Hoxton. I am got somewhat rational now, and don't bite anyone. But mad I was; and many a vagary my imagination played with me, enough to make a volume, if all were told.[24]

In his delusions Lamb had thought he was the young Norval, hero of the popular contemporary romantic tragedy *Douglas*, and, after his recovery, he told Coleridge that his madness had been in some ways a fortunate experience: 'I look back upon it at times with a gloomy kind of envy: for, while it lasted, I had many, many hours of pure happiness. Dream not, Coleridge, of having tasted all the grandeur and wildness of fancy till you have gone mad.'[25] But in spite of this brave pretence, in reality he must have been left with feelings of miserable despair.

Then, in the summer of 1796, Lamb began to worry about Mary. She was overburdened with the care of her semi-paralysed mother, spending her days and nights – they even shared a bed – in the closest proximity to the invalid, who had never been loving to her daughter and was now becoming increasingly querulous and difficult. Her father was senile; and an additional burden was an old aunt who lived with them and needed care. There was also the necessity for Mary to find time to earn some money to eke out Charles's meagre salary. She set up as a dressmaker, or, more specifically, a mantua maker, and employed a young woman, not much more than a child, as her apprentice. On 22 September 1796, only months after Charles's own episode of madness, which had left the young man frail and stammering, a terrible blow was struck, which was to change the course of his and his sister's life. Mary, overwrought by the strains of her life, became ominously excitable, and on that morning Charles, feeling anxious about her condition, went in search of a doctor. He did not find one and, fatally, went on to his office. He returned home at the end of the day in time to see his mother lying dead, his father wounded, and his sister standing with a knife in her hand in a state of frenzied madness. Charles removed the knife, and from that instant he assumed control of the family – there was no one else to whom he could turn.

Inevitably a good deal of public interest was aroused by Mary's case, which was reported at length and in sensational detail in the *Whitehall Evening Post* four days after the catas-trophe:

On Friday afternoon the Coroner and a respectable Jury sat on the body of a Lady in the neighbourhood of Holborn, who died in consequence of a wound from her daughter the preceding day. It appeared by the evidence adduced, that while the family were preparing for dinner, the young lady seized a case knife laying on the table, and in a menacing manner pursued a little girl, her apprentice, round the room; on the eager calls of her helpless infirm mother to forbear, she renounced the first object, and with loud shrieks approached her parent. The child by her cries quickly brought up the landlord of the house, but too late – the dreadful scene presented to him the mother lifeless, pierced to the heart, on a chair, her daughter yet wildly standing over her with the fatal knife, and the venerable old man, her father, weeping by her side, himself bleeding at the forehead from the effects of a severe blow he received from one of the forks she had been madly hurling about the room.

Lamb immediately took his sister to Fisher House, a small private lunatic asylum in Islington, determined that she should be spared what might well have been, once the authorities were in charge of her case, a life sentence in the horrors of Bedlam; and by his swift action he somehow managed to avert this worst of all fates. After the catastrophe Lamb, on the surface, was calm and made all the necessary arrangements. He then made a resolve, never to be broken, to devote his life to the care of Mary. Later, when he was still struggling to come to terms with what had happened, he wrote a poem, disturbing in its passion and misery. The first stanza was originally:

> I had a mother, but she died, and left me
> Died prematurely in a day of horrors –
> All, all are gone, the old familiar faces.

But Lamb later suppressed this, and the poem now opens with the more familiar:

> I have had playmates, I have had companions,
> In my days of childhood, in my youthful school-days –
> All, all are gone, the old familiar faces.[26]

It continues for six more strange and heartfelt stanzas, providing a rare glimpse directly into his state of mind, unprotected by his customary shield of wit.

Lamb's father did not live long after the horrors of 22

September, nor did his old aunt; his brother John, who seems to have been of no assistance to him, removed himself to separate lodgings; and so for brother and sister life settled down into a pattern that was to become all too familiar to them. Mary recovered from her frenzied outburst, and returned to Lamb's care, who reported to Coleridge: 'My poor, dear, dearest sister, the unhappy and unconscious instrument of the Almighty's judgments on our house, is restored to her senses, – to a dreadful sense and recollection of what has passed, awful to *her* mind, and impressive, (as it must be to the end of her life).'[27] Brother and sister now lived on the edge of a precipice, never knowing exactly when the next blow would fall. Mary's seizures began with a period of increasing excitement, escalating into frenzy. Both of them were then aware that an attack was under way, and Lamb would guard her against all company or other distraction in the hope that her symptoms might subside. If not, they made their preparations, Lamb packing for Mary a little parcel of her belongings, and they then set off on foot together for the lunatic asylum. Their friend Charles Lloyd saw them on one such occasion, walking along, both in tears, Lamb with Mary's straitjacket under his arm.

Ironically during her sane intermissions Mary's was the most calm and rational of natures, and many contemporaries noted her gentle manner and her intuitive kindness. Consequently the sudden switch to frenzy would come almost as a double-blow to Lamb, after the preceding happy period of quietness. The two loved one another almost to the exclusion of anyone else, and when Mary was incarcerated Lamb suffered intensely from loneliness as well as anxiety. He wrote to Sara Hutchinson in 1815 to tell her that Mary was ill once again, saying that such an interlude 'cuts sad great slices out of the time, the little time we shall have to live together'. In an attempt at cheerfulness, he continued:

I will imagine us immortal, or forget that we are otherwise; by God's blessing in a few weeks we may be making our meal together, or sitting in the front row of the Pit at Drury Lane, or taking our evening walk past the theatres, to look at the outside of them at least, if not to be tempted in. Then we forget we are assailable, we are strong for the time as rocks, the wind is tempered to the shorn Lambs.[28]

Like Lamb and Haydon, John Keats too had moved lodgings soon before the Immortal Dinner. The previous year had been a watershed in his life. By the summer of 1816 he had decided to abandon the profession of medicine, for which he was about to qualify, in order to devote himself entirely to the pursuit of poetry. He saw the poet's role as also one of healing, pouring out 'a balm upon the world'. When the examination for membership of the Royal College of Surgeons came up in February 1817, he did not sit it, although he continued to work at Guy's Hospital and St Thomas's for some months. He was pleased to leave his dismal lodgings in Southwark, which, though convenient for his hospital work, he found to be in 'a beastly place in dirt, turnings and windings',[29] and found rooms instead in the house of the local postman at 1 Well Walk, Hampstead, just large enough for himself and his brothers George and Tom. After Southwark, Hampstead appeared as a paradise of light, air and rural surroundings, with a lovely vista from the brothers' sitting-room window up an avenue of lime trees directly to the Heath. At first everything remained delightful, but with the coming of winter Keats began to find the noise of his landlord's children an increasing irritation, and he was depressed by the pervasive smell of drying underclothes and worsted stockings. An added inconvenience was having to share one small bedroom with George and Tom – hardly an ideal arrangement for one whose temperament necessitated peace and space.

11. The Upper Flask, Hampstead, *c.*1800. The name derives from a time when flasks were available at the old Flask Inn for filling with pure water from the Hampstead wells.

During the autumn of 1816 Keats had met Leigh Hunt, the poet and editor, who lived in the Vale of Health at Hampstead, where his cottage had become a meeting place for most of the young literary figures of the day. Among these were Shelley and the great critic and essayist William Hazlitt, admired for his acute literary perception, an admiration in which Keats soon joined. Hunt immediately took to Keats and quickly introduced him to many of those who were to become his closest friends. Foremost among these was Haydon, who was staying in Hampstead in order to rest his eyes, which had been causing him a good deal of anxiety, and spending much of his time at Hunt's. He and Keats began to see each other frequently, and a warm friendship developed between them. On 31 October, his twenty-first birthday, Keats wrote to a friend about an impending visit to Haydon's studio: 'I shall be as punctual as the Bee to the Clover – very glad am I at the thought of seeing so soon this glorious Haydon and all his Creation.'[30] For his part, Haydon had been immediately aware of his new friend's potential, forming, he said, a very high idea of his genius, and noting in his diary that he was 'the only man I ever met with who seemed and looked conscious of a high calling and is resolved to sacrifice his life or attain it, except Wordsworth', adding disarmingly, 'but Keats is more of my own age'.[31] Wordsworth at this time was forty-six and Haydon thirty-one. Keats soon fell into the way of calling on Haydon after he had finished his day's work at Guy's, and long talks went on deep into the night. After one of these evenings, 19 November 1816, Keats wrote the sonnet, 'Great spirits now on earth are sojourning', which he sent round to Haydon with a note: 'Last evening wrought me up, and I cannot forbear sending you the following. Yours imperfectly, John Keats.'

> Great spirits now on earth are sojourning;
>   He of the cloud, the cataract, the lake,
>   Who on Helvellyn's summit wide awake,
> Catches his freshness from Archangel's wing:
> He of the rose, the violet, the spring,
>   The social smile, the chain for Freedom's sake:
>   And lo! – whose steadfastness would never take
> A meaner sound than Raphael's whispering.
> And other spirits there are standing apart
>   Upon the forehead of the age to come;
> These, these will give the world another heart,
>   And other pulses. Hear ye not the hum
> Of mighty workings in a distant mart?
>   Listen awhile ye nations, and be dumb.[32]

'He of the cloud, the cataract, the lake' was, of course, Wordsworth; 'He of the rose' Leigh Hunt, and he who listened to

Raphael's whispering was Haydon himself. Haydon was so impressed that he told Keats, to the latter's delight, that he would show the sonnet to Wordsworth. Haydon suggested that the penultimate line should end after 'workings' – an alteration which Keats adopted. In the event Haydon did not send the poem to the older poet until 31 December, when he enclosed a persuasive letter:

I copy out a sonnet by a young poet, Keats, addressed to me, but beginning with you. I should wish very much to know what you think of it. He promises a great deal, and said in a letter to me, when I said I should enclose it to you, 'The idea of your sending it to Wordsworth puts me out of breath; you know with what reverence I should send my well-wishes to him.' He is quite a youth, full of eagerness and enthusiasm, and what greatly recommends him to me, he has a very fine head! . . . I need not say his reverence for you, my dear Sir, is unbounded.[33]

Wordsworth replied in a tone of guarded appreciation:

. . . your account of young Keats interests me not a little; and the sonnet appears to be of good promise, of course neither you nor I being so highly complimented in the composition can be deemed judges altogether impartial – but it is assuredly vigorously conceived and well expressed . . .[34]

Leigh Hunt and his brother, imprisoned for libel, had been sent to separate prisons, to make their task as editors of the *Examiner* more difficult or prevent the journal appearing at all. Leigh Hunt's cell in Horsemonger Lane Gaol became a place of pilgrimage for his friends and admirers. 'Cell' is not exactly the appropriate word for his apartment of two rooms, where he was allowed to install his family and which he decorated as a bower of beauty, containing a piano, pictures, bookcases and busts. Venetian blinds concealed the window bars and there was even a little garden. Haydon visited him frequently, on one occasion bringing one of his huge canvases to show the prisoner; and the Lambs were also stalwart friends, turning up in even the worst of the bitter weather of 1814 with little presents and many jokes. Hunt continued to edit the *Examiner* from prison, until his release in 1815. During that time he never moderated his tone. Keats, whose views were becoming increasingly radical, looked on Hunt in the light of this glamorous background as something of a hero, and was flattered by his friendship, spending much time with him in the Vale of Health cottage. Initially he was influenced by Hunt's ideas and style, but as his own developed and his confidence grew, the relationship began to cloy and he gradually detached himself from what he felt to be a somewhat over-intrusive intimacy.

During the winter of 1816–17 Keats began to collect together his poems, including 'On First Looking into Chapman's Homer', which had been generated by an evening spent with Charles Cowden Clarke, the son of his old headmaster. Cowden Clarke had invited Keats to come and see a 1616 folio edition of George Chapman's translation of Homer lent to him by the *Times* journalist Thomas Alsager. The result was electrifying. As the two read their way through some of the most famous passages, Keats's excitement increased, and at the shipwreck of Ulysses he rewarded Clarke with one of his 'delighted stares'.[35] In contrast to such privileged writers as Wordsworth, with a background of a university education in the classics, access to such works for Keats was rare, an unattainable luxury for one on a tiny budget, and consequently the impact of this evening was all the more acute. The reading continued until it was almost light, but by ten o'clock the same morning, when Cowden Clarke, who was staying in London with friends, came down to breakfast, he found the completed sonnet lying on the table.

This formed the highlight of Keats's small volume, *Poems (1817)*, which was published by the Ollier brothers on 3 March 1817, in spite of Shelley having cautioned against the dangers of a premature appearance in print. It was bound in grey boards, the frontispiece carried an engraving of Shakespeare's head with a quotation beneath from Spenser, and it was priced at six shillings – a copy in fair condition today would be expected to fetch about £10,000. Haydon gave a celebratory party in his painting room to honour the young poet, and Keats himself took the first copy up to the Vale of Health to show Leigh Hunt. The two spent an evening in Hunt's garden, drinking, versifying and crowning each other with laurel and ivy wreaths. When two ladies called unexpectedly Hunt had the presence of mind to snatch off his wreath, but Keats defiantly retained his, though feeling foolish and humiliated.

Keats's friends had been supportive and full of congratulations, and were distressed at the scant general interest excited by the little volume. Cowden Clarke remembered how they had all expected that the poems would create a sensation in the literary world, but 'Alas! the book might have emerged in Timbuctoo with far stronger chance of fame and approbation.'[36] Few copies were sold and after a while the publishers disposed of remainders and loose sheets to a bookseller who bundled these together and offered them for a few pence each.

Meanwhile Keats was already working on a new and ambitious project, which would become the now little-read *Endymion*. This task overshadowed most of the rest of 1817, and involved him in long exhausting periods of concentrated work, during which he became dismayingly aware that his hope of achieving a masterpiece was not to be realized. He spent most of his time moving from place to place, hoping for inspiration. He received a reassuring letter from Haydon, urging him not to give way to forebodings:

They are nothing more than the over-eager anxieties of a great spirit stretched beyond its strength, and then relapsing for a time to languid inefficiency. Trust in God with all your might, my dear Keats. This dependence, with your own energy, will give you strength, and hope, and comfort. Do not despair; collect incident, study character, read Shakespeare, and trust in Providence, and you *will* do, you must.[37]

Keats did not share Haydon's Christian faith, but he thanked him for his concern:

I remember your saying that you had notions of a good Genius presiding over you – I have of late had the same thought, for things which I do half at random are afterwards confirmed by my judgment in a dozen features of propriety – Is it too daring to fancy Shakespeare this Presider? When in the Isle of Wight I met with a Shakespeare in the passage of the house at which I lodged – it comes nearer to my idea of him than any I have seen – I was but there a week yet the old woman made me take it with me though I went off in a hurry – Do you not think this is ominous of good? I am glad you say every man of great views is at times tormented as I am.

He went on to tell his friend how difficult he found it to remain sanguine, feeling himself to be plagued by 'a horrid morbidity of temperament which has shown itself at intervals – it is I have no doubt the greatest enemy and stumbling block I have to fear' – but he was grateful for Haydon's affection, which comforted him in his periods of darkness: 'I am very sure that you do love me as your own Brother – I have seen it in your continual anxiety for me – and I assure you that your welfare and fame is and will be a chief pleasure to me all my life . . . Your everlasting friend John Keats.'[38]

One light-hearted holiday encounter during this time was with Mrs Isabella Jones, a young woman of about his own age, or so he thought, a rather mysterious figure whose presence brought him the very tonic he needed. Isabella Jones was with an elderly Irish peer, Donat O'Callaghan, in what capacity is not clear. She was widely read, lively and intelligent, and was attracted to the young poet, who soon found that he had 'warmed to her and kissed her'. Keats wrote her a poem whose tone does not suggest anything more than a mild flirtation:

> You say you love; but with a voice
> Chaster than a nun's, who singeth
> The soft vespers to herself
> While the chime-bell ringeth –
> O love me truly!
>
> You say you love; but then your lips
> Coral tinted teach no blisses,
> More than coral in the sea –
> They never pout for kisses –
> O love me truly![39]

Isabella Jones appeared again in Keats's life eighteen months later, when they met by chance in a London street. She took him back to her lodgings, but gently repulsed his tentative advances. Their friendship continued, however, and she had a role to play in his life, showing kindness to Tom, and suggesting subjects for Keats's later poems, most notably that of *The Eve of St Agnes*.

During his holiday Keats wrote a tenderly affectionate letter to his fourteen-year-old sister Fanny, who was away at school and, in the holidays, kept closely by her guardian, Richard Abbey. Keats's father had been killed in a riding accident in 1804 when his eldest son was nine, and his wife died six years later. The burden of the little family, John's two younger brothers George and Tom, his little sister Fanny, and their

mother, already ill with tuberculosis, devolved to a large
extent upon John's shoulders. He was fiercely protective of
his mother and would not let anyone but himself look after
her and procure her medicines. After her death the family fell
under the control of their grandmother's trustee, Richard
Abbey, and his wife. Keats found Abbey obstructionist in all
his suggested plans, most especially over the question of his
abandoning the fruits of his long apprenticeship to an apothecary, and his later medical training at Guy's, in order to
concentrate solely on writing poetry. It is not difficult to
understand the reluctance of a trustee in such circumstances.
Mr and Mrs Abbey both disapproved of the Keats boys and
made it difficult for them to see their sister, whom they kept
strictly under their supervision, and this was much resented
by Keats. He reported that Mrs Abbey considered 'that the
Keatses were ever indolent – that they would ever be so and
that it was born in them – Well, whispered Fanny to me "If
it is born with us how can we help it." '[40] Keats felt an anxious
responsibility for his orphan sister's welfare and happiness, and
was unhappy at her circumstances. The end of his September
letter looks forward to a future together:

Now Fanny you must write soon – and write all you think about,
never mind what – only let me have a good deal of your writing –
You need not do it all at once – be two or three or four days about
it, and let it be a diary of your little life. You will preserve all my
letters and I will secure yours – and thus in the course of time we
shall each of us have a good bundle – which, hereafter, when things
may have strangely altered and god knows what happened, we may
read over together and look with pleasure on times past – that are
now to come.[41]

But these times were never to be.

Having nursed his mother through her last illness, the

spectre of tuberculosis was never far from Keats's thoughts, and now his brother Tom's health was becoming a matter for concern: ominously he was spitting blood, although Keats tried to conceal the reality of the condition as long as he could. He himself had also been troubled for some time with sore throats, which he found difficult to throw off, and he tried for a while to avoid going out on wet evenings. He may have had other health problems: he was dosing himself with small amounts of mercury, a specific for venereal disease among other complaints. He thought of trying to ship Tom off to Lisbon, to winter in a better climate, but nothing came of the scheme, partly because of the brothers' lack of funds. Instead, George and Tom set off for Teignmouth in Devon on 14 December, leaving Keats relieved for the present of the full burden of responsibility. With the strain of the first draft of *Endymion* safely behind him, and his brothers for the moment away, he now felt the need for relaxation and society, and embarked on a frenetic social round.

Before that, a few days after saying farewell to George and Tom, and two weeks before Haydon's dinner, Keats first met Wordsworth. Tom Monkhouse arranged the encounter, which took place in his house in Queen Anne Street. Haydon and Keats walked there together, Keats tense with tremulous anticipation. Wordsworth's *The Excursion* seemed to him one of the 'three things to rejoice at in this Age'[42] – the other two being Haydon's paintings and Hazlitt's 'depth of taste' – and the idea of now meeting its creator face to face was awe-inspiring. Haydon recalled the occasion:

When Wordsworth came to town, I brought Keats to him, by his, Wordsworth's, request – Keats expressed to me as we walked to Queen Anne Street East where Mr Monkhouse lodged, the greatest, the purest, the most unalloyed pleasure at the prospect. Wordsworth received him kindly, and after a few minutes, Wordsworth asked him what he had been lately doing, *I* said he has just finished an exquisite ode to Pan – and as he had not a copy I begged Keats to repeat it – which he did in his usual half chant (most touching), walking up and down the room – when he had done I felt really, as if I had heard a young Apollo – Wordsworth drily said 'a very pretty piece of Paganism'. This was unfeeling, and unworthy of his high genius to a young worshipper like Keats – and Keats felt it *deeply* . . . and though he dined with Wordsworth after at my table – he never forgave him.[43]

Haydon was the only witness of this incident, which he did not write down until twenty-eight years later, shortly before his death, when his memory was distorted by increasing paranoia, so that it is difficult to know how much to rely on what he said occurred. There is no contemporary evidence to suggest that Keats was wounded by Wordsworth's manner. Much of the force of the anecdote depends, too, on the intonation that was given to 'pretty': at that date it often carried a complimentary emphasis, rather than the mildly derogatory sense with which it is now associated. He recited it in Wordsworth's presence again during the Immortal Dinner less than a fortnight later, and the two met on several further occasions before Wordsworth returned to Rydal Mount in the middle of January: on 31 December they saw each other on Hampstead Heath; on 3 January Keats called on Wordsworth in Mortimer Street; and on 5 January he dined with him there – a programme that hardly suggests any sense of grievance or hurt.

Almost immediately after meeting Wordsworth, Keats accepted an invitation to dine with Horace Smith, author with his brother James of *Rejected Addresses*, parodies of various well-known contemporary poets' styles which had become an overnight success when published in 1812. Thomas Hill, gossipy book collector and bon vivant who liked to feel himself a member of the fashionable literary world, was also at dinner, as were Horace Smith's brothers and John Kingston, the Deputy Comptroller of the Stamp Office who was later to figure as the butt of Lamb's ridicule at Haydon's dinner. Keats did not like the company. Such men convinced him, he told his brothers, 'how superior humour is to wit in respect to enjoyment':

These men say things which make one start, without making one feel, they are all alike; their manners are alike; they all know fashionables; they have a mannerism in their very eating and drinking, in their mere handling a decanter – They talked of Kean and his low company – Would I were with that company instead of yours said I to myself![44]

Keats found a cheerful dining club of middle-class young men who met on Saturdays far more congenial. They taught him some Regency slang:

I am getting initiated into a little cant – they call drinking deep dying scarlet, and when you breathe in your watering they bid you cry hem and play it off – they call a good wine a pretty tipple, and call getting a child knocking out an apple – stopping at a tavern they call hanging out – Where do you sup? is where do you hang out?[45]

About now he gave a little party himself, entertaining his friends Joseph Severn and Charles Wells; a good deal of claret was drunk and they all 'got very witty and full of Rhyme – we played a Concert from four o'clock till 10'.[46] This concert was an affair of imitating musical instruments with their voices, which the young men enjoyed and felt to be exquisitely funny.

After all these parties, and in the pleasant sense of détente brought by the completion of the first draft of *Endymion*, Keats was able to set off for Haydon's dinner in the early afternoon of 28 December in a light-hearted frame of mind. Hampstead in 1817 still kept the characteristics of a village, with a scattering of grand villas such as the early eighteenth-century Burgh House with its handsome wrought-iron gates in Well Walk itself, Fenton House in the Grove, and Frognal Grove with its celebrated lime walk. Most Hampstead dwellers were there to escape from the fogs and damp of London, and to benefit their health – Pond Street, which Keats would have crossed on his way south, was mostly lived in by doctors, who could make good livings by looking after these immigrants who had left it rather late to move out from the noxious atmosphere of the Thames and its surrounding congeries of warren-like streets. The villages on the approach to the city were beginning to increase in size and amalgamate, although for the most part Keats's walk still lay across fields and woods and along small lanes. As he approached the outskirts of the city this peaceful countryside presently gave way to market gardens, rapidly increasing in number as London spread and demand increased for fruit and vegetables. Artisans' workshops and little factories were springing up everywhere to supply the city's growing need for such wares as china, bricks, soap and chairs.

For this pleasant journey Keats would have worn a loosely fitted dark jacket, with slightly padded shoulders and cuffs whose wide turn-backs were fastened with two large buttons, the whole topped with his heavy greatcoat against the cold night air. Gas street lighting had not yet reached the areas of semi-suburbia he passed through as he neared Lisson Grove, and he would have needed to carry a lantern for the long journey back home in the dark at the end of the party. Arriving at Haydon's house in the already fading light of the winter afternoon, the young man stepped into the warmth of a bright fire and of his host's welcome.

3. The Guests Assemble

On December 28th the immortal dinner came off in my painting
room, with *Jerusalem* towering up behind us as a background.
Wordsworth was in fine cue, and we had a glorious set-to – on
Homer, Shakespeare, Milton and Virgil. Lamb got exceedingly
merry and exquisitely witty; and his fun in the midst of
Wordsworth's solemn intonations of oratory was like the sarcasm
and wit of the fool in the intervals of Lear's passion. He made a
speech and voted me absent, and made them drink my health.

Benjamin Robert Haydon, *Autobiography*[1]

Dinner on that last Sunday of December took place in
Haydon's painting room, which was light and airy, and, compared with the congestion of his old studio, palatial in dimension, being a good thirty foot long by twenty wide, with a
height of fifteen foot, allowing his largest canvases to be
accommodated without difficulty. A fire burnt throughout
the afternoon and evening, and above the diners hung the
host's work in progress, the enormous painting depicting
Christ's triumphal entry into Jerusalem. Haydon's working
table was covered with a white tablecloth and was meticulously
set, something necessary for the host's self-respect, and in line
with the almost obsessive nature of his attention to detail in
his paintings. He insisted that things must always be in a state
of perfect readiness for receiving such a grandee as Lord
Egremont. Haydon was proud of his silver spoons and forks,
and had had a falling out with Leigh Hunt over Hunt's wife's

failure to return the tableware after borrowing it for a dinner of her own, one consequence of this angry interchange being the exclusion of Hunt from the present party.

A famous example of his disgust at the absence of order and precision was that of a christening party given by the Hazlitts in April 1813, where all was chaos and discomfort, as Haydon indignantly recorded in his diary:

I dined on Friday last with a man of genius, William Hazlitt. His child was to be christened, and I was desired to be there punctually at four. At four I came, but he was out! his wife ill by the fire, nothing ready, and all wearing the appearance of neglect and indifference. At last home he came, the cloth began to cover the table, and then followed a plate with a dozen large, waxen, cold, clayy, slaty potatoes. Down they were set, and down we sat also: a young mathematician, who whenever he spoke, jerked up one side of his mouth, and closed an eye as if seized with a paralytic affection; an old lady of genius with torn ruffles; his wife in an influenza, thin, pale and spitty; and his chubby child, squalling, obstinate, and half-cleaned. After waiting a little all looking forlornly at the potatoes for fear they might be the chief dish, in issued a bit of overdone beef, burnt, toppling about on seven or eight corners, with a great bone sticking out like a battering ram; the great difficulty was to make it stand upright! But the greater to discover a *cuttable* place, for all was jagged, jutting, and irregular. Like a true genius, he forgot to go for a parson to christen his child, till it was so late that every parson was out or occupied, so his child was not christened. I soon retired, for tho' beastliness and indifference to the common comforts of life may amuse for a time, they soon weary and disgust those who prefer attentions and cleanliness.[2]

William Bewick remembered being taken by his master to see Hazlitt in his house in York Street, Westminster, once lived in by Milton. He was overawed at the idea of sitting in the very room 'where he probably hymned and sung of Paradise'; but surprised at its present state of chaos and the absence of furniture. He noticed that, over the mantelpiece, instead of a picture or looking-glass Hazlitt had written in a 'good bold hand' and as high up as he could reach and covering the whole space:

all manner of odd conceits (as they appeared to be), of abbreviations – words – names – enigmatical exclamations – strange and weird sentences, quotations – snatches of rhyme – bits of arithmetical calculations – scraps of Latin– French expressions – words or signs by which the author might spin a chapter, or weave an elaborate essay. The chimneypiece seemed to be his table of mnemonics – his sacred hieroglyphics – all jotted down without line, or form of any kind, some horizontal, some running up to the right, some down to the left, and some obliquely. They seemed thoughts and indications of things to be remembered, put down on the instant, and I concluded that this room might not be his study, but his living room.[3]

As Haydon's guests settled themselves at his dining table they made a disparate group. The host himself was as usual wearing his hair *à la* Raphael, parting it and letting it fall towards his shoulders – although not very far towards, according to portraits of him at the time, which show his hair already wispy and receding fast – with his shirt collar open and a velvet cap, also in imitation of the Master, perched on top of his head. His friends described his eyes as brilliant, penetrating but hooded; his legs rather short, the general appearance stocky, but with neat small feet. There are a number of surviving portraits, showing a baffling dissimilarity between his fine and sensitive profile view and the more aggressive full face with its bull-neck and strong square jaw.

Wordsworth, at forty-seven the oldest, was also the tallest of the group, standing at a precise five foot nine and five-eighths inches – measurements recorded by Haydon in his diary – and easily the most imposing figure present. Despite anxiety over his eyes, complaints about headaches and so forth, he was also without doubt the fittest, having climbed Skiddaw twice the previous summer without noticing any diminution of the vigour and strength of his youth. William Hazlitt described him as he appeared at their first meeting in 1798, just as the poet was concluding *Lyrical Ballads*, as looking more Don Quixote-like than he had expected. He noted

a severe, worn pressure of thought about his temples, a fire in his eye (as if he saw something in objects more than the outward appearance), an intense high narrow forehead, a Roman nose, cheeks furrowed by strong purpose and feeling, and a convulsive inclination to laughter about the mouth, a good deal at variance with the solemn, stately expression of the rest of his face.[4]

Writing about him in *The Spirit of the Age*, Hazlitt was reminded of one of Holbein's heads: 'grave, saturnine, with a slight indication of sly humour, kept under by the manners of the age or by the pretensions of the person. He has a peculiar sweetness in his smile, and great depth and manliness and a rugged harmony, in the tones of his voice.'[5] Wordsworth's most characteristic attitude was to sit with one hand thrust into his waistcoat, and no doubt this was how he bore himself at Haydon's party. Most observers remarked on the poet's eyes. Thomas De Quincey found them to be

not, under any circumstances, bright, lustrous or piercing; but, after a long day's toil in walking, I have seen them assume an appearance the most solemn and spiritual that it is possible for the human eye to wear. The light which resides in them is at no time a superficial light; but, under favourable accidents, it is a light which seems to come from depths below all depths; in fact, it is more truly entitled to be held 'The light that never was on land or sea',[6] a light radiating from some far spiritual world, than any the most idealizing light that ever yet a painter's hand created.[7]

Charles Lamb presented a strange contrast to his friend. His large and noble head was perched on a disproportionately tiny body, ending in little legs and feet, which looked unlikely to be able to support their burden. He was always dressed in the same way: until 1817 in a snuff-coloured outfit, which soon after he changed for a rusty black to which he remained faithful for the rest of his life. He always kept to long clerical-like gaiters, knee breeches and coat, all of an outmoded design. Leigh Hunt described his features as strong yet delicately cut in a face that carried great marks of feeling and thought; and all his friends commented on the special sweetness of his expression. He had a good deal of curly brown hair, dark skin, a high intellectual forehead and soft brown eyes which sometimes twinkled but in repose were more characteristically sad.

The French critic, Philarète Chasles, left a sympathetic portrait of Lamb:

I was at James Valpy's one evening in June, 1818, in his office where the candle must be lit at mid-day, and the fire in June, when a little, dark, old fellow came in; one could only distinguish a head, then big shoulders, then a delicate body, and finally two artistically slender legs, which were almost imperceptible. Under his arm was a green umbrella, and over his eyes a very old hat. Wit, sweetness, melancholy, and gaiety gushed in torrents from this extraordinary physiognomy. After first seeing him, you did not think any more of his ridiculous body; it seemed as if something purely intellectual was before you, soaring above matter, burning through the material form, like light, and overflowing everywhere.[8]

12. Charles Lamb working at his clerk's desk in East India House, inscribed in his hand 'Yours ratherish unwell, Chs Lamb'. From a contemporary engraving.

Yours ratherish unwell
Chs Lamb

Hazlitt described Lamb's head as a fine Titian head, and had earlier painted a portrait of him in a velvet Titian outfit, in keeping with the current craze for historical dressing-up. Like Haydon, Lamb found it difficult to keep still, and was inclined to walk up and down the room as he talked, seldom looking directly at the person he was addressing. He suffered from a slight stammer, and the delivery of his puns and jokes was further pointed by this impediment. Few of the recorded puns come to life for a modern reader but he was famous for them during his life, although even then they did grate on some. Henry Crabb Robinson often missed their point, and Keats spoke of them as atrocious.

Lamb smoked or took snuff continuously, in spite of his sister Mary's efforts to wean him from the habit, and guests at his regular Thursday evenings seldom saw him without snuff box or pipe in his hand. All these evenings, at one period of their lives on Wednesdays, at another Thursdays, ran to the same pattern, with fairly serious whist, presently giving way to general conversation. Refreshments, because of brother and sister's necessarily frugal habits, were simple, consisting of cold meats and large bowls of steaming hot potatoes. There might be just cold mutton, or in season the addition of a cold pheasant, a gift from a friend, or some venison, of which Charles was fond, or occasionally meat pies. Veal pie was a favourite. Mary was always at hand, urging people to help themselves to whatever they needed. Large jugs of porter accompanied the supper, and later in the evening hot water and gin and brandy were brought in. But the talk was what people had really come for. Charles did not like political discussion on these occasions, and if such a topic was raised he would kill it by not responding. There were a lot of jokes, some of them made by Charles at Mary's expense, after which he would suddenly jump to his feet and slap her on the shoulder, but much serious discussion as well. Hazlitt, remembering these famous evenings later on, wrote of Lamb as

the most delightful, the most provoking, the most witty and sensible of men. He always made the best pun and the best remark in the course of the evening. His serious conversation, like his serious writing, is his best. No one ever stammered out such fine, piquant, deep eloquent things in half a dozen half-sentences as he does. His jests scald like tears: and he proves a question with a play upon words. What a keen, laughing, hare-brained vein of home-felt truth![9]

Like Lamb, Keats was physically small, only just over five feet high, but of a more robust physique than his senior, with exceptionally broad shoulders. He tried to give an impression of greater height – a matter about which he was sensitive – by an erect carriage and by leaning slightly backwards. Before he was stricken by tuberculosis he was athletic and strong, with no resemblance to the pale effete poet of legend. He had rich auburn curly hair, which he wore rather long. About the time of Haydon's dinner he had been seen in what was described as a naval outfit, probably a dark jacket with gold buttons. All accounts of the poet's appearance focus on his expressive eyes, large, dark and sensitive and constantly changing with his mood. Haydon thought they had 'an inward look perfectly divine, like a Delphian priestess who saw visions'.[10]

Everyone agreed on the sweetness of Tom Monkhouse's nature, and Lamb spoke of his 'noble friendly face'. He wrote to Wordsworth of his sense of loss at his friend's early death: 'Monkhouse was a character I learned to love slowly, but it grew upon me, yearly, monthly, daily. What a chasm has it made in our pleasant parties!'[11]

The diners' accents were also widely varied. Hazlitt described Wordsworth as talking 'with a mixture of clear gushing accents in his voice, a deep guttural intonation, and a strong tincture of the northern *burr*, like the crust on wine'.[12] He would have pronounced *waters* to rhyme with *chatters*. Both Lamb and Keats were cockneys, but Keats's accent also had West Country inflections inherited from his father. Haydon's intonation matched his Devonshire origin, and Monkhouse came from Wales. Haydon once teased David Wilkie about his Scottish accent, and in return Wilkie imitated Haydon's Devonshire lilt: 'Well, and *yew tew* are *Devonsheere*, and fancy, like Northcote, that you speak pure English.'[13] And Leigh Hunt teasingly called Keats 'Junkets', in mimicry of his clipped way of pronouncing his name, a vivid and somehow surprising hint at how the poet must have sounded.

Haydon would not have provided his guests with the

enormous range of dishes customary at more luxurious dinner tables of the day, but there would certainly have been two courses. A course at that time meant a table spread with a large number of different dishes, as many as fifty for a grand dinner party, ready for diners to help themselves and their neighbours as they wished. The first course inevitably included tureens of soup, one set at either end of the table, and removed when people began to turn to the more serious part of the fare, including roast joints, whole fishes, meat pies and vegetables. The joint would have been set down in front of the host, who would be expected to do the carving. The soups usually included a well-flavoured consommé, and, for the lucky few, sometimes the great luxury of real turtle soup made from live turtles. These might weigh from sixty to 100 pounds and were brought from the West Indies in freshwater tanks. They were advertised ahead of their arrival at the docks and also in the newspapers, with size and weight and condition specified, ready for auction. But most people had to make do with mock turtle soup concocted from a calf's head liberally laced with madeira. The main fish dish would probably have been salmon, surprisingly inexpensive; oysters were also cheap and plentiful, as were eels, and sometimes lobsters and little crabs.

When people had taken all they wanted of this first course, the dishes were removed and a second course, the 'remove', set to replace the first, a manoeuvre which took some time. The new course was still a substantial affair, with pheasants, hares, partridges or other game, generally a gift from a land-owning friend, from whose property it would have come; savoury dishes made with such ingredients as sweetbreads, tongue, little mushrooms; and small meat patties. At this stage the desserts were also spread out: ornamental jellies, floating islands, blancmanges, 'jaune manges' and other 'soft' dishes and creams, often together with more elaborate concoctions bought in from pastry-cooks, although these last were expensive.

After Waterloo, when it was possible once more to travel with ease on the Continent, some grand hostesses began to copy the Parisian serving of dinner *à la russe*, that is to say in much the same manner as is still often the custom, with the food handed round to the diners. The food kept hotter, but the new fashion meant more hired hands to help with the service. This fresh idea took a good while to permeate society, and it is unlikely that Haydon would have departed from the convention of the two courses, ending with a dessert of fruit and nuts, and with a longish gap between the courses as Corporal Sammons and his assistants reorganized the table. Because it was only three days after Christmas, turkey would probably have formed part of the menu, or the traditional goose pie usually served on Boxing Day. Mince pies were popular Christmas fare, made with a mixture of meat and sweet ingredients; and of course plum pudding, always spelt *plumb* by Charles Lamb: 'I think it reads fatter and more suetty.'[14] Although these menus sound excessive, it should be remembered that the idea of luncheon (or nuncheon) was only just beginning, primarily as a snack for bored ladies to break up the long morning hours. But for most people, dinner in the late afternoon was the first meal since breakfast.

Lamb was the great gourmet of the party. Wordsworth did not take much interest in what he was given to eat, and his home fare, even when the family had moved to Rydal Mount and money was less tight than it had been, was kept plain and economical by Mary and Dorothy, both firm believers in the benefits of the simple life. The Wordsworth family supper in the early days had typically consisted of small basins of new milk and pieces of bread. In the first Dove Cottage years, when Dorothy had kept house for her brother, Wordsworth tended to allow her amateur attempts at providing nourishing dishes to stand while he composed a poem, regardless of the food growing cold and spoiling in front of him. Dorothy used to bake bread made with oats or barley, or occasionally wheat given by friendly neighbours; other presents of provisions included tea from John Wordsworth, their sailor brother, a barrel of flour, honey, a turkey, a calf's head, pork, giblets for a savoury pie, apple pie, gooseberry pie and a hare. And Dorothy sometimes made hasty pudding, an unappetizing gruel of oatmeal boiled in salted water. Wordsworth's dyspepsia and stomach pains stemmed, not surprisingly, from these Dove Cottage menus. But his appetite was also inclined to fluctuate with the state of his ability to compose verse.

Keats wrote to his brother George and George's wife Georgiana, now emigrated to America, about his enjoyment of the breast of a partridge, the back of a hare, the backbone of a grouse, the wing and side of a pheasant, and a woodcock, but these were seasonal and rare treats, and for the most part he took little interest in food. But claret was another matter: '. . . now I like claret, whenever I can have claret I must drink it.' He wrote in the same letter:

'tis the only palate affair that I am at all sensual in – 'tis so fine – it fills one's mouth with a gushing freshness – then goes down cool and feverless – then you do not feel it quarrelling with your liver – no it is rather a peace maker and lies as quiet as it did in the grape – then it is as fragrant as the queen bee; and the more ethereal part of it mounts into the brain, not assaulting the cerebral apartments like a bully in a bad house looking for his trull and hurrying from door to door bouncing against the waist-coat; but rather walks like Aladdin about his own enchanted palace so gently that you do not feel his step – Other wines of a heavy and spirituous nature transform a man to a Silenus; this makes him a Hermes.[15]

Haydon reported disapprovingly in his diary that Keats once 'covered his tongue and throat as far as he could reach with cayenne pepper, in order as he said to have the "delicious coolness of claret in all its glory"'.[16]

Keats's eulogy to claret is matched in Lamb's case with musings of a lyrical, even an ecstatic, nature on fine food. In his Elia essay, the 'Dissertation on Roast Pig', he insists that a suckling pig must be roasted, because

There is no flavour comparable, I will contend, to that of the crisp, tawny, well-watched, not over-roasted, crackling, as it is well called – the very teeth are invited to their share of the pleasure of this banquet in overcoming the coy, brittle resistance – with the adhesive oleaginous – O call it not fat – but an indefinable sweetness growing up to it – the tender blossoming of fat – fat cropped in the bud – taken in the shoot – in the first innocence – the cream and quintessence of the child-pig's yet pure food – the lean, no lean, but a kind of animal manna, or, rather, fat and lean (if it must be so) so blended and running into each other, that both together make but one ambrosian result or common substance.

Then, moving on to the question of the piglet's sauce,

Decidedly a few bread crumbs done up with his liver and brains, and a dash of mild sage. But banish, dear Mrs Cook, I beseech you, the whole onion tribe. Barbecue your whole hog to your palate, steep them in shalots, stuff them out with plantations of the rank and guilty garlic; and you cannot poison them, or make them stronger than they are – but consider, he is a weakling – a flower.[17]

The Lambs ate frugally when alone, but Lamb found great pleasure in writing with a lingering sensuous pleasure about the finer aspects of diet. 'I am no Quaker at my food,' he wrote in 'Grace before Meat':

Those unctuous morsels of deer's flesh were not made to be received with dispassionate services. I hate a man who swallows it, affecting not to know what he is eating . . . I shrink instinctively from one who professes to like minced veal. There is a physiognomical character in the tastes for food. C[oleridge] holds that a man cannot have a pure mind who refuses apple-dumplings.

He confessed to being 'impatient and querulous' if disappointed in his dinner: to arrive home, for instance, expecting 'some savoury mess' only to find one 'quite tasteless and sapidless. Butter ill melted – that commonest of kitchen failures – puts me beside my tenor.'[18] To his naval friend Charles Chambers he wrote a hymn to turbot:

With regard to a John Dory, which you desire to be particularly informed about – I honour the fish, but it is rather on account of Quin, who patronized it and whose taste (of a dead man) I had as lieve go by as any body's, Apicius and Heliogabalus excepted – this latter started nightingales' brains and peacocks' tongues as a garnish. Else, in itself, and trusting to my own poor single judgment, it hath not the moist, mellow, oleaginous, gliding, smooth descent from the tongue to the palate, thence to the stomach, etc., as your Brighton turbot hath, which I take to be the most friendly and familiar flavour of any that swims – most genial and at home to the palate.[19]

Louis Simond was interested in English domestic economy, but complained of the poor presentation of vegetables at English dinner parties: 'Vegetables are exhibited in all the simplicity of nature, like hay to horses, only a little boiled instead of dried.' He was interested in plum pudding, for which he gave a recipe, noting its useful capacity to improve with boiling, 'and this precious faculty of not suffering anything from waiting, has made it be named emphatically Hunter's Pudding, *Pudding de*

Chasseur. Simond noted that the wines generally served were 'port, high in colour, rough, and strong, madeira and sherry', but claret, burgundy and champagne were considered luxuries, the 'most usual drink during dinner was small-beer or sparkling ale, served in high-shaped glasses like champagne glasses'. Port was not fortified until much later in the century. And he admired the beauty of the 'crystal glasses called decanters'.[20] One aspect of a dinner party disgusted him:

Drinking much and long leads to unavoidable consequences. Will it be credited that, in a corner of the very dining room, there is a certain convenient piece of furniture, to be used by any body who wants it. The operation is performed very deliberately and undisguisedly, as a matter of course, and occasions no interruption of the conversation.[21]

Keats took a more robust view of this custom, writing to his brothers about a dance at Reddall the sword-cutler's when 'on proceeding to the pot in the cupboard it soon became full on which the court door was opened Frank Floodgate bawls out, Hoollo! here's an opposition pot – Ay, says Rice, in one you have a yard for your pot, and in the other a pot for your yard.'[22] Simond described another ritual of glasses of coloured water being placed before each diner at the end of the meal:

All (women as well as men) stoop over it, sucking up some of the water, and returning it, perhaps more than once, and, with a spitting and washing sort of noise, quite charming – the operation frequently assisted by a finger elegantly thrust into the mouth! This done, and the hands dipped also, the napkins, and sometimes the table-cloth, are used to wipe hand and mouth.[23]

An unpleasing picture: can it really have been true?
   A few years before Haydon's dinner, Robert Southey wrote

a study of contemporary customs under the guise of a fictional Spanish traveller, Don Manuel Alvarez Espriella. Espriella complained about the dishwashy English coffee, but praised the tea, 'made in a vessel of silver, or of a fine black porcelain: they do not use boiled milk with it, but cream instead in its fresh state, which renders it a very delightful beverage'.[24] He mentions the English insistence on excellence at their dinners:

Wherever you dine since peace has been concluded you see a Perigord pye; India supplies sauces and curry-powder; they have hams from Portugal and Westphalia; rein-deers tongues from Lapland; caviar from Russia; sausages from Bologna; macaroni from Naples; oil from Florence . . . Fish comes packed up in ice from Scotland for the London market, and the epicures here will not eat any mutton but what is killed in Wales. There is in this very morning's newspaper a notice from a shopkeeper in the Strand, offering to contract with any person who will send him game regularly from France, Norway or Russia.[25]

Southey's don is scathing about the quality of the table wines, but enjoys the soda water: 'the fixed air of which hisses as it goes down your throat as cutting as a razor, and draws tears as it comes up through the nose as pungent as a pinch of snuff . . . At great tables the wine stands in ice, and you keep your glass inverted in water.'[26]

Another observer of Regency life, Captain Gronow, thought little of the English 'mild but abortive' imitations of French dishes, was bored by the ubiquitous boiled potato and, like Louis Simond, complained about the vegetables, which, though the best in the world, appeared at table without sauce and frequently cold. After describing the shockingly rich consumption of both food and wine at the more aristocratic dinner parties, he commented wrily 'how all this sort of eating and drinking ended was obvious, from the prevalence of gout, and the necessity of every one making the pillbox their constant bedroom companion'.[27] George III's strategy to avoid overeating was to select one dish and stick to that only.[28] Then as now there were many diet fads, perhaps the nastiest being Byron's, which consisted of potatoes boiled in vinegar.[29] Haydon was subject to disabling dyspeptic attacks further exacerbated by anxiety, and his curious remedy was to keep to a regime of mutton chops and nothing else. On 14 June 1828, after one such attack, he reflected:

Feebly at work, but advanced. Buonaparte during the battle of Dresden, ate a tough leg of mutton. His digestion became deranged; and to his illness was attributed his subsequent misfortunes and loss of his campaign. This it is. Lord Castlereagh ate buttered toast, which encreased his disease, and he cut his throat an hour afterwards! – and the crust of a gooseberry pye has impeded these last three days the thinking of a still more illustrious individual, B. R. Haydon![30]

On 28 December 1817, however, Haydon's digestive system was in fine fettle as he prepared to enjoy his party and to listen to the post-prandial recitations of a relaxed Wordsworth and an excited and tremulously eager Keats. His omnivorous reading, his passion for books – 'my darling authors', as he called them – meant that at his party he was well able to compete on equal terms in any discussion on literary merit, even with such scholars as Lamb or Wordsworth. In spite of his concentration on his painting, Haydon had still found time to continue his studies so that he could write and speak in French and Italian, as well as having a good working knowledge of the classics. His passion was for Shakespeare, and on this occasion he can perhaps be thought of as being the Shakespearian apologist, Wordsworth the apostle of Milton, and Keats of Homer. Lamb, the most erudite of the assembled company, was able to contribute to the debate on all fronts.

The story of the evening as it proceeded to unroll is best described for the most part in Haydon's own words and with his sense of the occasion's high drama:

On 28th December, the immortal dinner came off in my painting room, with *Jerusalem* towering up behind us as a background. Wordsworth was in fine cue, and we had a glorious set-to – on Homer, Shakespeare, Milton and Virgil. Lamb got exceedingly merry and exquisitely witty; and his fun in the midst of Words-worth's solemn intonations of oratory was like the sarcasm and wit of the fool in the intervals of Lear's passion. He made a speech and voted me absent, and made them drink my health.

It was delightful to see the good humour of Wordsworth in giving in to all our frolics without affectation and laughing as heartily as the best of us.[31]

King Lear was Haydon's holy text. His first diary entry of all, in July 1808, had been about a pilgrimage he had made to Dover to find the cliff to which Gloucester had supposedly been led by Edgar. As he stood staring around him and picturing the scene, a terrific storm obligingly blew up, and Haydon at once imagined Lear on the heath raging against it. Later in his life, when things went badly and he felt himself to be wrongfully slighted, he probably thought of himself as Lear battling against terrible odds out in that storm. He always managed to avoid seeing the play performed, fearing it would distort his own private vision of it. And in the suicide note he left behind in 1846 he quoted, or misquoted rather, Kent on Lear's death: 'Stretch me no longer on this rough world.'

All accounts agree as to the powerful effect on his listeners of Wordsworth reciting Milton, and his performance at Haydon's party was evidently no exception. Some years before, Dorothy Wordsworth had recorded an occasion when she, with William and Mary and their children, spent a week or two in a cottage high above Little Langdale in the Lakes for the children to convalesce after bad attacks of whooping cough. The weather was perfect, and on the first morning after their arrival the little party sat on a rock to enjoy the sun and gaze around at the mountains, hamlets, woods, cottages and rocks while Wordsworth read part of the fifth book of *Paradise Lost* to them. Dorothy said that he read 'The Morning Hymn', as the mist slowly drifted upwards from the valley and melted away. 'It seemed,' she said, 'as if we had never before felt deeply the power of the poet.'[32] Here warmth, a sense of escape from what could so easily have been mortal illness, and the beauty of the surroundings to which the Wordsworths were so open, combined for Dorothy to enhance the impression of Milton's hymn. But in early December 1817, without any of these extraneous circumstances, Wordsworth had also made a deep impression on Haydon, as the poet sat for him shortly after his arrival in London for his portrait in *Christ's Entry*:

He read Milton and his Tintern Abbey and the happy Warrior, and some of his finest things. He is a most eloquent power . . . He sees his road and his object vividly and clearly and intensely, and never turns aside. In moral grandeur of soul and extension of scope, he is equal to Milton.[33]

Haydon later wrote of Mary Wordsworth as listening entranced while Wordsworth read out an altered passage in his 'Laodamia', 'moaning out the burthen of the line, like a distant echo. I never saw such a complete instance of devotion, of adoration.'[34]

Hazlitt, in 'My First Acquaintance with Poets', also described the impact of Wordsworth's mode of reading aloud:

13. Study of
Wordsworth for
*Christ's Entry into
Jerusalem* by
Benjamin Robert
Haydon, 1819.
Hazlitt considered
this image of the
poet 'the most like
his drooping weight
of thought and
expression'.

'There is a *chaunt* in the recitation both of Coleridge and
Wordsworth, which acts as a spell upon the hearer, and disarms
the judgment. Perhaps they have deceived themselves by
making habitual use of this ambiguous accompaniment.' Hazlitt described Coleridge's manner as 'more full, animated,
and varied' and Wordsworth's as 'more equable, sustained,
and internal. The one might be termed more *dramatic*, the
other more *lyrical*.' He said that Coleridge liked to compose
'in walking over uneven ground, or breaking through the
straggling branches of a copse-wood'; but Wordsworth preferred to write whenever possible 'walking up and down a
straight gravel-walk, or in some spot where the continuity of
his verse met with no collateral interruption'.[35] How well this
description accords with the characters of both poets.

Robert Southey was another poet who liked to compose in the Wordsworthian mode, walking straight up and down. The travel writer William Howitt remembered being told of a visitor to Southey's next-door neighbour, who exclaimed at hearing the mating, booming bitterns in the Laureate's garden. 'Bitterns!' replied his host; 'oh no; it is only Southey humming his verses in the garden walk.'[36]

In their early Dove Cottage years, Dorothy's journal recorded instances of Wordsworth reciting his own verse to her in his incantatory mood. The curious and almost erotic atmosphere of one such poem is, in its tone of mesmeric authority, reminiscent of Prospero's treatment of Miranda, or of one of the more benign spells of Merlin:

> This is the spot – how mildly does the sun
> Shine in between these fading leaves! the air
> In the habitual silence of this wood
> Is more than silent: and this bed of heath,
> Where shall we find so sweet a resting place?
> Come! – let me see thee sink into a dream
> Of quiet thoughts, – protracted till thine eye
> Be calm as water, when the winds are gone
> And no one can tell whither. – My sweet friend!
> We two have had such happy hours together
> That my heart melts in me to think of it.[37]

Dorothy herself used this piece to soothe her brother when he was overwrought after a struggle to compose, reading 'This is the spot' to him over and over again until he was calmed and she felt able to leave him.[38]

Hazlitt in *The Spirit of the Age* further described Wordsworth's appearance as he recited. His mocking tone here cannot obscure his impression of the poet's majestic presence:

His manner of reading his own poetry is particularly imposing; and in his favourite passages his eye beams with preternatural lustre, and the meaning labours slowly up from his swelling breast. No one who has seen him at these moments could go away with an impression that he was a 'man of no mark or likelihood'. Perhaps the comment of his face and voice is necessary to convey a full idea of his poetry. His language may not be intelligible; but his manner is not to be mistaken. It is clear that he is either mad or inspired . . . He shone most (because he seemed most roused and animated) in reciting his own poetry, or in talking about it . . . His standard of poetry is high and severe to exclusiveness. He admits of nothing below, scarcely of anything above, himself . . . Milton is his great idol, and he sometimes dares to compare himself with him. His sonnets, indeed, have something of the same high-raised tone and prophetic spirit.[39]

Keats recited poetry in a less magisterial manner than his august elder. Haydon spoke of his 'half chant' when he had declaimed his 'Hymn to Pan' for Wordsworth a few days before the dinner party. On later occasions Haydon used the words 'murmuring' and 'tremulous' to describe his friend's delivery; but on this exalted occasion, his confidence evidently in good order, he may have become more expansive. It is interesting that it was evidently the same passage from *Endymion* which Keats now chose to repeat: he would hardly have ventured upon it again if Wordsworth's response on the earlier occasion had caused him pain or humiliation. He liked to walk up and down the room as he recited, but, unlike Wordsworth or Coleridge, he sat at a table to compose, certainly in the case of his months of agonizing over *Endymion*, when he set himself the task of completing a certain number of lines each day. For the ode 'To a Nightingale', his friend Charles Brown recalled that Keats took his chair from the breakfast table out into the garden of Wentworth Place and sat writing

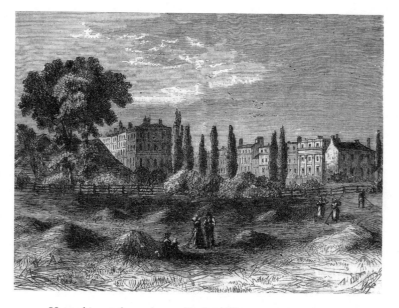

14. *Haymaking at the entrance to Portland Place,* 1815. Wordsworth and Monkhouse would have passed similarly rural scenes on their way to Lisson Grove.

under a plum tree, returning indoors with a completed draft after only two or three hours: a time span a little hard to credit.

The poets took their work with high seriousness and sense of mission. Wordsworth in particular never doubted his destiny and nor did his friends and admirers. In that context Haydon's comment on his guests does not seem exaggerated: 'it was indeed an immortal evening'.

4. Christ's Entry into Jerusalem

My great object is to form a school, deeply impregnated with my
principles of art, deeply grounded in all the means, to put the clue
into the hands of a certain number of young men of genius that
they may go on by themselves.

Benjamin Robert Haydon, *Diary*[1]

As the late winter light faded that afternoon, the focus narrowed
to the candle-lit figures seated round the table: Wordsworth,
Keats and Lamb with their backs to the fire, Haydon and Monkhouse opposite. Haydon, observing the three writers with his
acute sense of occasion and his painter's eye for structure, noted
in his diary entry at the end of the evening his satisfaction at the
tableau presented: 'There was something interesting in seeing
Wordsworth sitting, and Keats and Lamb, and my picture of
Christ's entry towering up behind them, occasionally brightened by the gleams of flame that sparkled from the fire.'[2] He was
pleased with the current state of the picture, which was to take
him six years in all to finish. It was now halfway towards completion. He had first rubbed in the overall structure in the early
summer of 1814, on an enormous canvas measuring thirteen
feet by fifteen, before setting out to visit Paris with David Wilkie, all ready for him to settle down to on his return. He told
John Scott before leaving England that it would represent

Christ's Triumphant Entry into Jerusalem, His Mother weeping for
joy; Magdalen pale with her eating passion; the mob in enthusiasm,

all expressing their various emotions. Never was there a finer subject; never was there one that left such scope to the painter's invention ... The whole scene rushed into my brain as if the sun had burst out at midnight.[3]

It is difficult to see quite how the picture could have taken so long to finish – Wordsworth told him jokingly but inaccurately that he ought to be called Teniers 'as it took you ten years to complete' – but when later in his life Haydon came to write his autobiography, in his memory it seemed to have occupied him to the exclusion of all else for the whole of that period, the other activities of those years, his meeting with his future wife and their passionate love for each other, his continued battles with his arch-enemies of the Royal Academy, his involvement in the long saga of the Elgin Marbles, his temporary but much-gloried-in position as a sought-after lion in the fashionable world of art, his visits to the country houses of patrons and so forth, were all blanked out of his mind, great though their importance had then been to him: 'My enthusiasm at this time was intense. I held intercourse only with my art and my great Creator. I shunned society. I looked on myself as called to produce a great reform, and I devoted myself to it with the passionate self-seclusion of an ascetic.'[4] The completion of the painting in 1820 did indeed mark a period of triumph and success, when he felt his importance to be such that he even thought of growing mustachios, but, he recorded, 'that passed off'.[5]

The picture hanging above the diners on 28 December 1817 showed a vast crowd pressing around the central figure of Christ and stretching away into the distance. To Haydon, the painting represented a declaration of his deeply held Christian faith and a challenge to sceptics and deists. Religion was a subject that his friends found dangerous to raise in his presence, and any mockery of his beliefs sent him into

*What ignorance of the animal! —
So much is the mind able
to conceive and do when uninformed
by practice & investigation!*

15. Preliminary sketch for Christ in *Christ's Entry into Jerusalem*,
1814, by Benjamin Robert Haydon. Corporal Sammons was the
model, although Christ's hands were drawn from those of David
Wilkie.

paroxysms of rage, as on the occasion when, dining with Leigh Hunt, he first met Shelley:

I seated myself in the place kept for me at the table right opposite Shelley himself, as I was told after, for I did not then know what hectic, spare, weakly, yet intellectual-looking creature it was carving a bit of broccoli or cabbage on his plate, as if it had been the substantial wing of a chicken. Hunt and his wife and her sister, Keats, Horace Smith, and myself made up the party. In a few minutes Shelley opened the conversation by saying in a most feminine and gentle voice, 'As to that detestable religion, the Christian . . .' I looked astounded, but casting a glance round the table easily saw by Hunt's expression of ecstasy and the women's simper, I was to be set at that evening *vi et armis*. No reply, however, was made to this sally during dinner, but when the dessert came and the servant was gone, to it we went like fiends. I felt exactly like a stag at bay and resolved to gore without mercy . . . We said unpleasant things to each other, and when I retired to the other room for a moment I overheard them say, 'Haydon is fierce.' 'Yes,' said Hunt; 'the question always irritates him.'[6]

In the foreground Haydon included portraits of his friends and also of two major figures from the past, Newton and Voltaire, his intention being to convey the continuing relevance of his subject down the centuries to the present time. Wordsworth was shown, head bowed in reverence; Keats in eager and loud colloquy with Haydon's pupil William Bewick, appearing to raise his voice above the noise of the crowd: it was for this portrait that Haydon took the famous life mask of the young poet. Hazlitt was also there. Another contemporary portrait was that of William Sharpe, the leading line engraver of the day, much admired by Haydon. Sharpe was a devoted member of the cult of Joanna Southcott, who predicted that she would give birth to the second Christ on 27 December

16. Bullock's Egyptian Hall, 22 Piccadilly, with its exotic frontage and imposing entrance. It was here that Haydon staged his triumphant exhibition of *Christ's Entry into Jerusalem* in 1820.

1814. In the event, the prophetess died childless on 19 October of that year. Haydon remembered that while Sharpe was sitting to him for his portrait he told Haydon that he believed that she would appear again on earth in July 1820. 'Suppose tho she does not, I replied, oh, said Sharpe – I don't care, nothing will shake my belief.'[7]

Voltaire was shown as a sneerer against Christianity and Newton, whom Haydon considered to be 'the greatest human mind that ever touched our sphere', as a believer. Christ's head presented the artist with his greatest problem, and he worked and re-worked it again and again without ever feeling completely satisfied with the result. Corporal Sammons was his model for the figure, and there is a fine drawing, commanding and impressive, of the naked Sammons,[8] which Haydon failed to transfer to his painting with an equal felicity. Wilkie's exceptionally beautiful hands were his model for Christ's.

David Wilkie was almost the only intimate artist friend that

Haydon ever made, and the two were very close, freely criticizing each other's work without causing offence. Wilkie had studied in Scotland for some years before coming south, and he never lost his Scottish accent. In contrast to Haydon, he was tall, slender and quiet, but with an air of concentrated energy about him. He enjoyed early popular success with *The Blind Fiddler* and *The Village Politician*, but Haydon was not jealous of him, welcoming his friend's triumphs almost as much as if they had been his own. Unlike Haydon, Wilkie had a shrewd nature, and avoided any falling out with the Academy, and he became in due course Sir David Wilkie and a respected Academician.

Wilkie was the critic upon whose judgement Haydon most relied, and after one of his sittings he spent some time contemplating *Christ's Entry* and finally gave it a favourable judgement. Haydon was relieved:

We then examined every head with a candle, and criticized each with the severity of the most acid critics. This is true human nature. It is what we always do to each other the moment that either has expressed a *decided approbation* of what the other has done. We could not bear it else.[9]

William Bewick remembered a later occasion when Haydon's turn came to criticize a picture of Wilkie's, and the two painters displayed a touching love for and confidence in each other:

Haydon praised what had been done since last he saw the picture, and Wilkie was delighted. Indeed I never saw him so light-hearted and playful. Haydon took hold of Wilkie's hands and said, 'Look here, Bewick, these are what I painted my Christ's hands from. Wilkie's hands are the only part of his person that are like his pictures, they are made for fine execution – my hands are very good, but they are not so tremulously nervous – so delicate or refined. You would never suppose that these hands would have made such a miserable mess upon the palette as you see there (looking down at Wilkie's dirty palette).[10]

On Boxing Day, two days before his dinner, Haydon successfully transferred Wordsworth's portrait from the preliminary drawing to the canvas, so on the 28th the paint would still have been wet. Hazlitt admired this drawing, feeling it to be of all portraits of the poet 'most like his drooping weight of thought and expression'.[11] Keats, having watched the picture's development with interest and admiration over a long period, told Haydon that he now felt it to be a part of himself. The artist's close friends all took a supportive interest in the picture's progress, and Lamb, in his Latin poem celebrating it, '*Tabulum egregii*', claimed a high place for his friend's work, concluding:

> Painters with poets for the laurel vie:
> But should the laureat band thy claims deny,
> Wear thou thy own green palm, Haydon, triumphantly.[12]

Wordsworth had also keenly watched the progress of *Christ's Entry*. He wrote to Haydon on 12 September 1815 to express the hope that it was going on to his satisfaction, adding, 'I cannot doubt but that picture will do you huge credit, and raise the reputation of the art in this country', so chiming precisely with the painter's own grandiose expectations. In reply Haydon reported that the picture continued to advance, and that he had got one of his characters, the penitent girl, done, as well as her mother and the centurion:

I hope to have the sister, who is leaning forward to encourage her, finished shortly. Behind, I intend putting a woman, who may have followed from curiosity, and in whose face I shall put a tender concern, a pity – an abstracted pity – as if she were musing on the frailties and the temptations of the lovely girl, as she looked at the penitent one. I had thought of another character instead of this woman, viz., the hard unfeeling prude, who looks with a sneer of cruel self-approbation at the penitent girl, chuckling that *she* has escaped the vice. It would be a strong character, and would be sure to excite one's feelings for the penitent, from its cruelty. Characters of this latter kind Raphael seems universally to have rejected. Perhaps he thought them incompatible with beauty and pleasure. All his men and women have one feeling of goodness and bene-volence.[13]

Haydon soon abandoned the idea of the prude, a decision with which Wordsworth agreed:

The feelings to be excited are adoration and exultation, and subordi-nate to them, astonished suspension of mind. You will infer that I think you have done well in rejecting the character of the supercili-ous prude. I cannot but think such a person discordant with the piece . . . A character like that of the haughty prude belongs rather to the higher kinds of comedy, such as the works of Hogarth, than to a subject of this nature, which to use Milton's expression is 'more than heroic'. I coincide with you as to Raphael's characters, but depend upon it he has erred upon the safer side.[14]

This is the voice of Wordsworth the pedagogue, but his generous tone and plainly genuine involvement with Haydon's problems were honey to his young friend, in whose eyes, at this stage in their relationship at least, such attention from the great man was the highest possible compliment. It was a time of increasing intimacy between the two. The letter quoted above ends 'Faithfully yours, W. Wordsworth', but a few months later he was signing himself 'Believe me with great respect and true affection' – a marked step forward for such a restrained correspondent.

William Hazlitt was in the picture, but not at the dinner table. His lack of an invitation is partly explained by Haydon's distrust of his attitude to religion and partly from resentment that he failed to support his friend in his continual attacks on the Royal Academy. He was also generally out of favour at the time because of some sharp criticisms he had made of Wordsworth, which had upset the poet and antagonized many of his friends. Haydon wrote soothingly to Wordsworth on 15 April 1817 about Hazlitt's attitude and its possible interpretations, adding that he seldom saw him and never asked him to his own home. The only members of Haydon's circle to remain faithful to Hazlitt just then were the Lambs, who insisted that they did not have so many friends that they could afford to lose even one.

That autumn Haydon's was briefly an irritable circle. Keats arrived back from a visit to his friend Benjamin Bailey at Oxford at the beginning of October and was dismayed by all the fractiousness he found. 'Everybody seems at loggerheads,' he reported to Bailey on the 8th:

There's Hunt infatuated – there's Haydon's picture *in statu quo.* There's Hunt walks up and down his painting room criticizing every head most unmercifully – There's Horace Smith tired of Hunt ... I am quite disgusted with literary men and will never know another except Wordsworth – no not even Byron – Here is an instance of the friendships of such – Haydon and Hunt have known each other many years – now they live *pour ainsi dire* jealous neighbours. Haydon says to me Keats dont show your lines to Hunt on any account or he will have done half for you – so it appears Hunt wishes it to be thought.[15]

At the time of his dinner party Haydon was full of confidence that he would be able to command a good price for *Christ's Entry* when it was finished, and free himself from his debts, which were beginning to reach alarming proportions; and so convinced was he that his paintbrush held the remedy to his difficulties that he continued to allow the debts to escalate. Three years later the picture was at last ready to face the public, and by March 1820 Haydon boldly rented the Great Room in Bullock's Egyptian Hall in Piccadilly to exhibit it for a whole year, at a cost of £300. William Bullock, an admirer of Haydon's work, accepted the gamble of recovering his money at the end of that time. Bullock had originally been a silversmith in Liverpool, where he had accumulated a heterogeneous collection of objects and natural history specimens bought from ships docking at the port. By 1812 he had moved himself and his collection to London, where he built a museum to display his treasures at 22 Piccadilly. He gave this the dignified name of the London Museum, but it soon became known as the Egyptian Hall, from the exotic nature of its façade, which was in the shape of a pylon and decorated with a giant scarab over the entrance, sphinxes, hieroglyphics, and two huge figures representing Bullock's idea of Isis and Osiris. This all reflected the cult of things exotic and Egyptian, fashionable at the time in homage to Nelson's victory at the battle of the Nile. William Bullock's brother George, sculptor and cabinet-maker, exhibited modern paintings on the grand staircase of his house in Tenterden Street, and in 1817 these were by Haydon, including his *Macbeth*, *Judgment of Solomon* and *The Assassination of Dentatus*,[16] bringing the artist welcome extra publicity.

When the moment came for *Christ's Entry* to be exhibited, it was rolled and carried to Piccadilly on the shoulders of three troopers of the Life Guards, lent for the occasion by their colonel and described by Haydon as 'my factotums'. There it was framed and put up. The frame weighed 600 pounds, and, at the first attempt to lift it into place, it snapped the iron ring. 'The strongest soldiers were as nervous as infants,' Haydon recalled in his autobiography, 'but at last we lifted it by machinery and pitched it without accident right on its proper support.'[17] All seemed set fair, and the painting ready for varnishing, 'when lo!' Haydon remarked, neatly dissociating himself from any responsibility in the matter, 'my money was all gone'. Sir George Beaumont came to the rescue with £30:

This soon went, and now with upholsterers, soldiers and journey-men in full work, the picture up and looking gloriously, everybody waiting for the word of command to buy the hangings and begin fittings, myself ready to glaze, oil staring me in the face, picture reproaching, the sun shining, my palette set, the landlord peeping in now and then, as if half suspicious [as well he might be] there was a halt. Sir George's gift was gone![18]

Undefeated, the artist set out breathlessly on the familiar search for further support, managed to raise £50, dashed off to the upholsterer's to buy fabric for hangings of a purple-brown colour, and returned to the Egyptian Hall, where he found his six-foot-three-inches Corporal Sammons shrunk like a child in a fright, and Bullock looking at the picture in doubt.

But my appearance with my mouth clenched five times fiercer than ever, the rolls of fittings actually bringing up, my stamping walk [his son Frederic later remarked on this curious walk] my thun-dering voice, put fire into all. Women began to sew, boys cleared away and bustled, fittings were tearing right and left, while I mounted the ladder, palette in hand, ordered the door to be locked, and let fly at the foreground figures with a brush brimming with asphaltum and oil, and before dark had toned richly one-third of the picture.[19]

His account leaves the reader as breathless as others around the painter must so often have been, but for him the whole occasion was exhilarating. His pupils were set to write out 800 invitations to the private view, Haydon drawing liberally on the Court Guide for names of all the ministers and their wives, foreign ambassadors, bishops, and 'All the beauties in high life, all the officers on guard at the palace, all the geniuses in town, and everybody of any note, were invited and came.'[20]

Haydon was at the gallery when the private-view day, Saturday 25 March, came at last, and found all arranged to his satisfaction. As the morning wore on, tension began to mount: would no one come? The best way to pass the time, he decided, was to go out and have a good lunch. On his return he was delighted to find Piccadilly blocked with carriages, the staircase of the Egyptian Hall full of waiting footmen, and Bullock's great room packed with viewers. This account of the crowds seems amazing; even the most prestigious of the Royal Academy's great exhibitions now would not bring Piccadilly to a halt. One factor in the great success was probably the then virtual absence of public art galleries for society or artists. The occasion sounds more like that at the opening of a twentieth-century musical rather than a staid picture exhibition.

Keats had loyally made the long journey down from Hampstead, braving the March winds, although he was really in no state to do so, having only just left his bed after a sudden attack of what his friend Brown described as 'violent palpitations at the heart', but he was so excited by the whole occasion that he managed the long trudge back to Wentworth Place without any evident harm. Haydon spotted him in a corner talking to Hazlitt. 'At this moment in came the Persian ambassador and his suite; his fine manly person and black beard, with his splendid dress, made a prodigious show, and he said, in good English and in a loud voice, "I like the elbow of soldier." '[21]

One fly in the ointment remained: the more he gazed at his picture, the more Haydon felt uncertain about Christ's head; and the general reaction was also uncertain, doubts were being expressed:

Everybody seemed afraid, when in walked, with all the dignity of her majestic presence, Mrs Siddons, like a Ceres or a Juno. The whole room remained dead silent, and allowed her to think. After a few minutes Sir George Beaumont, who was extremely anxious, said in a very delicate manner: 'How do you like the Christ?' Everybody listened for her reply. After a moment, in a deep, loud, tragic tone she said: 'It is completely successful.' And then, approaching the artist, she added her high admiration at the way he had so 'variously modified' the same expression. 'The paleness of your Christ,' she said, 'gives it a supernatural look.' This idea was passed from person to person: the expression was to be thought of as *supernatural*.[22]

Nothing in Haydon's life ever again came up to this moment of exultation. His *Jerusalem*, he now felt, had achieved a national triumph, showing that the public did care about High Art, and, further, that he had demonstrated that an Englishman could execute it. Thirty-one thousand people visited the exhibition during the whole run, giving him the publicity he so much loved. *The Times* and *Observer* were among the many publications carrying good reviews, the *Observer* devoting three columns of praise to the picture. One less than enthusiastic voice was that of Henry Crabb Robinson, who visited the Egyptian Hall on 11 May and found the picture unpleasing. 'Our Saviour has a face not of divine meekness but of sheer human lowliness – a sort of dreamy meditation, not of superhuman foreknowledge,' he wrote in his diary.[23] He also disliked the portrait of Wordsworth, which he thought made him look like a forlorn and haggard old man.

Haydon wrote to Mrs Siddons to thank her for her support, and was invited to call, which he duly did. It was, he felt, like speaking to the mother of the gods, and he revelled in the moment. Two years later Mrs Siddons and Haydon were still on friendly terms and he described one of her famous private readings, on this occasion from *Macbeth*.

It is extraordinary the awe this wonderful woman inspires. After her first reading the men sallied into a room to get tea. While we were all eating toast and tingling cups and saucers, she began again. Immediately like the effect of a mass bell at Madrid, all noise ceased, and we slunk away to our seats like boys, two or three of the most distinguished men of the day passed me to get to their seats with great bits of toast sticking out of their cheeks, which they seemed afraid to bite. It was curious suddenly to look up and see Lawrence's[24] face pass you in the bustle with his cheek swelled from his mouth being full, and then when he sat down, hearing him bite it by degrees, and then stop for fear of making too much crackle, while his eyes full of water told the torture he was in; at the same moment you heard Mrs Siddons say, 'Eye of newt, toe of frog'; then Lawrence gave a bite and pretended to be awed and listening. It was exquisite! At last I went away highly gratified, and as I was standing on the landing place to get cool, I overheard my own servant in the hall say, 'Why, is that the old lady making such a noise?' 'Yes,' said another. 'Why, she makes as much noise as ever,' said Sammons. 'Yes,' said the other, 'she tunes her pipes as well as ever she did.' What a bit of nature! Just like Shakespeare's porter in Macbeth, who says, 'We were carousing till the second cock', that is, they were drinking the King's health and talking of their Master's exploits by the kitchen chimney while Duncan was murdering above! And why should not this be, as well as the wind blow and the rain scatter?

While upstairs we were awed and Mrs Siddons was talking like a pythoness, a servant says, 'is that the old lady making such a noise!' It awakened me out of a dream, and made one think perhaps that the old lady *was* making a noise.[25]

The fame of *Christ's Entry* had its drawbacks: creditors began to crowd round Haydon again, but no firm offers to buy the picture materialized, despite the efforts of Sir George Beaumont and various other patrons and friends. Beaumont urged the directors of the British Gallery to buy it, and there was a degree of interest at this idea; but a senior Academician, Richard Payne Knight, always antagonistic to Haydon, was emphatically in opposition to any purchase, arguing that in exhibiting the painting under his own aegis Haydon had behaved badly in ignoring the established art authorities, and that he should now be made to feel his dependence on them. Another unrealized project was that the government should buy the picture to adorn the new Chelsea church.

In an attempt to raise at least some money from exhibiting it, Haydon had the picture taken down from the Egyptian Hall, rolled and sent by sea to Edinburgh, at the beginning of an extensive and successful tour. In Edinburgh Haydon met John Gibson Lockhart, son-in-law and biographer of Sir Walter Scott and a major contributor to *Blackwood's Magazine*. The *Maga*, as it was affectionately known, had been founded as a Tory counterblast to the *Edinburgh Review*, and early in its career became notorious for a damaging series of diatribes on the 'Cockney School of Poetry', directed chiefly against Leigh Hunt, Hazlitt and Keats. Haydon and Lockhart took to each other at once, and Lockhart made amends for past persecutions by writing warmly of Haydon in *Blackwood's* as being 'by far the greatest historical painter that England had yet produced'.[26]

But the amounts raised by the tour were not enough to fend off his creditors, and the picture remained on Haydon's hands until, in April 1823, he suffered a cruel blow: he was arrested and imprisoned for debt, his goods seized and a sale of his belongings arranged. On 1 July he wrote from prison to Sir Walter Scott:

Such scenes in the house, my dear Sir Walter! Reptiles, intoxicated with tobacco and beer, rolling about under the 'Ilyssus'[27] and jesting upon its naked beauty! My painting room, where none but rank and talent had ever trod, was now stenched with the sleeping heat of low-lived beasts, slumbering in blankets! At the foot too of the Crucifixion which I had just rubbed in! They drank my wine; they plundered the property they were protecting; they quarrelled with the servants! My blood was boiling half the day, and I declare solemnly, one night, infuriated with anxiety and agony at seeing the state of my wife and the pining look of my infant in consequence of its mother's condition, had I met either of the parties, I would have strangled him like a rabbit. I set out to look for them, and lucky for myself I met none! I really would have done it. I would have crushed him like paper! I was obliged to surrender, and was transferred to this sink of dimness and gamblers.[28]

At the forced sale of his belongings one of his pupils bought *Christ's Entry* for £220, but later he too went bankrupt, and in 1831, to Haydon's dismay, it was sold to Childs and Inman of Philadelphia, and shipped to America. He went to see it before it was crated up for its long voyage.[29]

It was melancholy thus to look, for the last time, at a work which had excited so great a sensation in England and Scotland; the progress of which had been watched by all the nobility, foreign ministers and people of fashion, and on the success of which all prospect for the historical art of the country at that time appeared to hang. It was now leaving my native country for ever, where I had hoped to have seen it placed triumphantly in some public building.[30]

In an attempt to comfort himself, he reflected on the fine state of the painting. 'Its condition is admirable. It was painted in pure linseed oil, and not a single atom of gum in it, or on it since. God bless it, and the result of its mission.' Searching for someone other than himself to blame for its departure, he added, 'What a disgrace to the aristocracy!'[31]

William Bewick was one of several who had joined Haydon as pupils in 1815. Haydon had already taught Charles Eastlake, who came to him for instruction at the early age of fifteen; but two years before the Immortal Dinner he had decided to open a proper school. 'My great object,' he recorded in his diary,

is to form a school, deeply impregnated with my principles of art, deeply grounded in all the means, to put the clue into the hands of a certain number of young men of genius that they may go on by themselves. O God, grant that I may form a complete school, grant that I may impregnate some glorious spirits with my views so that they may complete them if I am not destined, but grant I may be destined to complete them, and grant the spirits I impregnate may assist me. Let me not be treated with ingratitude, let them be firmly attached to me, and by proving their sincerity, induce me to persevere.[32]

On this occasion his prayers were answered, his school was a success, his pupils talented, grateful and loyal to their master, and useful to him as assistants. The first to apply to him were the three Landseer brothers, Charles, Thomas and Edwin, who were brought by their father John, the distinguished landscape engraver, to apply for entrance. John Landseer, an immediate contemporary of Wordsworth's, had been trying in vain to coax the Royal Academy schools to give engraving the same status as that enjoyed by the other arts, as was already the case on the Continent. At the time of Haydon's party he had just published a work on engraved views. There is a portrait of him by his son Edwin, holding an open book of engravings and looking sweetly benign, with flowing white locks. This may have given a misleading impression: he was said to have had a short temper with his pupils. His eldest son Thomas was to follow his father and become an engraver of power and originality. He devoted much of his career to the etching and engraving of the more famous Edwin's drawings and paintings. Charles, influenced by Haydon, chose to become a history painter. The youngest member of this gifted family was a daughter, Jessica, a landscape and miniature painter. Their father felt a formal education was harmful to artists, so his children did not receive any. Instead he sent them out to sketch in the fields, which then still extended from Marylebone to Hampstead.

That John Landseer, experienced and well known in the art world, should have taken his sons to Haydon was a significant step: his more conventional move would have been to apply to the Academy schools, but in deciding not to do this he underlined the need for a separate establishment such as Haydon planned to provide. He had asked Haydon, 'When do you let your beard grow and take pupils?' and Haydon replied, 'If my instructions are useful or valuable, now.'[33]

Edwin's talent for animal painting was already evident at the age of thirteen, and Haydon lent him his dissections of a lion, 'and I advised him to dissect animals – the only mode of acquiring their construction – as I had dissected men, and as I should make his brothers do'.[34] Edwin, although he admitted his debt to his old master, was the only one of Haydon's pupils who later voiced feelings of anger against him, his attitude apparently being the result of Haydon's having borrowed money from him, which he no doubt failed to repay. While understandable, this also showed a lack of sympathy. Haydon had not only been extremely kind to him as a young untried artist, but had also gone out of his way to bring his name to the attention of possible future patrons, on one occasion taking a portfolio of Edwin's work to a large dinner party at Sir George Beaumont's, where he showed the drawings round after coffee to Beaumont's influential and distinguished guests. The effect of Haydon's teaching can be plainly seen in one of Landseer's most celebrated paintings, *The Hunting of Chevy Chase*, where the central rider and horse derive from the rider and horse in Slab II of the Panathenaic Procession of the Elgin Marbles.[35] The marbles were to Haydon the absolute epitome of beauty, and he insisted that the secret of their overawing presence was the deep understanding of nature displayed in the minutely accurate representation of the figures, combined with the most imaginative artistry. All his pupils were encouraged to make studies of them.

The Academy schools in the early nineteenth century were in an unsatisfactory state. The atmosphere in Somerset House, where the Academy was then housed, was one of faction and intrigue, and, worse, the teaching methods were outdated and perfunctory and the schools inadequately equipped. Prince Hoare, one of the Academy officials, complained of the lack of models and plaster casts. Such casts as did exist were kept huddled together in a small space, so that students had difficulty in getting an unimpeded view of them. Drawing instruction was minimal, painting nil, and there were no original pictures on the walls. In the sculpture school there were no marble statues; and there was only a tiny collection of engravings. In the lecture rooms, notorious for their poor acoustics, the best seats were kept for visitors, students being crowded at the back. For the most part lectures were monotonously delivered, read out from regularly repeated scripts. The most incoherent and inaudible of all the lecturers was J. M. W. Turner, to the despair of students eager to learn from the great man. Contemporary complaints about his mode of delivery from the rostrum included that he read too fast; that he spoke with

1 (*Above left*) Benjamin Robert Haydon in a fashionable Van Dyck costume of red velvet, painted by G.H. Harlow *c.*1816, a few months before Haydon's party.

2 (*Above right*) Haydon's portrait of William Wordsworth, drawn a fortnight after the Immortal Dinner as a present for Mary Wordsworth. The poet himself referred to it as 'The Brigand'.

3 (*Below*) Lisson Grove in winter, at the junction of Marylebone Road and Stingo Lane, *c.*1849, by T. Paul Fisher. The tall building on the left would not have been there at the time of the Immortal Dinner.

4 Tom Monkhouse, successful merchant of Budge Row, and 'dearest coz' of Mary Wordsworth and Sara Hutchinson. A universal favourite, gentle and loving, he was always happy to run errands and make purchases for his Grasmere cousins.

5 Charcoal drawing of John Keats, *c.*1816, by Joseph Severn. This earliest surviving portrait of the poet captures something of what Severn described as 'the almost flamelike intensity of Keats's eager glance when he was keenly excited or interested'.

6 *Lane at Hampstead*, a la eighteenth-century watercolour by Thomas Girtin. It was here that Leigh Hunt once met Keats, who presented hi with a copy of his poems. The lane was also favourite walk for Lamb Hazlitt and Coleridge.

8 Chalk sketch of Hazlitt by Haydon's pupil William Bewick, painted in Scotland in 1824. Hazlitt was flattered by the portrait and made Bewick prop it up on his mantelpiece with two forks so that he could admire it at his leisure.

7 An 1815 drawing by Thomas Charles Wageman of the poet, essayist and radical editor Leigh Hunt, shortly after his release from prison after serving a two-year sentence for libel.

9 The east side of Regent Street, *c.*1824, by Thomas Shepherd, engraved by W. Wallis.

10 *Turner on Varnishing Day*, oil painting by S.W. Parrott, 1830–40. Turner, in his famous high hat, is surrounded by the tools of his trade and, as always, an admiring audience, as he adds several layers of varnish to enhance the luminous effect of his canvas.

11 *River Scene with Rainbow* by J.M.W. Turner. Turner is said to have written out Wordsworth's 'My heart leaps up when I behold/A rainbow in the sky' and pinned it to his easel before beginning work on such a painting.

encil portrait, attributed to W.E.
t, believed to be of the youthful
arles Lamb, at about the time of
lary Lamb's fatal attack on her
mother.

13 The actress Frances Maria (Fanny) Kelly.
Engraving by J. Thomson after a painting by
William Derby, 1823. Fanny was the love of
Charles Lamb's life. He spoke lovingly of her
'divine plain face'.

14 *Interior of the Sale Room, East India House*, an aquatint by J.C. Sadler
after T. Rowlandson and A.C. Pugin, 1808, from Ackermann's *Microcosm
of London*. One of Charles Lamb's duties as clerk to the East India
Company was to attend such auctions. He may well have been one of
the figures seated below the auctioneer.

15 *Christ's Entry into Jerusalem*, the huge picture Haydon took six years to complete and which hung, unfinished, above the guests in December 1817.

16 Detail of *Christ's Entry into Jerusalem* showing Wordsworth, head bent in worship, Voltaire and Newton immediately to his right, and above, William Bewick and Keats engaged in an animated exchange.

17 A chalk drawing of a bespectacled and endearingly vulnerable-looking Haydon asleep, by David Wilkie, 1815. The two friends were on holiday together in Brighton.

18 *Clare Market, 1815.* This old market, dating from the seventeenth century, was near the Lambs' lodgings, where it formed just such a maze of miscellaneous stalls as would have been Lamb's delight on his city wanderings.

19 *(Above)* Voltaire in his study, by an unknown artist. Haydon was troubled about whether to include the philosopher in his *Christ's Entry*, but decided it was appropriate to show him as a mocker of the Christian religion in contrast to Newton, a believer.

20 *(Below)* Thomas Bruce, seventh Ea[rl of] Elgin, *c*.1795, by G.P. Harding afte[r] Anton Graff. A portrait painted bef[ore] Elgin set off for Constantinople on [his] appointment as Ambassador to th[e] Sublime Porte.

21 *(Below) The Temporary Elgin Room* (British Museum), painted in 1819 by A. Archer, seated sketching on the right. Benjamin West, president of the Royal Academy, is seated in the centre; and, significantly separated from the establishment figures of the art world, Haydon is working on the extreme left.

much hesitation and difficulty; and that there was too much umm-ing and err-ing. On one occasion Turner mounted the rostrum to deliver one of his lectures on perspective, only to descend again at once, saying that everyone might as well go home as he had left all his notes in a hackney carriage. His close friend and biographer, Walter Thornbury, said that his remarks at the Academy council meetings were difficult to follow because of his indistinct voice:

You saw the great man's mouth move, and imperfectly heard certain sounds proceed therefrom; but out of them you seldom caught more than 'Mr President' and 'namely', the two verbal forms to which the speaker had recourse when he had hopelessly entangled himself in the subtleties of his own rhetoric.[36]

In contrast, Haydon selected only pupils whom he felt to be sufficiently promising and temperamentally suited to appreciate his methods. By now he owned a considerable collection of engravings and drawings, and a growing number of casts from which they could learn. Just as importantly, he inspired his students with his own infectious enthusiasm and sense of high mission. It must have been difficult not to love a master whose attitude to his work was so passionately wholehearted. 'Another day of work, God be thanked!' he once wrote in his diary:

Put in the sea – a delicious tint. How exquisite is a bare canvas, sized alone, to paint on; how the slightest colour, thin as water, tells; how it glitters in body; how the brush flies – now here, now there. It seems as if face, hands, sky, thought, poetry, expression, were hid in the handle, and streamed out as it touched the canvas.[37]

He was also generous to his pupils with his time, and treated them for the most part as if he were their father. One of them,

Edward Chatfield, ended a letter to him, 'I remain, dear Sir, your devoted son (for you have ever been a father to me).' He charged his first pupils no fee, although Landseer, for one, could well have afforded to pay for his sons; and later on he never worried about a pupil's ability to pay the premium, provided he showed sufficient talent. One such, the fruit painter George Lance, asked nervously what his terms were, and Haydon replied that when he took pupils he didn't ask the length of their fathers' purses; if a pupil's drawings showed promise, and if he was industrious, then he would be taught for nothing. And he told Bewick, who arrived in London nearly penniless, 'Only be industrious and succeed in your art, and *that* is all I require.' This attitude was generous but did not help to pay his rent, and presently he found he must be more businesslike in his approach to the school, charging as a rule a premium of £200 for a three-year course. Every Monday morning he saw all his pupils and told them what work they were to do that week. 'I guide them,' he said, 'but not with the bit in their mouths', adding that they were under his control 'morally and absolutely'.[38] His course was designed to emphasize in particular the crucial importance of an understanding of anatomy, and pupils were set to work at once on the dissection and drawing of animals and of the human body in Sir Charles Bell's anatomy theatre. The course was rigorous and in the summer often most unpleasant as the young men hung over rotting carcases for hours at a stretch, long after the surgeons themselves had given up in disgust.

William Bewick had first heard of Haydon through reading the *Examiner* in the house of a friend who was encouraging him to paint. Here Haydon's *Judgment of Solomon* was praised as 'above any other historical work of the English school'. He longed to reach London and become a part of the glittering life described in the *Examiner*, but his father was adamant in his opposition to the plan, and it was not until the young man had saved £20 from painting portraits of neighbours that he was able to set off. During the three-day journey he dreamt of the joys ahead: 'London appeared to me the heaven of youthful hopes and expectations, that Armida's garden of enchantment where all bright visions must be realized or disappointed.'[39] Almost his first visit was to the Elgin Marbles. 'One morning, while visiting the Elgin Marbles (then at Burlington House),' Haydon remembered:

I saw a youth with a good head drawing in a large way. I spoke to him and was pleased by his reply. It ended in an invitation to breakfast. The next day he came and told me his name was Bewicke [*sic*]; that he came up from Darlington to find me out, and that after I was gone somebody told him who I was, and he was very much agitated. He entered my school at once, was introduced to the Landseers, proceeded to copy all my dissection drawings, and soon became the most prominent pupil of the whole set.[40]

Bewick was overwhelmed by his good fortune, and wrote to his brother about his first visit to Haydon's painting room, where he was shown the painter's drawings and told to borrow anything from his collection that he was not using himself. He worked at Haydon's every day, and was introduced to 'all kinds of known characters, authors, poets, painters, sculptors, etc., not only of this, but of every other country of Europe'.[41] Haydon made much use of Bewick's 'good head', employing him as a model in various paintings, including *The Raising of Lazarus*, which he was working on in 1823 when one of his imprisonments for debt was imminent. Bewick remembered that he had to pose mounted on a box, upon a chair, upon a table, and his master had to leave him twice to get rid of the duns.

When he came back a third time and mounted the steps, he said to me in accents not to be forgotten, 'Bewick, if I am called out again, it will be impossible for me to go on; that is the third time this morning I have been arrested.' He painted the head, hands, and drapery all in that day! and it has never been touched since.[42]

Haydon, too, remembered the occasion only too vividly. After he succeeded in preventing the first threatened arrest of that day, he found his mind too hurt to be capable of immediately settling down again to work.

At last, in scrawling about the brush, I gave an expression to the eye of Lazarus; I instantly got interested, and before two I had hit it. My pupil Bewicke sat for it, and as he had not sold his exquisite picture of Jacob, looked quite thin and anxious enough for such a head. 'I hope you get your food regularly,' said I. He did not answer; by degrees his cheeks reddened, and his eyes filled, but he subdued his feelings. This is an illustration of the state of historical painting in England. A master and his pupil – the one without a pound, the other without bread![43]

   Bewick was another who became a casualty in Haydon's fall, but, unlike Edwin Landseer, he never blamed Haydon, though he wrote miserably to his brother of the mess in which he had allowed himself to be embroiled, and which drove him from London to begin all over again as a portrait painter in the North. Bewick's memoirs give the impression that he was a sweet-natured, modest and loving character, and his must have been a calming presence in Haydon's frenetic life. Haydon told Keats that he and Bewick 'are the only men I have ever loved with all my heart', and Bewick was the only pupil ever to be allowed to watch Haydon painting. He soon found himself included in his master's most intimate circle and was amused by the antics of Haydon's distinguished friends, remembering how they would meet at one another's houses and romp like schoolboys, tell inexhaustible stories, and always laugh at each other's jokes. Their interest in art, in literature, in politics and religion, he noted, was on quite another level. Here they were deeply serious, debating over the classics, fighting Napoleon's battles with the fierceness of partisans, Hazlitt, of course, being for the French emperor, Haydon for Wellington.

By 1816 Haydon felt his pupils had progressed sufficiently well to embark on a new project: he coaxed William Seguier, who would later become the first director of the National Gallery, to ask the Prince Regent for permission to have two of Raphael's cartoons from Hampton Court Palace brought to London for them to copy. Haydon's enemies were jealous and made a great to-do over how dangerous it was to move such precious treasures, they were bound to be damaged by careless treatment, and so forth; but Haydon himself was triumphant. Cylinders were made to transport *The Miraculous Draught of Fishes* and *Paul at Athens* to the British Gallery, and he settled down at once to make full-size drawings of St Paul and of all the other heads. His students followed on and, said Haydon complacently, 'We all set to work and made such studies and cartoons as had never been seen in England before.'[44] Later two more of the cartoons were brought to London for the school to work on: *The Blinding of Elymas* and *The Death of Ananias*, and early in 1818 a cartoon appeared in *Annals of the Fine Arts* entitled *A Master in the Grand Style and His Pupils*, which showed Haydon's pupils perched on various tables, chairs and ladders working on one of the cartoons. The central figure is Bewick, shown using a compass, a practice forbidden by Haydon and frowned on by all art exponents of the time. Bewick wrote to his brother, describing the caricature, in which, he said:

17. *A Master in the Grand Style and His Pupils.* Caricature of Haydon's
school by John Bailey for *Annals of the Fine Arts*, 1818. Haydon's
pupils – with Bewick as the central figure – are copying Raphael's
cartoons while Haydon, in the shape of an owl, hovers over them.

Your brother is made most conspicuous, being placed in the centre,
and figuring away in a most energetic style. I have had an impression
given me. Haydon is flying in the shape of a bird [a bespectacled
owl], he has kicked his palette and colours behind him, and is
blowing a trumpet as director of the public taste, with two large
pens before him denoting his authorship. It will be the best thing
for us that has happened, for it connects us altogether – brings us
into public notice, and if we produce anything, it will make it tell
so much the more.[45]

At the beginning of 1819 Haydon staged a private exhibition of his pupils' studies from the Raphael cartoons in the Great Room in St James's Street. Although some visitors grumbled at having to pay not only to see the chalk drawings, but also a further sixpence for Haydon's catalogue, the private view was a triumph, crowded out with notables, including Turner and Coleridge. Haydon felt it to be the proudest day of his life. The occasion provoked another caricature, *St James in an Uproar or the Quack Artist and His Assailants*, which showed the artist, his young students and his pamphlet being attacked by angry geese.

From work on the cartoons Haydon set his school on to make drawings from the Elgin Marbles. They created a stir as they swept through the galleries, led by their master, in their Raphaelesque costumes to match his, their long hair hanging in curls behind them and their little velvet caps perched on top of the whole. At first, astonished visitors took them for Italians, to Haydon's delight, one of his chief aims being to re-create the atmosphere and appearance of a Renaissance master class, from which had emanated the great fresco cycles which for him represented the pinnacle of artistic achievement. The resultant cartoons of some of the chief figures of the marbles were much admired, their fame even reaching Goethe in Weimar, who wrote for a set for his house. Here they were preserved after his death, when the house became a museum to the great man's memory. In spite of his successes with his school, Haydon's aims for transforming English art remained unrealized. Portraiture continued to rule the day, and it was not until the appearance of the Pre-Raphaelites, to all intents and purposes Haydon's spiritual heirs, that historical and biblical painting once more came into its own.

The year before the Immortal Dinner Haydon had embarked on another new venture. His architect friend, James Elmes, set up as editor of a new quarterly, *Annals of the Fine*

18. Study of horses' heads by Benjamin Robert Haydon, engraved by Thomas Landseer for *Annals of the Fine Arts*. The head on the left is copied from the Elgin Marbles, that on the right from one of the horses from St Mark's, Venice, removed by Napoleon to Paris, where Haydon had seen it.

Arts, which ran for the next four years. Elmes was a devoted admirer of Haydon's and, although he was the titular editor, a large proportion of the content of the *Annals* was either written by Haydon or at his instigation. This was the first periodical to be devoted exclusively to the fine arts, and its aims were to encourage both the study of Renaissance and classical art and modern historical painting on a grand scale:

Thinking to help my views of founding a school, and to put the editor in the right road of sound art, I flung some of my best writing into it, and upheld through its pages the necessity for public encouragement. Elmes backed my views with all his might, and as the Academy had sneered at me the instant it appeared, I opened my battery against that stumbling block and coiled snake.[46]

Haydon admitted shamelessly that he had unlimited control of the *Annals*, and was responsible for its strident and endlessly repeated attacks on the 'stumbling block and coiled snake', which make tiresome reading, although it certainly ensured that his name was constantly before the public. 'The art,' Haydon said with relish, 'was soon in an uproar, and the quarterly appearance of the *Annals* was watched for with the same sort of anxiety as a shell in the air during a siege. "Here it comes; now for it." '[47]

Annals of the Fine Arts had one claim to the greatest possible distinction. It was here, in the surrounding cacophony of Haydon's trumpet-blowing and target-shooting, that Keats's odes 'To a Nightingale' and 'On a Grecian Urn' made their first appearance.

The winter of 1817 saw Haydon at one of the most successful points of his career. *Christ's Entry into Jerusalem* was eliciting a good deal of sympathetic interest and his pupils showed a growing and pleasing talent. But the greatest part of his fame, or notoriety is perhaps the better word in this context, was due to what he himself saw as his triumphant role in the affair of the Elgin Marbles. He was convinced that it was entirely because of his tireless hammering at the relevant authorities that the government had finally agreed to purchase Lord Elgin's collection for the nation. And although this was not an entirely accurate picture of events, certainly Haydon, more than any other single person, had succeeded in bringing the controversy out of the grey area of a select committee of the House of Commons into the bright glare of the public eye. By the time of the Immortal Dinner all was resolved, the marbles suitably housed, and crowds were visiting them every day.

The story of Lord Elgin's marbles began in 1799, when he was appointed Envoy Extraordinary to the Porte. Wondering how best to use this opportunity to improve English knowledge of architecture and sculpture, he consulted an architect called Thomas Harrison, who had been working on his estate in Scotland, who advised him to focus attention on the sculptures on the Parthenon at Athens. There his first priority should be to take plaster casts and measurements and make accurate drawings. William Pitt, then prime minister, was opposed to the idea of the government financing any such scheme and Elgin decided to go ahead on his own account, working with an ardent enthusiasm prefiguring Haydon's own reaction when the marbles eventually arrived in London. Recruiting English artists proved difficult: those Elgin would have liked to employ demanded fees far beyond his means – among them, tantalizingly enough, being Turner, who thus deprived the world of his vision of sunsets over the Parthenon.

On their journey to Constantinople, the Elgins visited Sir William Hamilton and his wife Emma, then in Palermo, where Hamilton was British Minister to the Kingdom of the Two Sicilies. Nelson was also in attendance. Lady Elgin wrote to her mother describing the legendary Lady Hamilton: 'My father would say, "There is a fine Woman for you, good flesh and blood." She is indeed a Whapper!'[48] Hamilton recommended an Italian painter, Giovanni Battista Lusieri, who was entrusted with the engagement of a team of artists, architectural draughtsmen and makers of plaster casts.

In spite of difficulties with the local Turks, in the summer of 1800 work began on the Acropolis, but after a while this was halted by the authorities. In 1801 Philip Hunt, Elgin's chaplain, visited Athens and reported back to Elgin in Constantinople that it was imperative to obtain a written authorization, or 'firman', from the Turkish government to ensure restored access to the Parthenon. Hunt, having seen for himself the destructive effects of the Turkish occupation of the Acropolis, now made a crucial recommendation. Initially Elgin's intention had simply been to make a detailed record of the site, but Hunt now added a suggested proviso that the firman should also include permission to remove pieces of sculpture. Elgin seems to have been easily persuaded to accept this extra dimension to what he passionately felt to be his mission. He was well aware of the imputations of greed that were likely to be levelled at him at home, but felt morally bound to rescue what he could of the precious sculptures.

What Philip Hunt had seen in 1801 was the evidence of a long history of depradation by the Turks living on the Acropolis, who had been in the habit of using the marble ruins as building materials for their houses on the slopes leading up to the summit, and also as reinforcements for what had now become a military complex. In the seventeenth century the Acropolis had suffered a series of disasters. In 1645 the Propylaea, used as a storehouse for gunpowder, was struck by lightning and exploded. Forty years later the temple of Athene Nike was pulled down in order to clear the bastion for an artillery position. And in 1687 the Parthenon itself, now the chief gunpowder magazine, received a direct hit from Venetian cannon and the whole building exploded, the roof was blown out and much of the sculpture turned into piles of rubble. The small pieces of marble lying around were ideal for rendering down into lime for building purposes, and this became their fate. Even the lead which the original builders had used to hold the column sections in place was removed to make bullets. In addition to this, the Turkish soldiers fired at the statues from the plain, using them for target practice; and they also polished marble heads into round shot.

As the eighteenth century developed, a new threat appeared in the form of tourists, eager to take home precious fragments from classical Athens; and this escalated during the Napoleonic

wars, when access to western Europe was restricted and travellers needed to find further fields to explore. Trade in marble
fragments became brisk, but much that was then removed
from the Acropolis was subsequently lost, although various
pieces eventually surfaced in museums all over Europe, and in
private collections, including some in the great English
country houses. It was with this in mind that Hunt made his
momentous recommendation to Elgin. The required firman
was granted, which included the phrase 'that no one meddle
with their scaffolding or implements, nor hinder them from
taking away any pieces of stone with inscriptions or figures'.[49]
Elgin's team together with 300 local labourers then resumed
their interrupted work, as well as their more ambitious new
task of dismantling the Parthenon, although it seems question-
able whether permission was actually intended to cover the
removal of pieces still *in situ*. Bribes helped to ease the situation.

Not surprisingly the enterprise ran into constant difficulties,
notably when a consignment of marbles, transported in the
only cart in the whole of Athens strong enough to carry
them, was unloaded at Porto Leone, some five miles from the
Acropolis, and embarked for England. The ship, the *Mentor*,
ran into a storm two days out, struck a rock off Cythera and
sank. Seventeen cases of marbles lay on the sea bed, where
they remained for the best part of two years, during which
time sponge divers from nearby islands struggled to bring them
to the surface. Eventually all were recovered. Nelson sent a
ship to collect them, and in time they found their way back to
England. Meanwhile Lord Elgin himself, recalled to London at
the conclusion of his mission, began to travel home across
France during the short-lived Peace of Amiens, only to find
himself seized as a prisoner of war on the resumption of
hostilities. He was not released on parole until 1806, but work
on the Acropolis continued steadily in the interim and there
were further shipments from the port.

When Elgin eventually returned to London, he found the marbles had been given temporary refuge in the Duke of Richmond's garden. His first move was to rent a large house on the corner of Park Lane and Piccadilly with a good garden at the back, and here he built a shed about fifty foot square so that the sculptures could be unpacked and arranged in some kind of order, and this temporary museum was completed and the sculptures ready for display by June 1807. On his way home Elgin had asked the Italian sculptor Canova his advice on whether or not to restore the figures, and Canova gave it as his opinion that this would be wrong, suggesting that if Elgin remained set on restoration, then the sculptor John Flaxman, soon to become the first Professor of Sculpture at the Royal Academy, would be the best person to approach. Fortunately Flaxman was reluctant to touch the sculptures, feeling that to do so would amount to sacrilege. In any case, his estimate of the likely cost of restoration was way beyond Elgin's means, who was deeply in debt after the huge sums incurred in removing and transporting the marbles, already amounting to £39,000.

Flaxman's immediate reaction to the sculptures was that they were undoubtedly of the fifth century BC, and far superior to what had been accepted until then as the greatest remaining embodiment of ideal beauty of the classical age, such works as the Apollo Belvedere and the Medici Venus. This opinion was generally shared by the few artists who were now allowed to view the display in Piccadilly, including the president of the Royal Academy, Benjamin West, David Wilkie, Henry Fuseli, Thomas Lawrence and also John William Mallord Turner, who wrote to Elgin 'to pay my homage to your lordship's exertions for this rescue from barbarism'.[50] But some of the influential art connoisseurs of the day, whose opinions were accepted by patrons and collectors, were slower to realize the nature of Lord Elgin's acquisitions. Chief among these was

Richard Payne Knight, collector of bronzes, powerful art critic and senior member of the Society of Dilettanti. Payne Knight immediately launched an attack on the authenticity of the marbles which he maintained for the next ten years, although he was gradually compelled to modify his views as they became increasingly untenable. His first and most notorious statement came a few days after Lord Elgin's return from captivity in France. The two met at dinner at Lord Stafford's, and Payne Knight, aggressively raising his voice, proclaimed across the table: 'You have lost your labour, my lord Elgin. Your marbles are overrated: they are not Greek: they are Roman of the time of Hadrian.'[51] Elgin, behaving with admirable dignity, bowed but remained silent. At this point Payne Knight had not even seen the marbles, yet to be unpacked from their crates, but his remark made an immediate and widespread impact. His animosity against Elgin seems to have been personal, and certainly the arrival of the marbles posed a threat to his long-held and hitherto unchallenged opinion as to the paramount supremacy of the later Italian works. His hostile attitude could hardly have been more damaging to Elgin's chances of selling them to the government as, given his status, both connoisseurs and authorities were hesitant to go against his powerful voice.

At this point Haydon entered the story. Although only twenty in 1806, he had already made his mark as a promising artist, and this had been emphasized by Lord Mulgrave's commission to paint *The Assassination of Dentatus*. The picture, once completed, was sent to the Academy at Somerset House where, to Haydon's joy, it was hung in an important position in the main gallery. And now an incident took place which was to colour the whole of the rest of the artist's life. For some reason, possibly that his patrons Lord Mulgrave and Sir George Beaumont had antagonized the hanging committee by exerting too much pressure to give their protégé's picture a prominent position, or whether, as was suggested, the president had decided that it needed more light, or, and most likely of all, that the young man had already irritated his elders and betters in the Academy, Haydon returned one day to the Academy to find that his picture had been moved to the ante-room. The fact that it now occupied the central place there was as nothing to him – he chose to feel that he had been offered an intolerable insult, worked himself up into a towering passion of rage out of all proportion to the occasion, and behaved in the ridiculous manner of a spoilt child, shouting and denouncing all concerned, and deaf to all reason. For the rest of his career he became the committed enemy of the Academy and, in return, the Academicians remained implacable in their determination to exclude him from their elite circle. Haydon's *Dentatus*, gallantly fighting the servants of a corrupt regime against overwhelming odds, now represented for the painter a symbol of himself as persecuted genius.

During the painting of his picture Haydon had soon discovered that to produce a tragic figure on a heroic scale which was also true to nature presented almost insuperable difficulties. One day, as he was struggling with his dilemma, painting, scratching out, and trying again, Wilkie called in at his studio, listened to his problems and suggested they should go together to see the Elgin Marbles, for which he had a permit. The two friends made their way to the Park Lane house, passed through the hall to the yard at the back, and entered the damp shed where the marbles were ranged in a semicircle facing the door. For Haydon the moment was of seminal importance, and began his love for the marbles, which soon amounted to adoration:

The first thing I fixed my eyes on was the wrist of a figure in one of the female groups, in which were visible, though in a feminine form, the radius and ulna. I was astonished, for I had never seen them hinted at in any female wrist in the antique. I darted my eye to the elbow, and saw the outer condyle visibly affecting the shape as in nature. I saw that the arm was in repose and the soft parts in relaxation. That combination of nature and idea which I had felt was so much wanting for high art was here displayed to midday conviction. My heart beat![52]

Next he saw what he took to be the figure of Theseus[53] and felt again a sense of revelation beyond anything he could have anticipated:

I felt the future, I foretold that they would prove themselves the finest things on earth, that they would overturn the false beau-ideal, where nature was nothing, and would establish the true beau-ideal, of which nature alone is the basis. I shall never forget the horses' heads – the feet in the metopes – I felt as if a divine truth had blazed inwardly upon my mind and I knew that they would at last rouse the art of Europe from its slumber in the darkness.[54]

Here, by the 'false beau-ideal', Haydon was referring to the then accepted belief that the highest and unsurpassed examples of classical excellence were those of the Italian masters, a belief for ever shattered for him by the sight of the contents of that dingy shed on a dreary winter's afternoon.

Haydon hurried home and attacked his picture, dreading that his comprehension of the mysteries he had seen might fade before he could incorporate them on canvas, working on late into the night, and sleeping only in fits and starts. The next morning he returned to Park Lane, having managed to obtain a pass. Then in a great state of excitement he rushed – his favourite mode of locomotion – to find Fuseli, and so infected him with his enthusiasm that the two set off at once:

I remember that first a coal-cart with eight horses stopped us as it struggled up one of the lanes of the Strand; then a flock of sheep blocked us up; Fuseli, in a fury of haste and rage, burst into the middle of them, and they got between his little legs and jostled him so much that I screamed with laughter in spite of my excitement. He swore all along the Strand like a little fury. At last we came to Park Lane. He strode about saying, 'De Greeks were godes! de Greeks were godes!' Immortal period of my sanguine life! To look back on those hours has been my solace in the bitterest afflictions.[55]

Haydon's next move was to ask Mulgrave to request permission for him to draw from the marbles, to which Elgin agreed, only stipulating that the drawings were not to be engraved. Haydon was almost the first to be allowed such freedom to copy, and for the next weeks he spent long hours each day, sometimes as much as fourteen or fifteen hours, working at his drawings, holding a candle and his board in one hand and drawing with the other, eventually returning home

cold, benumbed and damp, my clothes steaming up as I dried them; and so, spreading my drawings on the floor and putting a candle on the ground, I have drunk my tea at one in the morning with ecstasy as its warmth trickled through my frame, and looked at my picture and dwelt on my drawings, and pondered on the change of empires, and thought that I had been contemplating what Socrates looked at and Plato saw, and then, lifted up with my own high urgings of soul, I have prayed God to enlighten my mind to discover the principles of those divine things, and then I have had inward assurances of future glory, and almost fancying divine influence in my room have lingered to my mattress bed and soon dozed into a rich, balmy slumber.[56]

This account of events in his autobiography telescopes time, and the revelation Haydon experienced, described by him in the manner of St Paul on the road to Damascus, must in reality have evolved over the ensuing weeks as he worked on his drawings and realization dawned and grew of the scale of the achievements he was recording, and particularly of the wonder of the sculptures' anatomical precision combined with their creators' power to convey emotion. But this does not detract from the validity of his response, and his teaching and writing about the truths he then learnt constitutes his most valuable contribution to artistic knowledge, which he first passed on to his pupils by word and by demonstration, and which they in their turn handed down to a later generation of nineteenth-century artists.

By the time Haydon first saw them, the marbles were the sensation of London, and permits to view them were eagerly sought. In June 1808 a popular prize-fighter posed naked in various attitudes to an invited audience, allowing the viewers to compare his perfect physique with that of the sculptures. On another occasion Mrs Siddons, in her role of arbiter on matters of aesthetics, also agreed to pay a visit to Lord Elgin's shed, and was moved to tears by the impact of what she saw. By the end of the following year Payne Knight was having to moderate his tone, no longer claiming that the marbles only dated from the age of Hadrian, although his attitude remained grudging.

The growing fame of the collection encouraged Elgin to apply to the trustees of the British Museum to consider his petition that the government should purchase the marbles for the nation, and the reaction seemed hopeful. His estimated expenses had by now grown to the huge sum of more than £62,000. But the Paymaster-General let Elgin know that the most he could hope for would be £30,000, a sum which Elgin indignantly rejected. Meanwhile his troubles increased when the lease of the Park Lane house ran out and he had to find a new home for his collection as a matter of urgency. Eventually the Duke of Devonshire agreed to provide a temporary lodging place behind Burlington House. The removal of the enormously heavy marbles from the other end of Piccadilly proved another large expense. Then, in May 1812, the prime minister, Spencer Perceval, was murdered in the lobby of the House of Commons and all hope of further negotiation with the government was necessarily abandoned for the time being.

To add to Elgin's woes, Lord Byron, who had journeyed back from his travels in Greece as a guest on one of the ships carrying the marbles, and who had been guided round the Acropolis by Elgin's own agent, Lusieri, now published *Childe Harold's Pilgrimage*, which contained a violent attack on Elgin as a despoiler and plunderer. The immediate and phenomenal success of the poem meant that it was read and discussed by all fashionable London. Byron overnight became the lion of the era, and his views, to Elgin's detriment and frustration, were accepted by the majority of his readers. Later in 1812 Byron published another poem, *The Curse of Minerva*, which contained a more overtly virulent attack on Elgin, including references to the break-up of his marriage and his facial disfigurement from syphilis. Almost immediately he decided to have the edition suppressed, but a few copies were privately printed to give to friends, and these naturally soon found their way into public awareness. In 1815 a pirated edition appeared, adding fuel to the flames of anti-Elgin fever. As a result of Byron's poems and his philhellenic emphasis, a new dimension was now added to the debate on the marbles: what right had Elgin to remove such a precious part of Greek heritage from that oppressed nation?

During these years Haydon continued to praise the sculptures, to canvass for their acceptance and to revile and ridicule Payne Knight, antagonizing as he did so one of the most powerful voices of the art world. His passion for the beautiful objects increased as he continued to work from them, and to insist that his pupils did so too, and nothing could have diverted him from his persistent course of seeking to influence public opinion in their favour and of shaming the government into purchasing them for the good of the nation and at a realistic price. He repeatedly emphasized the views of Ennio Visconti, the director of the Louvre, who was a fervent supporter of Elgin's achievement, and whose views were necessarily listened to on the Continent, so that, as Haydon pointed out, London would become the envy of the European art world as possessor of these treasures. Haydon corresponded with Elgin, and at one point was offered the curatorship of the marbles.

Wordsworth supported Haydon's cause, writing to him at the end of 1815 after Canova's visit to London and the publication of his laudatory report: 'I am not surprised that Canova expressed himself so highly pleased with the Elgin Marbles. A man must be senseless as a clod, or perverse as a fiend, not to be enraptured with them.'[57] Louis Simond was also among their earliest enthusiasts, and felt that their removal had been the best way to impress the 'barbarous' Turks with their value, so that they might be influenced into respecting the remaining parts of the Parthenon and refrain from destroying them. Simond made a perceptive comment on Mrs Siddons's tears on seeing the marbles:

She may have been so affected – there is no knowing what ideas might arise in her mind – but certainly it was more what she thought than what she saw: Phidias – the Parthenon – so many centuries – and those precious remains of the arts of Greece transported into regions which had hardly a name in the days of the glory of Athens![58]

Early in 1815 a new problem arose: Burlington House was sold to Lord George Cavendish, who intended to start work on his new acquisition within a few weeks. The marbles, many of them lying out of doors and becoming increasingly damp, must be moved once more, and the obvious move, Elgin decided with reluctance, was to apply again to the British Museum. A committee was set up and an offer was made for their acquisition at the derisory sum of £15,000–20,000, far less than the earlier estimate. Elgin then appealed to the government to replace the British Museum committee with a select committee of the House of Commons, and this was duly arranged. But a few days before the matter was about to be debated, Napoleon was defeated at Waterloo, the House was unable to find time for such a relatively parochial affair, and Elgin's petition was relegated for consideration to February 1816. At last, on 23 February, the debate took place. By now the effects of the aftermath of war were making themselves felt, and there was much distress among the men discharged from the armed forces and reduced to beggary; a series of ruined harvests had resulted in a sharp increase in the price of bread, and the government was in no mood to spend large sums of money on the arts, particularly in such a disputed area. Henry Brougham, the radical lawyer and politician, with his usual felicity of phrase, said that as the government seemed unable to help these unfortunates, or afford to give them bread, 'we ought not to indulge ourselves in the purchase of stones'. His point was immediately taken up by George Cruikshank in a cartoon entitled *The Elgin Marbles! or John Bull buying Stones at the time his numerous Family want Bread!!*

Elgin's petition was accepted, though only after a sticky passage through the House, and the select committee set to work the following week. The painters and sculptors called for their opinions were West and Lawrence, Nollekens, Flaxman, Chantrey, Rossi (who by the following year was to become Haydon's landlord) and Westmacott. As the committee's examinations proceeded, it became clear that the overall majority of artists' and art connoisseurs' witnesses were in

19. *The Elgin Marbles! or John Bull buying* Stones *at the time his numerous Family want* Bread!! Caricature by George Cruikshank, 1816. Castlereagh is telling an unimpressed John Bull: 'Here's a Bargain for you Johnny! Only £35,000!! I have bought them on purpose for you! Never think of *Bread* when you can have Stones so wonderous *Cheap*!!'

favour of government purchase. Less clear was the question of how much should be paid, and here estimates differed widely. Finally the sum recommended for Elgin was fixed at £35,000, less than half his incurred expenses.

At Lord Elgin's request Haydon had been one of the artists chosen to testify.

With three others he named me, but day after day passed and I was never called. Lord Elgin became impatient, because his other friends had been called and dismissed after a very few words, while all witnesses inimical to the marbles were questioned and cross-questioned at a length which gave them a full opportunity of impressing their peculiar opinions on the members of the committee. At last Lord Elgin received a promise that I should be called, but the day passed and I was never sent for.[59]

This was too much for Haydon:

'This is Knight's influence,' I said to Hamilton. 'I have seen it is,' said he. 'Banks says that you will not be examined out of delicacy to Knight.' 'Very well,' I replied, 'I'll appeal to the public. It is unjust and unfair to Lord Elgin, and to myself also, and I'll appeal to the public.'[60]

It is understandable that the select committee should wish to avoid submitting itself to a scene of the kind of blustering and exaggerated rhetoric that had become Haydon's hallmark in the affair, or to expose the by now discredited Payne Knight, who had made a pathetically inadequate showing at his examination, to further humiliation; but at this stage Haydon was in no frame of mind to make allowances, even if he had been aware of the unfortunate effect of his interventions.

I told Lord Elgin I would make Knight remember the Elgin Marbles as long as he lived; Lord Elgin smiled incredulously, but I knew my power, and retiring to my painting room with my great picture of Jerusalem before me, I dashed down on the paper thoughts and truths which neither nobility nor patrons ever forgave.[61]

The result of this dashing down was a long and impassioned piece which was published simultaneously in the *Examiner* and the *Champion*, entitled 'On the Judgment of Connoisseurs being Preferred to that of Professional Men'. The effect of the letter was gratifying to Haydon's vanity and craving for fame – he did indeed for a while become the centre of attention, and the letter was widely read and discussed, and translated into French and Italian, and attracted the notice of Goethe. But for his career it was a disaster, as it confirmed the Royal Academy in its determination to exclude him from membership. Haydon did have a brief moment of doubt about this, wondering if he could not have achieved his aim of validating the marbles without infuriating and antagonizing the Academicians.

By January 1817 the marbles were installed in the British Museum and the public admitted. Crowds came to see what all the fuss had been about, and one day there was a record of more than 1,000 visitors. The sculptures were well displayed, some on pivots so that they could be viewed from all sides, and the general interest continued to mount. Two hundred permits to copy were issued to students during the first year.

On 1 March, the publication day of Keats's first volume of poems, Haydon took him to see the marbles. The young man's response was unexpected: rather than the experience of revelation which Haydon expected, Keats was overwhelmed by a sense of oppression and inadequacy in the face of such marvels, his fragile self-confidence dangerously shattered. He wrote two sonnets for Haydon on the subject, which appeared in the *Examiner* the following week, and gave his friend the fiercest pleasure. The first, 'Haydon! forgive me that I cannot speak', ended

> In this who touch thy vesture's hem?
> For when men star'd at what was most divine
>   With browless idiotism – o'erwise phlegm –
> Thou hadst beheld the Hesperean shine
>   Of their star in the East, and gone to worship them.

Keats returned to the museum many times by himself, sitting for hours sunk in thought, as ideas began to evolve which two years later would result in the 'Ode on a Grecian Urn', where 'the heifer lowing at the skies' was almost certainly inspired by the heifer of the south frieze being led to the sacrifice. He was amused when one afternoon he was approached by a dandified man with whom he had a slight acquaintance, who had been peering at the marbles through his eyeglass, and who finally announced, 'Yes, I believe, Mr Keats, we may admire these works safely.'[62] The marbles, which had so overwhelmed the poet by their self-evident beauty, remained for many other viewers hostage to the judgement of public opinion.

Haydon remained blissfully regardless of the dangers of his published diatribes, and basked in his fame. His diary entries are full of his feelings of triumphalism:

In a week my painting room was again crowded with rank, beauty and fashion, to such excess that I ordered the front doors to be left open . . . My views were now completely before the world. Wilkie said I should carry all before me. I was an object of curiosity whenever I appeared in a public place. My vanity was tickled; and the Academicians when I met them at a conversazione, or a rout, slunk by, pale and contemptible, holding out a finger as they passed.[63]

5.   The Mystery of the Rainbow

'Now, you rascally Lake poet,' said Lamb, 'you call Voltaire a dull
fellow.' We all agreed there was a state of mind when he would
appear so – and 'Well, let us drink his health,' said Lamb. 'Here's
Voltaire, the Messiah of the French nation, and a very fit one.' He
then attacked me for putting in Newton, 'a Fellow who believed
nothing unless it was as clear as the three sides of a triangle'. And
then he and Keats agreed he had destroyed all the poetry of the
rainbow, by reducing it to a prism. It was impossible to resist
them, and we drank 'Newton's health, and confusion to
mathematics!'

Benjamin Robert Haydon, *Diary*[1]

The dinner table was by now cleared except for wine and
dessert, and the time had come for the drinking of toasts. One
of Haydon's guests drew attention to the presence of Voltaire
and Sir Isaac Newton in his picture, and Lamb, excited by the
wine, rashly raised the question of the appropriateness of
including Voltaire in the presentation of such a sacred
occasion. This was a sensitive topic to Haydon, and as a rule
he would have reacted angrily to Lamb's teasing tone, his
partisan rage at any hint of mockery of the revealed religion
of the Anglican Church being one of the most virulent bees
in his capacious bonnet. But tonight nothing could disturb his
equanimity. He had agonized over the question of portraying
the philosopher during the previous two years, conscientiously
exploring Voltaire's works for proof of the blasphemous anti-

Christianity bias he felt sure he would find, eventually reaching the conclusion that 'Voltaire was the worst of hypocrites because under the mask of impartiality, he was the most maliciously prejudiced of any human being. Every page I read adds confirmation to this truth.'[2] Page after page of his diary was devoted to making out a case against Voltaire, drawing largely mistaken deductions from his reading of the philosopher's works. One element, however, in all this searching about for an excuse to include Voltaire in his picture may simply have been that Haydon enjoyed painting his strange Hogarthian features as a respite from his greater problem, never really to be solved, of how he was to convincingly portray the head of Christ.

Haydon was not alone in his opinion that night. Wordsworth also had an antipathy to Voltaire. Lamb's teasing accusation, quoted above, of his having described Voltaire as dull refers to a passage in *The Excursion* where the poet had dismissed *Candide* – that brilliant masterpiece of Voltaire's maturity – as 'this dull product of a scoffer's pen'.[3] Haydon would have accepted William Blake's view as expressed in a poem which in 1817 was still lying unpublished in his notebook:

> Mock on, Mock on, Voltaire, Rousseau!
> Mock on, Mock on – 'tis all in vain!
> You throw the sand against the wind,
> And the wind blows it back again.
>
> And every sand becomes a Gem
> Reflected in the beams divine;
> Blown back they blind the mocking Eye,
> But still in Israel's paths they shine.[4]

Haydon's conclusion that Voltaire was an atheist and vicious sneerer at the Christian religion, and therefore suitable to be

portrayed as the anti-Christ figure in his picture, was a distor-
tion of the philosopher's actual beliefs. His prime target had
been the then authoritarian rule of the Catholic Church in
France, with its rigid conviction of its own exclusive possession
of the truth, its intolerance of the views of others, its injustices
and cruelty, and the venality of a large proportion of its
priesthood. And during the three years of exile he spent in
England from 1726, he certainly came to feel that the Anglican
Church shared in some of the failings of the French priesthood,
particularly those of excessive luxury and lazy abrogation of
pastoral duties. At the other end of the doctrinal spectrum
Voltaire also disliked the moral intolerance of the Presbyterians
with their harsh belief in predestination and their condem-
nation of the simple pleasures of life. The only English religious
persuasion he felt able to admire was that of the Quakers,
whose simplicity and lack of rigid dogma best represented the
basis of his own lifelong search after truth. In his *Letters on
England* (or *Lettres philosophiques*) he wrote at length about the
sect, gently mocking their eccentricities but praising their
tolerance, and admiring their freedom of thought as being
closest to his own view of a man's right to his own opinion
on the likelihood of the existence of a supernatural being. No
amount of reasoning, he argued, could prove if there was a
God, and therefore nobody had the right to force anyone to
subscribe to one specific belief, or indeed to any dogmatic
belief at all.

   The discussion about Voltaire at Haydon's dinner influenced Keats the next month to settle down to read some of
his work, and he also went to listen to Hazlitt lecturing on the
philosopher, admiring his 'very fine piece of discriminating
criticism'.[5] The following year he reported to George and
Georgiana Keats that he was reading Voltaire's *Siècle de Louis
XIV*; and the Frenchman was still in the forefront of his mind
in the summer of 1820 when he went to see an exhibition of

English portraits, including one of George II looking 'very like an unintellectual Voltaire, troubled with the gout and a bad temper'.[6]

The question of science versus religion was one factor in the party's general discussion about the inclusion of Voltaire and Newton in Haydon's picture. Another concerned the threat posed by increasing scientific knowledge to the status of the poetic imagination. Lamb and Keats used as an example of this Newton's great work on optics, which had destroyed, or so they protested, 'all the poetry of the rainbow, by reducing it to a prism'. Later Keats wrote, in *Lamia*, of his consequent sense of loss:

> Do not all charms fly
> At the mere touch of cold philosophy?
> There was an awful rainbow once in heaven:
> We know her woof, her texture; she is given
> In the dull catalogue of common things.
> Philosophy will clip an Angel's wings,
> Conquer all mysteries by rule and line,
> Empty the haunted air, and gnomèd mine –
> Unweave a rainbow . . .[7]

Newton had been much in Haydon's thoughts all the week. A few days earlier, on 22 December, after Wordsworth had sat for him, his mind turned to Newton as his next subject. Later on the same day he went to the British Museum to consult Chalmers's *General Biographical Dictionary* for details of Newton's appearance, where he learnt that the great man had been 'of a middle stature, and rather plump in his latter years: he had a very lively and piercing eye; a comely and gracious aspect, and a fine head of hair, as white as silver, without any baldness. To the time of his last illness he had the bloom and colour of a young man.'[8] Chalmers's description may stem

20. The young Isaac Newton conducting an experiment on the nature of light, from Guillaume Louis Figuier's *Les Grands Savants*.

from an uncharacteristic late portrait by John Van der Bank, which goes against the evidence of previous portraits showing him with sharp features and a stern abstracted gaze. By 26 December Haydon could write: 'Got in Newton's head. Voltaire, Newton and Wordsworth make a wonderful contrast.'[9] He considered Newton to have had the 'greatest human mind that ever touched our sphere, the circle of whose intellect in its range almost reached the outermost circle of the influence of Divinity'.[10] He might have been taken aback to learn that Voltaire agreed with him, considering Newton to be the greatest man who ever lived, 'the very greatest, the giants of antiquity are beside him children playing with marbles'.[11] Voltaire had attended the great man's state funeral in Westminster Abbey, and wrote admiringly of him in his *Letters on England*, as being

always tranquil, happy and honoured in his own country . . . His great good fortune was not only to be born in a free country, but at a time when, scholastic extravagances being banished, reason alone was cultivated and society could only be his pupil and not his enemy.[12]

Although he never met him, it was Voltaire who made Newton famous in France, and he was the author of the famous story of the apple falling from a tree, from an anecdote told him by Newton's half-niece, Catherine Barton, in a conversation about her uncle's profound meditations on the laws of gravitation.

Three years after his dinner party, on the eve of the private view day of the finally completed *Christ's Entry into Jerusalem*, Haydon still had a tremor of rage at the sight of Voltaire's 'sneering, diabolic face' beside that of Newton, 'humble, pious, mild, gentle in his temper and deep, profound, almost immortal in his faculties'.[13] But it is not easy to reconcile this idea of a benign figure with the rebarbative recluse of reality. Newton's nature was complex and difficult, and he was obsessively secretive – it was always a painful effort for him, postponed as long as possible, to make any of his work public, although it was often in his best interest that he should do so. He strongly believed in Arianism, the denial of the doctrine of the Holy Trinity. But the greatest shock to Haydon would have been today's knowledge of Newton's most closely kept secret, that parallel with his scientific researches he was a passionate alchemist, devoting the larger part of his time to the pursuit of the philosopher's stone that would turn other metals into gold. This aspect of his work did not become generally apparent until 1936, when John Maynard Keynes bought a collection of Newton's papers up until then dismissed as of no particular interest. Keynes was astonished by the contents of his purchase, which overset the conventional idea of the great scientist as the propounder of the supremacy of reason over imagination, and in 1942 he gave a lecture on his discoveries and the conclusions to be drawn from them:

Newton was not the first of the age of reason. He was the last of the magicians, the last of the Babylonians and Sumerians, the last great mind which looked out on the visible and intellectual world with the same eyes as those who began to build our intellectual inheritance rather less than ten thousand years ago. Isaac Newton, a posthumous child born with no father on Christmas Day 1642, was the last wonderchild to whom the Magi could do sincere and appropriate homage.[14]

Over a million of Newton's words on alchemy survive, a large number written in coded Latin, and there may have been many more, as a quantity of his papers were destroyed in a fire in his Cambridge rooms in 1677. The practice of alchemy in the seventeenth century constituted a felony, and that of the black arts, with which it is thought he may also have flirted, was still a capital offence, which helps to explain his obsessive secrecy. His voracious investigation of any fact which baffled him, however irrelevant to his scientific explorations it may have seemed, was often concerned with his alchemical experiments. Not only were Newton's alchemy and his scientific studies deeply interwoven, but the fruit of his alchemical work became the forerunner and enabling factor of much of his greatest scientific work, rather than a block to its progress. His *Opticks* and even his *Principia mathematica* owed much to his immersion in such esoteric studies as the chronology of the Bible, the investigation of early prophecies, the hermetic tradition, and the doctrines of the Rosicrucians. The members of this latter secret society believed themselves to be superior to the general run of humanity: among other skills they could, they said, make themselves invisible and converse with spirits. Their strongest emphasis was upon the need for an absolute purity of spirit before they could acquire their supernatural powers. They also insisted upon the truth of the Christian religion. Newton shared their mystical orientation, agreeing that moral purity was a crucial factor for successful chemical experimentation.

Newton's central purpose was to discover the unifying principle which he believed underlay the constitution of the universe. Keynes remarked that Newton regarded the universe as a cryptogram set by the Almighty, and this happy phrase sums up the purpose of his life. If he could once crack that cryptogram, the *prisca sapienta* of ancient lore, all else, he felt, would fall into place. He believed that the early alchemists had acquired this precious wisdom, but that it had been lost, and that he had been appointed to recover the secret. His experiments with mercury were slanted in this direction, Newton being convinced that if he could discover the way to transform base metals into gold, the solving of the cryptogram would almost certainly follow, and late in his life he was deluded into thinking he had achieved this aim.

Newton was created Lucasian Professor of Mathematics at Cambridge at the age of twenty-six. It is an extraordinary fact that this brilliant man, who came to be widely recognized as the possessor of the most powerful intellect in the world, should find himself, as he did, in the ridiculous position of lecturing on his theories on optics, and later on the laws underlying the *Principia mathematica*, to an empty room in the university. At first a sprinkling of students attended, but after a while, baffled and bored, they abandoned him. Time after time Newton punctiliously fulfilled his lecturing duties to thin air, speaking as briefly as possible and then hurrying back to what he regarded as his real work in his laboratory.

It is Wordsworth's cool vision of Newton which comes closest to the reality of this strange solitary genius rather than the benign figure portrayed by Voltaire or Haydon. In *The Prelude* the poet looked back to his Cambridge days, when, lying awake in his St John's College room overlooking Trinity College antechapel, he meditated on Newton's isolation:

And from my pillows, looking forth by light
Of moon or favouring stars, I could behold
The antechapel where the statue stood
Of Newton with his prism and silent face,
The marble index of a mind for ever
Voyaging through strange seas of Thought, alone.[15]

As a boy Wordsworth had first become fascinated by
Newton's *Opticks* and the beautiful clarity of the book's expo-
sition when it was lent to him by his Hawkshead schoolmaster.
Newton's subtitle is *A Treatise of the Reflexions, Refractions,
Inflexions and Colours of Light,* and it sets out what he was the
first to understand, that white light is composed of a continuous spectrum of seven colours. To demonstrate this he forced
light through a prism, the refraction breaking it down into its
constituent colours, then back again, returning it to white.
Similarly the phenomenon of the rainbow, also discussed in
the *Opticks,* is shown as the refraction of light downwards
through the top of raindrops, which form minute prisms as
the sun behind the viewer projects light at an angle of 42
degrees above the horizon, this most commonly occurring in
the late afternoon. The eye then sees one separate colour of
the spectrum through a single raindrop, so that the whole
spectrum results from seeing a complex of drops, and consequently no two viewers see precisely the same rainbow. The
perception of the rainbow as being at a considerable distance
is illusory, the raindrops often being quite close to the eye of
the viewer. For Newton as alchemist the rainbow would have
had special significance as heralding the end of a period of
disharmony, an auspicious moment when it should be possible
to turn base elements into gold, and, as some alchemists
believed, at the moment of translation the molten residue
would give off a rainbow-hued glow.

Wordsworth's pleasure in the beauty of the rainbow

remained untroubled despite his awareness of Newton's scientific explanations, as he showed in his famous declaration, published in 1807 when he was thirty-seven:

> My heart leaps up when I behold
>   A rainbow in the sky:
> So was it when my life began;
> So is it now I am a man;
> So be it when I shall grow old,
>   Or let me die!

He was one of those who felt that a fusion between science and the imagination enriched rather than destroyed the latter faculty. In 1815 he reinforced this impression by using the poem again as the epigraph to 'Ode: Intimations of Immortality'. Before beginning to paint a rainbow, Constable, whose approach to his art was for the most part of a scientific nature, copied out Wordsworth's lines and pinned them to his easel as a source of inspiration.

Charles Lamb's accusation of Newton as 'a Fellow who believed nothing unless it was as clear as the three sides of a triangle' was a fairly representative idea at the time of Haydon's dinner. Blake, in his picture of a naked Newton leaning forward with his dividing compasses to measure precise angles, was making this point. This was the picture which would most likely have been in Lamb's mind as he voiced his protest. But the beauty and nobility of Blake's figure of Newton tends to give his protest a disturbing ambivalence.

Hazlitt was another who voiced doubts about the effect of the advances of scientific knowledge on the poetic imagination:

We can no more take away the faculty of the imagination, than we can see all objects without light or shade. Let the naturalist, if he will, catch the glow-worm, carry it home with him in a box, and find it next morning nothing but a little grey worm; let the poet or the lover of poetry visit it at evening, when beneath the scented hawthorn and the crescent moon it has built itself a palace of emerald light . . . It cannot be concealed, however, that the progress of knowledge and refinement has a tendency to circumscribe the limits of the imagination, and to clip the wings of poetry . . . There can never be another Jacob's dream. Since that time, the heavens have gone farther off, and grown astronomical. They have become averse to the imagination, nor will they return to us on the squares of the distances, or on Doctor Chalmers's Discourses.[16]

Perhaps Wordsworth's story of the glow-worm in 'Among all lovely things my Love had been' had crossed Hazlitt's mind as he wrote his 'On Poetry in General' lecture quoted above. Hazlitt's glow-worm had been wantonly destroyed for scientific advance, but Wordsworth's had been carefully cherished, carried on a leaf by the narrator to his love's orchard and left there under a tree as a surprise, knowing she longed to see one. Would it survive until the next evening?

> The whole next day, I hoped, and hoped with fear;
> At night the Glow-worm shone beneath the Tree:
> I led my Lucy to the spot, 'Look here!'
> Oh! joy it was for her, and joy for me![17]

Newton and the rainbow were popular topics in December 1817. On Sunday 14 December, a fortnight before Haydon's party, the *Champion* carried a report on the lecture of the president of the Royal Academy, Benjamin West, entitled 'Observations on the principle of colour, and on the application of those principles to the art of painting'. West was generally considered a poor speaker. His American accent and stumbling diction made his lectures an irritating ordeal for his audiences, and his pronunciation of the Royal *Hackademy* is said to have made George III laugh.[18] On this occasion West began his lecture by saying that 'light is the source of colour, and that the colours of the rainbow are to be considered as a rule for the distribution of colour in a picture'. He then produced a painting of two globes, one colourless and the other with the prismatic colours. He used the first to demonstrate 'the existence of central light, shade and reflection, of which all natural objects partake, as they are all in some degree round'. The second, he explained, was to show 'how the colours of the rainbow expressed the different degrees of light, half-tints and reflection; and showed how perfectly well the arrangement of these colours was adapted to the purpose of painting. Titian understood this, and earlier Raphael.'

West then reminded the students of the great advantages they possessed in the Elgin Marbles and the cartoons of Raphael, which must have given Haydon great satisfaction, particularly as coming from such an important figure in the enemy's camp. It is reports such as this which underline how mistaken Haydon had been to alienate himself from the mainstream of the art establishment of the day. With a little more flexibility and tact he might have shone in the Royal Academy, as had his friend Wilkie. And he could have enjoyed the comforting sense of support in his endless troubles which membership of that charmed circle would have brought him. Despite Haydon's hostile attitude, West had been most kind to him when he was first battling with money troubles, which the younger man never forgot.

Keats's dislike of demystification was not a typical one in the heady atmosphere of the early nineteenth century, when limitless possibilities were opening up for the enquiring mind. For the most part, scientists, poets and artists felt that they were travelling forward together on a roller-coaster of new knowledge towards new horizons, and there was no atmosphere of compartmentalism or of barriers between cultures, the world of science and the arts intermingling as a matter of course. Turner, for example, was a fervent explorer of the latest scientific inventions in the techniques of colour and medium for his wonderful visionary canvases. And Wordsworth's friend, the electrochemist Sir Humphry Davy, a prime example of this duality, was not only the greatest chemist of his time, but also a not inconsiderable poet, whose literary judgement had led Wordsworth to ask him to oversee the publication of the 1800 edition of *Lyrical Ballads*. This was at a time when Davy was working at Beddoes's Pneumatic Institution in Bristol as superintendent of the laboratory, and making experiments, some of them extremely dangerous, but also on occasion highly pleasurable, into the nature of nitrous oxide, on the use of voltaic batteries and the elements of chemical composition. On one occasion he nearly died in an attempt to breathe carburetted hydrogen gas, but he did not allow this mishap to interfere with his investigations. In spite of his own preoccupations, he accepted Wordsworth's commission good-naturedly and spent time he could ill afford over such matters as the correction of the poet's punctuation, 'a business at which I am ashamed to say I am no adept', as Wordsworth told him. Davy admired *Lyrical Ballads* but could not resist writing a parody of Wordsworth's simple style in that volume, which he called 'My Cousin Matthew Brown':

> He then became a farmer true
> And took to him for aid
> A wench who though her eye was blue
> Was yet a virgin maid.
>
> He married her and had a son
> Who died in early times
> As in the churchyard is made known
> By poet Wordsworths Rymes . . .[19]

But in his more serious moments his feeling for nature was Wordsworthian in its scope. 'Oh, most magnificent and noble nature!' he exclaimed:

> Have I not worshipped thee with such a love
> As never mortal man before displayed?[20]

He felt that his chemical work in no way weakened the power of his imagination, but rather served to exalt it. And he experienced visionary states which would have been sympathetic to both Wordsworth and Coleridge. In one such, he described himself lying on top of a rock:

The wind was high, and everything in motion; the branches of an oak tree were waving and were rapidly floating over the western hills; the whole sky was in motion; the yellow stream below me was flowing (agitated by the breeze) . . . Everything seemed alive, and myself part of the series of visible impressions; I should have felt pain in tearing a leaf from one of the trees.[21]

In 1817 Davy was at the height of his powers, having become Professor of Chemistry at the Royal Institution in 1802 and Fellow of the Royal Society in 1803, and gained the Prix Napoléon from the Institut de France for his discoveries in 1807. He had been knighted in 1812, and successfully invented the miner's safety-lamp, the practical invention for which he is now most remembered, in 1815. By 1820, less than three years after Haydon's dinner, Davy became president of the Royal Society, so crowning his extraordinary career at the age of forty-one. Throughout these years poetry remained of central importance to him, as did his Romantic conception of nature; and from time to time he continued to experience visionary states. In his Preface to the 1802 edition of *Lyrical Ballads*, Wordsworth wrote of the relationship between science and poetry in a manner which suggests the possibility of some influence from Davy's ideas, insisting that 'The remotest discoveries of the chemist, the botanist, the mineralogist will be as proper objects of the poet's art as any upon which it can be employed.' Davy twice visited Dove Cottage. He and Wordsworth shared a pleasure in fishing, and much time was dedicated to this pursuit; on Davy's second visit to the Lakes, Southey reported that he was 'stark-mad for angling'. Later in life he wrote a treatise on fish and fishing, *Salmonia*. This was more a meditation on the pleasures of fishing and of rivers he had loved than in any way a handbook; its great interest lay in what it revealed of its author in his private persona and general philosophy of life. When with Sir Stamford Raffles he became co-founder of London Zoo, he hoped, but in vain, to find a way of acclimatizing exotic fish to life in British rivers.

Once installed at the Royal Institution Davy began his lectures, which soon established him as the most successful scientist – chemist, rather, or natural philosopher, the term 'scientist' not being used until 1833 – of his age. Tickets for the lectures were almost impossible to secure, carriages jammed Albemarle Street on lecture evenings and Davy became the lion of the day and London's most sought-after intellectual dinner guest. He and his assistant rehearsed the lectures well in advance, so that the demonstrations, a vital part of his lecturing technique, could be perfected. The impression he gave was theatrical in the extreme. He was a small man whose quietly hypnotic voice enhanced the impression he intended to make in his lectures, and he had brilliant eyes: everyone commented on these. The smallness of stature, the dark burning eyes and the excitement generated by his presence, all sound reminiscent of his contemporary Edmund Kean, the tragic actor. His audiences were entranced by the excitement of the experiments, always dramatic and sometimes near to fireworks. He recorded of one such occasion that 'the globules flew with great velocity through the air in a state of vivid combustion, producing a beautiful effect of continued jets of fire'.[22] Another successful effect was the setting off of an eruption of a model volcano, received with rapturous applause.

Louis Simond attended some of the lectures when he was in England in 1815, and noted Davy's provincial accent and air of natural bashfulness, which did not prevent him from filling the lecture hall to capacity. Simond was amused to see that half the audience was female, 'and it is the most attentive portion. I often observe these fair disciples of science taking notes timidly, and as by stealth, on small bits of paper.'[23] He disapproved of the unrestricted applause, remarking that uncontrolled clapping could sometimes turn to hissing – not that that ever happened in Davy's case. Some of his admirers among the ladies in the audience sent Davy poems and presents, and their husbands paid as much as fifty guineas for Davy's course. Simond returned the following year to find the Royal Institution even more crowded than before, 300 people were crammed in, and 'the lecturer himself more than ever sought-after by the great and the fair'. He commented that

the elocution of this celebrated chemist is very different from the usual tone of men of science in England; his lectures are frequently figurative and poetical; and he is occasionally carried away by the natural tendency of his subject, and of his genius, into the depths of moral philosophy and of religion. The voice and manner of Mr Davy are rather gentle, than impressive and strong; he knows what nature had given him, and what it has withheld, and husbands his means accordingly. You may always foresee by a certain tuning or pitching of the organ of speech to a graver key, thrusting his chin into his neck, and even pulling out his cravat, when Mr Davy is going to be eloquent.[24]

Haydon first met Davy at a dinner party in 1807. 'Mr Davy was announced, and a little slender youth came in, his hair combed over his forehead, speaking very dandily and drawlingly.' Haydon found him very entertaining: 'I well remember a remark he made which turned out a singularly successful prophecy. He said: "Napoleon will certainly come in contact with Russia by pressing forward in Poland, and there probably will begin his destruction." This I heard myself five years before it happened.'[25]

Davy shared Haydon's love of a lord, but he was not quite so endearingly candid about it. He loved the grand parties to which he was invited, and would dash to them from his laboratory at the Royal Institution at the end of a long day of concentrated work, struggling into his evening shirt as he went, sometimes forgetting to remove the working shirt beneath it. This was the general pace of his life, as also seen, for instance, when he climbed Helvellyn with Wordsworth and Sir Walter Scott. Wordsworth moved slowly to accommodate Scott's lameness, and there was much pausing while Scott told stories and anecdotes. On reaching the summit Davy could not stand this loitering for another minute, and bounded downwards ahead of the other two, soon vanishing from their sight into the mist. His brain, too, worked at such a pace that onlookers who watched him moving towards an answer to a problem would be startled to see that his mind would flash to a conclusion before he had finished speaking. Wordsworth was always interested in Davy's inventions, but towards the end of the great chemist's career the poet was sad to find that 'his scientific pursuits had hurried his mind into a course where I could not follow him; and had diverted it in proportion from objects with which I was best acquainted'.[26] The divide between the two cultures had begun.

Davy's father had been a woodcarver, often unemployed, and his mother had to support the family by opening a milliner's shop. The young Davy was taught the rudiments of science by a saddler in Penzance. He had every reason to be proud of the position in society he attained, his early eminence as a brilliant young chemist, and of the benefits to his fellow men stemming from the practical results of his inventions. His early experiments with potentially dangerous gases such as nitrous oxide, for example, led on, after his death, to the blessed use of anaesthetics in operations. At the Royal Institution, Davy's electrochemical research resulted in his isolation of the new metallic elements potassium, sodium, barium, strontium, calcium and magnesium. No matter how abstruse this may sound to the lay ear, he easily succeeded in infecting his audiences with his own enthusiasm for his triumphant forward progress, his unveiling of new and beneficial discoveries.

Thomas De Quincey was much struck by Davy, although there was some mockery in his description of the chemist:

I must say that nowhere, before or since, have I seen a man who had so felicitously caught the fascinating tone of high-bred urbanity which distinguishes the best part of the British nobility. The first time of my seeing him was at the *Courier* office, in a drawing room then occupied by Mr Coleridge, and as a guest of that gentleman: this must have been either in 1808 or 1809. Sir Humphry (I forget whether then a baronet, but I think not) had promised to drink tea with Mr Coleridge, on his road to a meeting of the Royal Society; before which learned body he was on that evening to read some paper or other of his own composition. I had the honour to be invited as sole 'respondent' to the learned philosopher; sole supporter of the antistrophe in our choral performance. It sounded rather appalling to be engaged in a glee for three voices with two performers such as these; and I trepidated a little as I went upstairs, having previously understood that the great man was already come. The door was thrown open by the servant who announced me; and

I saw at once, in full proportions before me, the full-length figure of the young *savant*, not perhaps above ten years older than myself, whose name already filled all the post-horns of Europe, and levied homage from Napoleon. He was a little below the middle height, agreeable in his person, and amiable in the expression of his countenance. His dress was elaborately accurate and fashionable – no traces of soot or furnace *there*; it might be said, also, that it was youthful and almost gay in its character. But what chiefly distinguished him from other men was the captivating – one might call it the *radiant* – courtesy of his manner. It was at once animated and chastised by good-breeding; graceful, and, at the same time, gracious.[27]

Of Haydon's dinner guests, Wordsworth felt that science was a good thing if 'imaginatively pursued', which in Davy's case it certainly was, but Charles Lamb was not so sure. Writing to his friend George Dyer in December 1830 about an arsonist who had set fire to the barns and haystacks of an Enfield farmer using the new phosphorus matches, he exclaimed:

What temptation above Lucifer's! Why, here was a spectacle last night for a whole county – a bonfire visible in London, alarming her guilty towers and shaking the Monument with an aguefit – all done with a little vial of phosphor in a clown's fob! How he must grin, and shake his empty noddle in the clouds, the Vulcanian Epicure! Can we ring the bells backwards? Can we unlearn the arts that pretend to civilize, and then burn the world? There is a March of Science. But who shall beat the drums for its retreat?[28]

One indirect offshoot of Davy's work was the creation of the monster in Mary Shelley's *Frankenstein*. Mary was eighteen when she began to write her novel. Davy knew and visited her father William Godwin when she was a child, and in the autumn of 1816 she was reading his works. That year she was living with Shelley at a villa near Geneva, which he had taken to be near to Byron in the Villa Diodati. Shelley, Mary and her half-sister Claire Clairmont spent long evenings at the Diodati, sometimes sleeping there. They talked late into the night, ranging over topics such as the current theories of the source of electricity, the use of galvanic impulses, and experiments with voltaic batteries, all central to Davy's work. The Diodati party also began to argue about what they called the nature of the principle of life, and to wonder whether the secret of the generation of life could soon be discovered, perhaps by the reanimation of a corpse. During a time of persistent storms the little group spent an evening reading a rare volume of German horror stories, discovered by Shelley. Afterwards it was decided that each of them should try their hands at writing such a story to help pass the time. Mary was anxious to comply, but was lost for a topic, until a few days later she had a terrible dream in which she saw 'the hideous phantasm of a man stretched out, and then, on the working of some powerful engine, show signs of life, and stir with an uneasy, half vital motion'.[29] In the aftermath of her nightmare she realized that here lay the genesis of her story, and set to work immediately, incorporating the figure she had seen with the conversations of the earlier part of the month to produce the tale of the medical student Frankenstein, creator of the monster destined to become the cause of his own death, presented in the novel as merited retribution for unlawful meddling with forbidden mysteries. During 1817 Shelley wrote the introduction, and the novel was published in March 1818, just too late for Haydon and his guests to have read it before the party at the end of December 1817, although it may well have been talked about in literary London during the previous months.

Turner knew Davy, their friendship being facilitated by the fact that the Royal Academy, of which Turner was a pillar, and the Royal Society were housed alongside each other in

Somerset House, on the Strand, looking out on to the Thames, London's most important thoroughfare with its ceaseless busy traffic. Their respective entrances were on either side of the great portico, and there was much coming and going between the two organizations, scientists wandering into Academy lectures and vice versa, to the benefit of both. Davy may have looked in on some of Turner's famous lectures on perspective, which rivalled his own in dramatic interest. One very deaf enthusiast of the series, Thomas Stothard, on being asked what benefit he could derive from the lectures as he could not hear a word of them, said that it was because there was so much to *see*. He particularly enjoyed, as did everyone else, the illustrative brilliance of Turner's perspective drawings. Turner usually spoke for about half an hour, and seemed uncomfortable in front of his audience, not looking in their direction but either down at his notes or towards the porter who was displaying his illustrations, to whom he muttered contradictory instructions about which one to hold up next.

Turner was already Professor of Perspective at the Royal Academy when the young Haydon began his lifelong campaign of rage against that institution. Naturally, as a devoted Academy supporter, Turner resented Haydon's inveterate hostility, and when he was told years later the news of Haydon's death, he repeated several times, 'He stabbed his mother! He stabbed his mother!' referring to Haydon's behaviour towards the Academy. But when Haydon's *Judgment of Solomon* was exhibited, Turner said, 'Tell Haydon I am astonished'; and Haydon wrote in his diary with some satisfaction that Turner had done well in making the effort to come to see his picture.

Turner was one of those who made the fullest use for his own purposes of the many technical inventions of the time, in his case particularly in the area of the chemical constituents of pigments and the creation of new colours, notably chrome yellow, cobalt blue and emerald green – yellow being of the greatest importance as the basis of much of his work. He was always fascinated with how things worked, and had a great love of gadgetry: one of his most prized possessions was an umbrella with a two-foot-long dagger concealed in the handle. He had a circular table constructed on a pedestal so that he could turn it round to reach the colour he needed; and in his Harley Street corner house he installed a water closet, a very novel idea.[30] Turner knew Davy and shared with him a love of poetry. And like him he had a visionary capacity, a quality existing in both men in happy parallel with absolute dedication to matters scientific and of practical application. Turner's interest in the minutiae of industrial inventions, for example, is clear in many of his paintings.

Like Wordsworth, and indeed Keats, Turner had a tremendous capacity for close observation of nature and his environment. Even as a child he demonstrated this characteristic:

When I was a boy I used to lie for hours on my back watching the skies, and then go home and paint them; and there was a stall in Soho Bazaar where they sold drawing materials, and they used to *buy* my skies. They gave me 1s 6d for the small ones and 3s 6d for the larger ones. There's many a young lady who's got my sky to her drawing.[31]

Turner was a founder member of the Athenaeum. Club life was beneficial for the scientists and inventors of the day, who could meet and discuss their work in relaxed surroundings. In such places Turner could listen and question theories of the properties of light, always a subject of central importance to him. In time this was to become an obsession, as were his feelings about the sun as the source of light.

When Turner built his own gallery in the back part of his Harley Street house, just round the corner from Tom

Monkhouse in Queen Anne Street, he used his knowledge of light effects, constructing a series of skylights, immediately under which he spread herring netting covered with pieces of tissue paper, with a resultant harmonious diffusion of light, exactly as he had desired. He guarded his pictures jealously: when the gallery was open to visitors he would watch them through a spyhole in the next room, and if anyone was foolish enough to touch or try to copy any of the paintings, out he shot and warned off the startled viewer. Another innovative use of light, learnt in Italy during his travels, which he demonstrated to Academy students, was to place a model in front of a white sheet, so creating reflections all over the naked body.[32] At the time of Haydon's party Turner's *Decline of the Carthaginian Empire* was completed, and *England: Richmond Hill on the Prince Regent's Birthday*, his largest canvas to date, was on show in Somerset House. Everyone stared at him as he progressed round the gallery, a stumpy, cross-looking figure wearing, as always, his famous high hat.

In his diary entry after the dinner party Haydon wrote of Lamb and Keats agreeing that Newton had destroyed all the poetry of the rainbow by reducing it to a prism. This phrase, 'all the poetry of the rainbow', was not entirely newly minted for the occasion, a parallel phrase having appeared the previous week in a review by Keats of Kean's Richard III in the *Champion*, a liberal Sunday newspaper much favoured by the dinner-party guests. Keats had been standing in for his friend John Hamilton Reynolds, the paper's regular drama critic, who wished to spend the Christmas holidays with his fiancée's family in Devon. Reynolds was in Haydon's bad books, having been invited to the dinner party, but having failed to answer the invitation or to turn up. Haydon regarded this, unreasonably in the circumstances, as an unforgivable defection, and nursed a sense of grievance against Reynolds for some time. Keats, on the other hand, was delighted to be given the opportunity of Reynolds's absence to write a eulogy of Kean, to him the prince of Shakespearian tragic actors. Reynolds had lent Keats his silver ticket, which guaranteed free entry to the theatre for life, and Keats also used the pass to see his hero as Luke in Sir James Bland Burgess's *Riches*. He was by now a fervent and experienced theatre-goer, visiting the pit at Drury Lane as often as he could, often borrowing a silver admittance pass from another friend, Charles Brown, and feeding his passion for Shakespeare. Now here, a few days before the Immortal Dinner, was an opportunity to voice his opinion of the greatest Shakespearian actor of the day in a widely read Sunday newspaper.

Kean, the idol of the minute, probably had gypsy blood; he had been abandoned by his actress mother in infancy, and had worked his way in the course of an adventurous childhood slowly towards fame on the stage of Drury Lane via ventriloquism and tumbling work in a circus, and as a strolling player around the country. By a happy chance Dr Drury saw him playing in Dorchester, and introduced him to the stage manager of the Drury Lane Theatre, where on 26 January 1814 he made his debut as Shylock to a sparse audience of devoted theatre-goers who were undeterred by the terrible cold of the winter of the Great Frost. After the performance Arnold, the stage manager, is said to have reproached Kean, saying, 'This will never do, Mr Kean, it is an innovation, Sir, it is totally different from anything that has ever been done on these boards'; to which Kean coolly replied, 'I wish it to be so.'[33] Hazlitt, who was present, realized at once that he was watching the acting of a genius who was casually oversetting the accepted classical mode of his predecessor Charles Kemble for a startlingly new realism and a passion all his own.

It was this quality of passion which drew Keats to him three years later. Kean, like himself, was of small stature and with somewhat similar features, and his darting intensity matched

Keats's own. Off stage Kean lived a dissolute and drunken life, drawing disapproving comments from the more conventional; but for Keats this freedom from social restraints, together with the actor's libertarian views, added to his attraction.

Henry Crabb Robinson, another experienced theatre-goer, initially found little to admire in Kean's approach to the great tragic parts, and pronounced his declamation to be 'very unpleasant, his words and syllables are too distinctly separated', though as Othello he found him surpassing any male actor he had ever seen: 'I could hardly keep from crying – It was pure feeling.'[34] But in his *Champion* review Keats described the actor's diction as one of his salient qualities, with its 'elegance, gracefulness and music of elocution':

There is an indescribable gusto in his voice . . . his exclamation of 'blood, blood, blood!' is direful and slaughterous in the deepest degree, the very words appear stained and gory. His voice is loosed on them, like the wild dog on the savage relics of an eastern conflict; and we can distinctly hear it gorging, and growling o'er carcase and limb. We could cite a volume of such immortal scraps, and dote upon them with our remarks; but as an end must come, we will content ourselves with a single syllable. It is in those lines of impatience to the night, who 'like a foul and ugly witch, doth limp so tediously away'. Surely this intense power of anatomizing the passion of every syllable, of taking to himself the wings of verse, is the means by which he becomes a storm with such fiery decision; and by which, with a still deeper charm, he 'does his spiriting gently' . . . He feels his being as deeply as Wordsworth, or any other of our intellectual monopolists.

Kean had been absent, ill, from the Drury Lane stage for some time, this production of *Richard III* marking his triumphant return, and Keats referred to this in his peroration, using the image about the demystification of the rainbow which was

J.GRIMALDI
Song in Character - "All the world's in Paris".

21. Grimaldi the clown in the role of an English tourist singing 'All the world's in Paris', in 1814, the year of Haydon's visit to the French capital.

destined to provide such a central topic at the following week's dinner party:

Kean! have a carefulness of thy health, an in-nursed respect for thy own genius, a pity for us in these cold and enfeebling times! Cheer us a little in the failure of our days! for romance lives but in books. The goblin is driven from the heath, and the rainbow is robbed of its mystery![35]

On Boxing Day and on 2 January Keats again went to the theatre for the *Champion*, seeing the Christmas pantomime, including the famous clown Grimaldi, and a tragedy. After

the pantomime he walked home with his friends Charles
Wentworth Dilke and Charles Brown, and had 'not a dispute
but a disquisition with Dilke, on various subjects'. Writing to
his brothers about this, he described how during the talk
'several things dovetailed in my mind', and went straight on
to make his famous pronouncement:

at once it struck me, what quality went to form a man of achievement especially in literature and which Shakespeare possessed so
enormously – I mean negative capability, that is when man is
capable of being in uncertainties, mysteries, doubts, without irritable
reaching after fact and reason – Coleridge, for instance, would let
go by a fine isolated verisimilitude caught from the penetralium of
mystery, from being incapable of remaining content with half-
knowledge. This pursued through volumes would perhaps take us
no further than this, that with a great poet the sense of beauty
overcomes every other consideration, or rather obliterates all consideration.[36]

By 1817 the Theatre Royal had endured a particularly
chequered career. Nell Gwynn made her debut there in 1665;
it was burnt down in 1672 and swiftly rebuilt by Christopher
Wren during 1672–4 at a cost of £4,000. In 1742 Garrick
appeared on its boards, and made the theatre famous for its
Shakespeare revivals. In 1775 the building was extensively
altered by the Adam brothers, and it was here that Mrs Siddons
first appeared as Portia, followed a year or two later by her
brother Charles Kemble as Hamlet. Here, too, the Duke of
Clarence first saw his mistress, the actress Mrs Jordan. The
building was later declared unsafe and a new one by Henry
Holland built on the site. The Theatre Royal was burnt down
for a second time in 1809, within a year of the Covent Garden
Theatre conflagration, leaving the public bereft of serious
entertainment as the two theatres were the only ones licensed

to perform classical drama. Kean's great success at the rebuilt
Drury Lane after the fire of 1809 helped that theatre's fortunes,
but not sufficiently so as to create a healthy profit, and Samuel
Whitbread, the manager in 1815, was driven to suicide largely
because of the problems confronting him. By 1817 his suc-
cessor Robert Elliston had installed gas lighting, which people
found disconcertingly bright, the portico was added and the
interior remodelled, but despite all his efforts he became
bankrupt. This was the era of sensational stage sets, scenery
painted on a gigantic scale so as to be seen from the back of
the auditorium replacing the lesser impact of the painstakingly
detailed former mode. The scenic artists enhanced their effects
with a new glaze, spectacularly highlighted by the overhead
gas candelabra. Disconcertingly detracting from the splendour
of the sets, the house lights were left undimmed during performances, as people came to stare at each other as much as at
the unfolding drama on the stage.

In his *Letters from England* Southey gives an account of
a visit to Drury Lane in 1807 by his fictitious Portuguese
protagonist, Don Manuel Alvarez Espriella, for a performance
of *The Winter's Tale* with Kemble and Mrs Siddons. He complained, as many others did, of the excessive size of the auditorium – it seated 3,000 people – which had the unfortunate
result that most of the spectators lost the finer facial expressions
and much of the dialogue of the actors, who were driven to
respond to this problem by overemphasis, loud, distorted
diction and extravagant gesture. Soldiers were stationed at the
entrances to keep order, arriving theatre-goers were pestered
by women selling oranges and boys hawking playbills. Southey's Don Manuel was taken to the pit in order to get the
best view of the house. Here tickets cost three shillings and
sixpence for a seat on a bench, and he was surprised to see
that the random seating meant no segregation between the
sexes. His visit took place two years before the Sheridan

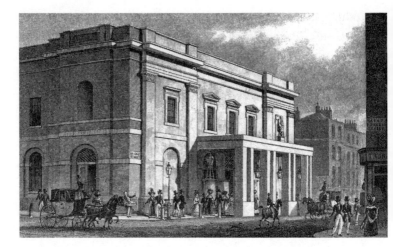

22. *The Theatre Royal, Drury Lane, c.*1825, by Thomas Shepherd.
The new theatre by Rowles and Wyatt, built within three years of
the old theatre's destruction in the fire of 1809. From 1814
Edmund Kean revived the theatre's fortunes by force of his acting
genius and his compelling new style.

conflagration of 1809, and the auditorium he then saw astonished him by its size, the pit alone seating 1,000 people. He
admired the decorations in blue and silver and the splendid
cut-glass chandeliers, which 'made every part as distinctly seen
as if in the noon sunshine', but disliked an appearance of
flimsiness in the architecture, particularly the over-slender
iron pillars, which produced a feeling of insecurity:

The people in the galleries were very noisy before the representation
began, whistling and calling to the musicians; and they amused
themselves by throwing orange peel into the pit and upon the stage:
after the curtain drew up they were sufficiently silent. The pit was
soon filled; the lower side-boxes did not begin to fill till towards
the middle of the first act, because that part of the audience is too
fashionable to come in time; the back part of the front-boxes not
till the half-play; they were then filled with a swarm of prostitutes,

and of men who came to meet them. In the course of the evening there were two or three quarrels there which disturbed the performance, and perhaps ended in duels the next morning.

The don found this behaviour disgusting, but was full of praise for the performers and particularly impressed, as well he might have been, by Mrs Siddons as Hermione:

The actress who personated the queen is acknowledged to be perfect in her art; she stood leaning upon a pedestal with one arm, the other hanging down – the best Grecian sculptor could not have adjusted her drapery with more grace, nor have improved the attitude; and when she began to move, though this was what the spectators were impatiently expecting, it gave every person such a start of delight, as the dramatist himself would have wished, though the whole merit must be ascribed to the actress.[37]

He enjoyed his evening, although he found the strange custom of playing a comedy after the main piece tiresome – on this occasion a performance of *Don Juan* in mime. And he disliked the late hours of a performance which did not begin until seven o'clock, so preventing him from getting home to bed before midnight. At that time a usual evening at the theatre consisted of a brief one-act play, followed by the main piece, and succeeded as a rule, though not on this occasion, by a two-act farce: a marathon evening by any standards, although people did not necessarily attend the entire programme.

Henry Crabb Robinson went to see the new Drury Lane in November 1812, a month after its reopening, and found it, he recorded in his diary, 'a magnificent object':

The Proscenium is the most splendid scene I ever beheld. It is certainly quite enough adorned but it would be absurd to reproach the architect with making a theatre gorgeous. Let the prison be dry and rude so as to excite a sense of severity, let the temple and the hall of justice be majestically simple, but the public theatre should be pompous and profusely adorned ... The boxes capped by a Statue of Comedy and Tragedy are placed over an elegant tripod bearing a brilliant white-flamed lamp of numerous wicks in a circle. And beyond this on each side a superb column of verde antique. The audience part of the Theatre I had little opportunity of observing, but the roof displeased me – instead of being arched and lifted above the walls, it lies as it were a weight upon them. And the shilling gallery is cut out of the ceiling, so that the whole produced in me an impression of imperfection and insecurity.[38]

Mrs Siddons had first achieved the status of London's acknowledged queen of tragic and heroic actresses at the age of twenty-six, a position which she held unchallenged until her official retirement in 1812. Hazlitt, the most influential drama critic of the time, idolized her. 'Power was seated on her brow,' he wrote, 'passion emanated from her breast as from a shrine. She was tragedy personified.' On her retirement he asked, 'Who shall make tragedy stand once more with its feet upon the earth, and its head above the stars, weeping tears and blood?' She was particularly admired for the resonance of her voice and the nobility and expansiveness of her gestures. At the height of her fame she became an arbiter of taste, not only with reference to things theatrical, but also, as was seen in her anxiously awaited judgement on Haydon's *Christ's Entry*, to all things artistic. Adored on the stage, she was less popular behind the scenes, where she had the reputation of being distant and parsimonious, and, because of a dislike of publicity, she was apt to be snubbing to her crowds of admirers. After her retirement she injudiciously returned to the stage on various occasions. Crabb Robinson went to see her as Queen Katherine in *Henry VIII* and found her delivery laboured, as if she was afraid that her power of expression was gone. He

23. *Interior of Drury Lane*, 1813, by W. Hopwood after
N. Heideloff, showing innovations, including the slender pillars
disliked by Crabb Robinson. Haydon and his friends mostly made
use of the pit, partly because it was the cheapest area, but also
because it was the best area for watching Kean's changing facial
expressions, which were lost on those further back in the
auditorium.

also thought she moved less majestically than she used to.
Hazlitt agreed, and thought it undignified that once retired
she should reappear all over again.

Haydon, who later became one of Mrs Siddons's most
fervent admirers, was not impressed by her Lady Macbeth,
her most famous role, when he saw her perform it in 1808,
four years after his arrival in London. He felt particularly let
down when she emerged from Duncan's chamber saying,
'That which hath made them drunk hath made me bold',

finding that she spoke this with 'very little spirit', in a passage when she 'should have been in a blaze':

I, who had been accustomed to read *Macbeth* at home, at the dead of night, when every thing was so silent that my hair stood up, could not at this moment put up with such a laceration of feeling as to be roused from contemplation by the slamming of a box door, when I almost fancied Duncan was groaning – I grew quite enraged and disgusted and left the house before the third act.[39]

In fact, he decided in the light of his experience on this occasion never to go again to see any performance of a Shakespeare play, because 'you always afterwards associate the actors with the characters. Thank God, *Lear* I can read with purity as I have never seen it, nor never will.'[40] But in spite of his resolution never to return to the theatre, he was soon back, and in April 1820 he was overawed by Mrs Siddons's presence when she invited him to pay her a visit. It gave him

something of the feeling of visiting Maria Theresa. The tone of her voice, her air, and action were calm and grand. They had something of a subdued feeling, as if she feared to speak too powerfully. She seemed the Mother of the Gods, adapting her powers to converse with a mortal.[41]

In October 1814 he saw Kean as Hamlet in the reopened Drury Lane, and felt his whole conception and execution of the part to be perfect: 'The longer he acts, the more will he bring the World to his principles, and the time is not far distant when his purity, his truth, his energy, will triumph over all opposition.'[42]

At the end of June 1817 Haydon was present at Kemble's farewell dinner, an occasion which put him in a fury, as he perceived the eulogies for the retiring actor as masked slurs upon the genius of Kean. Kean himself, who was also present, made a speech, to Haydon's admiration: 'Kean sprung into the midst of them and with one flash of his vigorous eye, dwindled the stately march and solemn heartlessness of the Kemble mockery into its real insignificance.'[43] Or so it seemed to him.

All Haydon's guests were devoted theatre-goers, though Wordsworth necessarily had fewer opportunities than those living in London, and three of them, Wordsworth, Lamb and Keats, themselves wrote plays. Wordsworth's tragedy, *The Borderers*, was written in 1797 when his mind was full of his recent experiences in revolutionary France, and at a time when the Terror had escalated to its greatest extremes. He submitted it to Covent Garden in the autumn of that year, but it was at once rejected, causing him pain both from wounded pride and also from the frustration of his hopes of earning some much-needed money. The play was to remain unpublished until 1842, towards the end of the poet's life. Keats wrote *Otho the Great*, also a tragedy, two years after the Immortal Dinner, in collaboration with his friend Charles Brown. His intentions were partly that the venture might increase his popularity as a writer, and partly that he longed to write something worthy of performance by Kean. The play was accepted by the management of Drury Lane, but Keats did not live to see it appear.

Perhaps the most appreciative theatre-goer of all to visit Drury Lane was the child Charles Lamb attending his first play:

I remember the waiting at the door – O when shall I be such an expectant again! – with the cry of nonpareils, an indispensable playhouse accompaniment in those days. As near as I can recollect, the fashionable pronunciation of the theatrical fruiteresses then was, 'Chase some oranges, chase some numparels, chase a bill of the play;' – chase *pro* chuse. But when we got in, and I beheld the green curtain that veiled a heaven to my imagination, which was soon to be disclosed – the breathless anticipations I endured! I had seen something like it in the plate prefixed to *Troilus and Cressida*, in Rowe's Shakespeare – the tent scene with Diomede – and a sight of that plate can always bring back in a measure the feeling of that evening. The boxes at that time, full of well-dressed women of quality, projected over the pit; and the pilasters reaching down were adorned with a glistering substance (I know not what) under glass (as it seemed), resembling – a homely fancy, but I judged it to be sugar candy – yet, to my raised imagination, divested of its homelier qualities, it appeared a glorified candy! – The orchestra lights at length arose, those 'fair Auroras!' Once the bell sounded. It was to ring out yet once again – and, incapable of the anticipation, I reposed my shut eyes in a sort of resignation upon the maternal lap. It rang the second time. The curtain drew up – I was not past six years old – and the play was *Artaxerxes*! . . . All feeling was absorbed in vision. Gorgeous vests, gardens, palaces, princesses, passed before me. I knew not players . . . It was all enchantment and a dream. No such pleasure has since visited me but in dreams.[44]

Lamb's own first play, *John Woodvil*, was rejected by Kemble in 1800. In 1806 he tried again, and his new play, *Mr H—*, was accepted by Drury Lane, where it failed. Poor Lamb! He had written to his friend Thomas Manning, the Chinese scholar and traveller, in a tone of mockery masking his real excitement at the prospect of success, although he recognized, or tried to make himself believe, that 'there never was a more ticklish thing'. As with Keats and Wordsworth, he hoped to earn some money – possibly £300, he estimated. But it was not to be. He wrote to Wordsworth the following morning:

Dear Wordsworth, – Mr H came out last night and failed. I had many fears; the subject was not substantial enough. John Bull must have solider fare than a *letter*. We are pretty stout about it; we have had plenty of condoling friends; but, after all, we had rather it should have succeeded . . . The number of friends we had in the house – my brother and I being in public offices, etc. – was astonishing, but they yielded at length to a few hisses.

A hundred hisses! (Damn the word, I write it like kisses – how different!) – a hundred hisses outweigh a thousand claps. The former come more directly from the heart. Well 'tis withdrawn, and there is an end. Better luck to us, C. Lamb[45]

The evening had begun rather well, with a good volume of applause for the prologue; but as the farce got under way the hissing began, and after a while the hapless Lamb joined in to hiss his own play, owning afterwards that he did so in order to conceal that he was the author.

This disappointment did not alienate Lamb from the theatre, and he wrote a large body of essays and criticisms of drama over the years. But the greatest magnet that drew him to performance after performance was the presence of Fanny Kelly, the great love of his life. Fanny had first appeared on the Drury Lane stage at the age of seven, as one of the Princes in the Tower, was admired as Arthur in *King John*, and later made a success as Ophelia to the Hamlet of her old fellow actor Kean. Lamb admired her acting, about which he wrote on a number of occasions, and addressed several poems to her, but probably did not meet her off stage until about 1813. On one dramatic occasion, in February 1816, Fanny Kelly was shot at on the Drury Lane stage, some of the shot falling into the lap of Mary Lamb, who was watching the performance with her brother – a dangerous incident for Mary's precariously balanced mental equilibrium. Fanny Kelly emerged unhurt and calm, and her assailant, George Barnett, a disappointed admirer who was said to have given her the choice of either marriage to him or the fighting of a duel, ended his life in a lunatic asylum. The impact of this incident made Lamb anxious at the thought of Fanny's vulnerability. By 1817 she occupied a central place in his thoughts, the naturalness of her performances was especially attractive to him, and she became a popular member of his circle, well able to join in the intellectual give-and-take of the Lambs' regular evening parties, always showing herself, according to Crabb Robinson, as 'calm, sensible and warm-hearted'. On one occasion, when Fanny Kelly and the Lambs were fellow guests at Thomas Hood's, an American friend of the Cowden Clarkes' remembered the talk turning to a comic scene in a new play in which Fanny had performed the character of a low-bred lady's maid passing herself off as her mistress:

She arose, and with a kind of resistless ardour repeated a few sentences so inimitably, that everybody laughed as much as if the real lady's maid, and not the actress, had been before them; while she who had so well personated the part, quietly resumed her seat without the least sign of merriment, as grave as possible. Most striking had been the transition from the calm lady-like person, to the gay, loquacious soubrette; and not less so, the sudden cessation of vivacity, and resumption of well-bred decorum.[46]

Mary Lamb was fond of her, and even undertook to give her Latin lessons. For Fanny the stage was a necessity, as she was the main support of her own fatherless family. With her rational temperament and kindly nature, she sounds as if she would have been the perfect complement to the more frenetic Lamb, who alternated between wild optimism and bouts of despair. 'Hers is the joy of a freed spirit,' he wrote lovingly, 'escaping from care as a bird that has been limed; her smiles seemed saved out of the fire, relics which a good and innocent heart has snatched up as most portable.' In 1818 he wrote to Mary Wordsworth of 'the gleam of Fanny Kelly's divine plain face';[47] and in one review of her he exclaimed in a famous phrase, 'What a lass that were . . . to go gipsying through the world with.' On 20 July 1819 he plucked up the courage to write to her with a proposal of marriage, phrased with the most delicate tact, so that a refusal would be easy for her to make if she so wished:

I am not so foolish as not to know that I am a most unworthy match for such a one as you but you have for years been a principal object in my mind. In many a sweet assumed character I have learned to love you, but simply as F. M. Kelly I love you better than them all. Can you quit these shadows of existence, and come and be a reality to us? can you leave off harassing yourself to please a thankless multitude, who know nothing of you, and begin at last to live to yourself and your friends?

But Fanny felt unable to accept. She told a friend years later that she felt she could not enter into a relationship with a family so tainted with insanity, although she never allowed Lamb to know that this was her reason, pleading instead with great delicacy the existence of an 'early and deeply-rooted attachment', adding:

I am not insensible to the high honour which the preference of such a mind as yours confers upon me – let me, however, hope that all thought upon this subject will end with this letter, and that you will henceforth encourage no other sentiment towards me than esteem in my private character and a continuance of that approbation of my humble talents which you have already expressed so much and so often to my advantage and gratification.

The tone of her suitor's acceptance of her rejection is moving in its attempt at light-heartedness:

Dear Miss Kelly – *Your injunctions shall be obeyed to a tittle.* I feel
myself in a lackadaisical no-how-ish kind of a humour. I believe it
is the rain or something. I had thought to have written seriously,
but I fancy I succeed best in epistles of mere fun; puns and *that*
nonsense. You will be good friends with us, will you not? Let what
has past 'break no bones' between us. You will not refuse us them
next time we send for them? C.L.
Do you observe the delicacy of not signing my full name?
N.B. Do not paste that last letter of mine into your Book.[48]

It is impossible to gauge from the evidence of his letter of
proposal, with its calm and realistic outlining of his financial
ability to support her and the mutual benefits each could
expect from such a union, whether Lamb was really in love,
or just indulging in another of his comforting daydreams, but
however that may have been, he and Fanny remained close
friends for the rest of his life. Fanny never married.

6. Medicine and Poets

By this time other visitors began to drop in, and a Mr Ritchie, who is going to penetrate into the interior of Africa. I introduced him to Wordsworth as such, and the conversation got into a new train. After some time Lamb, who had seemingly paid no attention to any one, suddenly opened his eyes and said, alluding to the dangers of penetrating into the interior of Africa, 'and pray, who is the gentleman we are going to *lose*?'

Benjamin Robert Haydon, *Diary*[1]

'If you have not seen the poems of J. Keats, a lad of nineteen or twenty – they are well worth your reading. If I am not mistaken he is to be the great poetical luminary of the age to come.'

Joseph Ritchie to Richard Garnett, 1817[2]

The time had now come for the party to leave the dinner table and move to another room to welcome friends invited for the second part of the evening. The first of these to arrive was a young surgeon, Joseph Ritchie. He had just returned to London from his work at the British Embassy in Paris to arrange his affairs and make preparations for a small expedition he had been commissioned to lead to Africa. His brief was to travel south from Tripoli to Timbuktu in search of the source, course and outlet of the river Niger. Haydon introduced him to Wordsworth as such, and, he said, 'the conversation got into a new train'. African exploration had been much in the public eye since the two expeditions of Mungo Park a few years earlier; and the horror of the African slave trade was also a topic much aired at the time in liberal circles, so that the evening's conversation probably now turned for a while to the likely problems and challenges facing the young and inexperienced explorer. This was soon interrupted by Lamb's sudden interjection from the fireside where he had been half asleep of 'and pray, who is the gentleman we are going to *lose*?' Ritchie joined in the roar of laughter that followed from the company.

Very little has been known about Ritchie, except as leader of what was to prove a fatal expedition. But eight letters addressed to Richard Garnett, in the possession of today's Richard Garnett, his great-great-grandson, now provide a considerable amount of information about the earlier part of his life. Joseph Ritchie was born in 1788 or 1789 at Otley in Yorkshire, where his father and grandfather had both been surgeons – a term roughly approximating to today's general practitioner – and when the surviving letters begin, in 1811, he was studying medicine in York with a view to joining the family practice. No portrait of Ritchie has been found, but he is known to have been very fair and slender. He had some congenital weakness, possibly asthma, which he insisted, when interviewed for the African expedition, he well understood and was able to manage. He and Garnett, the son of a paper manufacturer, had been friends at Otley grammar school. After leaving school Garnett had spent some time learning French, German and Italian, his father intending him for a mercantile career. But when the correspondence with Ritchie opens, having come to the conclusion that such a career was not for him, he was employed at a Nottinghamshire school as assistant master, learning Latin and Greek in his spare time with a view to entering the Church; and within an unusually brief period he was ordained curate by the Archbishop of York. Later in life he became known as a philologist and linguist. In 1838 he was appointed assistant keeper of printed books at the British Museum, but philology always remained his overriding pre-occupation.

The letters between the two young Yorkshiremen came to light in 1933, when David Garnett, novelist great-grandson of Ritchie's Garnett, inherited a japanned metal box containing family papers. Reading through the contents, Garnett came on the letters from Ritchie, and was so struck by the prescience with which he forecast in one of them that the then largely unknown Keats would be counted among the greatest poets of the age that he published the letter in the *New Statesman and Nation* in June of that year. The rest of the little cache remained undisturbed in its tin box until now.

Ritchie's earliest surviving letter to Garnett, dated 26 November 1811, when both young men were in their early twenties, was written from the hospital in York where he was then working. A common interest in literature was already a central concern. Ritchie told Garnett of his new acquaintance with William Ireland, the notorious Shakespeare forger, who had been successful in passing off works of his own as Shakespeare's, using old parchments stolen from the lawyer's office where he worked. His forgeries were published in 1795, and Boswell is said to have kissed the documents. By the time Ritchie arrived in York, Ireland had been rumbled and forced to confess, afterwards settling down to write under his own name. Ritchie was amused by him: 'He is a man of very engaging manners and extremely communicative, but talks rather too much of what books he has published and what he intends to publish.'[3]

The next letter is dated 10 February 1813, by which time Ritchie had moved to London to acquire further medical qualifications. He found himself impressed by the superior quality of the London libraries, chemical laboratories and dissecting rooms, and, most especially, by the 'profound lectures, on almost every branch of science'. But he was disappointed in the quality of the literary life available to a young and friendless medical student. He had literary aspirations himself, wrote quantities of unremarkable poetry, and longed to meet others of the same mind. Garnett had evidently pictured his friend being catapulted into the company of the brilliant galaxy of writers then in the capital, but this had not been the case, and Ritchie felt frustrated and depressed that he was learning nothing from his new companions:

In literature generally, London is not a place to acquire knowledge, but to display the acquisitions which you have already made. I am frequently thrown into the company of literary pretenders, whose learning is perhaps sufficient to cover a sixpence at the bottom of a basin, and nothing is easier, nor more seducing to a raw country boy, than to chatter with them, and to obtain a share of their applause.

He knew that somewhere in the London world there was literary society of the first eminence, 'but the access to this is difficult, extremely difficult'. He went on to tell Garnett about the most talked-of success of the previous year, James and Horace Smith's *Rejected Addresses*. A competition had been announced for the most appropriate address to use at the opening of the newly rebuilt Drury Lane Theatre, and the Smiths wrote a collection of bogus addresses as from Wordsworth, Byron, Thomas Moore, Southey, Coleridge, Walter Scott and others, of such brilliance that they found themselves immediately famous, their identity being soon widely known, though perhaps not in the circles in which Ritchie found himself. At the beginning of his letter Ritchie was not aware of the authorship of the *Addresses*, though he had discovered it before he finished writing. There is a hint of homesickness

24. *The Lock Hospital, Grosvenor Place*, 1825, watercolour by
Thomas Shepherd. Here Joseph Ritchie finished his medical
training and qualified as a surgeon.

in this letter, and 'to tell the truth', he concludes, 'I shall always
be happy to receive a letter from you, write what you will'.

On 10 May he wrote again, more cheerfully, to tell Garnett
that he had moved his lodgings from St Martin's Lane to the
Lock Hospital, Grosvenor Place (later to become St George's)
'where I figure away as House Surgeon'. He found his medical
studies in the capital engrossing. He told Garnett that 'my
present opportunities are very great, and if I do not greatly
improve by them, I know well where the fault will be':

Mr Brande, our Chemical Lecturer, has succeeded Sir Humphry
Davy as Professor at the Royal Institution and to the Board of
Agriculture and now stands unrivalled as a teacher of chemistry in
this town. He is a very young man, very affable and very accessible,
and if I do not flatter myself, shews towards me a little extra
condescension. I have entered as a subscriber to the Royal Insti-

tution having procured his recommendation, where we have an
excellent scientific library.

He then went on to express a growing anxiety:

All this is very charming, but it will not last for ever. How I am to
leave my Lectures and Institutions and Brandes and Campbells and
quietly set to work manufacturing boluses in a country town is what
I really cannot tell. I leave my present situation next June, where I
shall next go I know no more than the pen that I am writing with.

This slight touch of arrogance appears to have been justified,
Ritchie having evidently been a brilliant student. He had
indeed been fortunate in attracting the notice of William
Brande, who coincidentally was later to examine Keats for his
apothecary's certificate. After Sir Humphry Davy, Brande was
the foremost chemist of the day, and the connection was
shortly to prove of great importance to Ritchie, who was now
achieving some success and beginning to feel the prickings of
ambition. No doubt there was family pressure for him to
return to the Otley family practice in the steps of his father
and grandfather, but it is understandable that he already felt it
too late to settle down happily to such a life after the heady
experience of medical opportunity in the capital.

For the moment there were other things to think of: his
hospital work kept him busy and he was enjoying London
more than he had at first. He caught a glimpse of Lord Byron,
now at the height of his fame: 'I watch'd his carriage a
considerable time and at last had the satisfaction of seeing him
step into it. He is lame – has a very youthful appearance and a
countenance which I fancied very expressive of tenderness
and melancholy. He sets out again for Greece in a very short
time.' And he wrote out a parody of one of Thomas Moore's
Irish Melodies, 'Love's Young Dream', for Garnett's amuse-

ment. Moore, an enormously popular songwriter, felt himself to have 'an instinctive turn for rhyme and song', which indeed he had. The *Irish Melodies* collection also included 'The Harp That Once through Tara's Halls', 'The Minstrel Boy', 'Believe Me If All Those Endearing Young Charms' and 'The Last Rose of Summer'. Ritchie's parody introduces the figure of Eliza, who appears in three of his surviving poems, but it is idle now to wonder if she was an imaginary figure or if Ritchie did love someone of that name.

In July 1814 Ritchie was in Sunderland, having passed the examination qualifying him as a surgeon: 'I am now duly authorized to kill and cure *secundum artem*,' he announced offhandedly, but without altogether concealing his pleasure in the newly acquired status. He had been reading more Wordsworth, had seen Byron's *English Bards and Scottish Reviewers* in the local library, and found himself disagreeing with its attitude to the Lake Poets, 'knowing a little more of these than I once did and wishing to know still more'. He had also been working on a commission for the editor of a London medical journal 'analysing some French medical and physiological works'. He was still brooding on his future, 'but what great designs lie in embryo I need not inform you'. He continued: 'I long to do something to make myself known. Now excuse all this egotism if you can.'

During those holiday weeks in Sunderland Ritchie had come across the sixteenth-century Portuguese writer Camoëns's account of his adventurous life fighting against the Moors, and being shipwrecked off the coast of Cochin China. Camoëns's exploits chimed in well with the current fascination, which Ritchie shared, with all things exotic and oriental, from Coleridge's *Kubla Khan* and Byron's *Mazeppa*, *The Giaour* and *The Bride of Abydos* to the gigantic and apocalyptic paintings of John Martin. In London Eastern-style costume, too, had become fashionable for a while, as had anything Egyptian. But in 1817 the great literary success in the genre was to be Thomas Moore's extravaganza, *Lalla Rookh*, which was immensely popular, running in the next few years into forty editions. In London Lady Holland was almost alone in her ignorance of it, and at one of her dinner parties she is reputed to have said to Moore: 'Mr Moore, I have not read your *Larry O'Rourke*, I don't like Irish stories.'

Ritchie was one of Moore's admirers. 'Have you seen *Lalla Rookh*?' he asked Garnett:

It is a most magnificent fairy palace. I never met with anything that carried me so completely away into the midst of roses, and bulbuls, and perfumes, and humming birds, and jewels and all manner of precious stones . . . And what beautiful sparkling prose! I have finished the whole at a sitting except the Fire Worshippers, which I have only dipped into.[4]

It was at about this time that he decided to try to use his newly acquired professional qualification in a wider context, perhaps to gain a place as surgeon on some foreign expedition. It may have been that reading of Camoëns's exploits proved the catalyst that turned Ritchie's thoughts in such an entirely new direction. With a view to extending his medical and scientific knowledge to that end in Paris, then at the height of its fame as the centre of scientific excellence, he began to search for an opening in the French capital. Here he had the good fortune to obtain a post as secretary to Sir Charles Stuart, the British ambassador, arriving to take up his duties in the city a few months after the battle of Waterloo. Sir Charles, then in his mid-thirties, was a genial and popular figure. Captain Gronow in his *Reminiscences* described the British Embassy of that era as the congregating point of all British visitors to Paris. There were dinners, balls and receptions in profusion, and in fact, Gronow said, 'Sir Charles spent the whole of his private income in these noble hospitalities.' He also remarked that the attachés, 'as is always the case, took their tone and manner from their chief, and were not only civil and agreeable to all those who went to the Embassy, but knew everything and everybody, and were of great use to the ambassador, keeping him well supplied with information on whatever event might be taking place'.[5] Ritchie now found himself in this privileged circle, a wonderful change from the rather dreary existence he had endured outside his working hours in London. By the time he arrived at Haydon's party two years later, he must have acquired something of the polish of a practised diplomat, a far cry from the Yorkshire youth who had first made his way to London, longing but failing to gain acceptance into the prestigious artistic and literary circles of which he had heard so much.

Paris's fame as the scientific capital of the world derived from the work and teaching of men of the calibre of André Ampère, whose name was given to the basic unit of electric current, and who taught at the Polytechnic schools where Ritchie was now to study; and the chemist Michel Chevreul, at that time director of the Museum of Natural History, an institution much admired by Humphry Davy. Chevreul invented margarine, and was also a director of the Gobelins tapestry works. Georges Cuvier, who came to be known as the father of comparative anatomy and palaeontology, was another illustrious Parisian scientist, as was Humphry Davy's rival, Joseph Gay-Lussac, chemist and physicist, who made balloon ascents, following in the steps of the Montgolfier brothers, to test the laws of terrestrial magnetism. In the months before Ritchie's arrival Gay-Lussac had succeeded in isolating oxygen, having earlier worked with Alexander von Humboldt, the great naturalist and traveller, to discover the ratio of oxygen to hydrogen which would form water. Two more Parisian scientific notables of the day were Jean Lamarck, naturalist and pre-Darwinian evolutionist, whose monumental *History of Non-vertebrate Animals* began to appear in 1815, and Pierre Laplace, whose study of the planets was the most important work on celestial mechanics since Newton's *Principia*. Such a constellation of scientific stars attracted students from all over the world to the Paris schools, and Ritchie could not have chosen anywhere to rival the opportunities with which he was now presented.

Ritchie's sixth surviving letter to Garnett was written from Paris at some point during 1817: this was the letter which was to impress David Garnett more than a hundred years later: 'If you have not seen the poems of J. Keats, a lad of nineteen or twenty — they are well worth your reading. If I am not mistaken he is to be the great poetical luminary of the age to come.' The tone of this letter is more relaxed and confident and less tentative and out to impress than that of the earlier letters. Though there are still naive remarks, there is also evidence of a shrewd perception. He wrote about Byron's latest work, including the third canto of *Childe Harold*, which he considered superior to the first two. But his greatest enthusiasm was for the poetry of Wordsworth:

I think I have met with finer poetry in his two volumes of minor poems than anything I have read except some of the best passages of Milton and Akenside. If you will begin by reading his sonnets, his lines on Tintern Abbey, the Intimations of Immortality from recollections of early Childhood – the story of Michael and his son – and of the two brothers, and after reading them three times each, differ with me in opinion, I will promise you to reconsider my verdict.

He then wrote out quotations from 'Tintern Abbey' and the 'Immortality Ode', in the hope of winning his friend into sharing his admiration of the great man and his work. 'I hope,' he added, 'these two extracts will go some way towards convincing you that all Wordsworth is not so ridiculous as our friends of Dun Edin would have it to be' – referring to the hostile *Edinburgh Review*. The letter goes on to rejoice in what Ritchie rightly perceived to be the changing climate of English poetry, about which he wrote with sympathetic understanding. He concluded: 'and now a man would as soon think of building a castle with sugar plums as of writing poetry by the rule line square and compasses of Aristotle Boileau and . . .' Tantalizingly, at this point the rest of the original letter is torn off, but enough remains to give an impression of a perceptive and gifted young man, full of excitement at the marvels of his literary discoveries.

Ritchie used his ample leisure from his Embassy duties to make an intensive study of natural history, astronomy and chemistry – subjects he felt would be relevant for his projected career as explorer – and for the same reason also learn the use of astronomical instruments at the famous Observatory. Meanwhile he applied to join an expedition to Senegambia but, although he had impeccable introductions, by the time his application reached London another surgeon had already been appointed. Through his position at the Embassy, however, he met many of the most distinguished people in Paris, including, by a happy chance, Alexander von Humboldt. Ritchie, with his gifts of tact and sympathy, made himself useful to Humboldt, procuring him books he needed when convalescing after an illness, and the great naturalist was impressed with the young man, telling him that he would 'always be happy to pursue an acquaintance with one so knowledgeable and obliging'.[6] So that when the British government began to plan a new expedition to chart the course of the Niger, Humboldt, visiting London at just the right moment, successfully put forward his young friend's name as a candidate for its leadership.

Reports had been reaching the British government of the threat of a French expedition being mounted to steal a march on their British rivals in the race to discover the course of the Niger, particularly its outlet. In 1805 Mungo Park had set out for the second time to solve the riddle, but he did not return, nor was his body recovered. This had been the last British attempt for over a decade, and now Sir Joseph Banks was urging further action on the government.

Humboldt's recommendation of Ritchie was further supported by Ritchie's chemistry professor, William Brande, who was an intimate friend of Sir Joseph Banks. Banks was the great naturalist of the day – the Banksia rose was named after his wife – his fame stemming initially from his botanical discoveries in the South Pacific, made when accompanying Captain Cook on his voyage on the *Endeavour* in 1768. In 1817 Banks was the country's leading scientific adviser. He was the great benefactor of the Kew Botanic Gardens; active in the founding of the Linnean and Horticultural Societies, one of the founders of the African Association and president of the Royal Society, which position he held for forty-one years. In short, he was the best patron any young man such as Ritchie, whose interests included botanical research, could hope to find.

Louis Simond painted an attractive picture of Banks in 1815, having attended two meetings of the Royal Society over which Banks presided. The Society met on Thursday evenings in Somerset House, and Banks got through the business, according to Simond, in record time. Meetings began at precisely eight o'clock, and Banks closed them within at most three-quarters of an hour, having conducted them with such expertise that, Simond said, 'this very short space of time' was sufficient. Simond was impressed by the president's open hospitality:

He receives such persons as have been introduced to him, on Thursday mornings and Sunday evenings. His friends are always admitted in the morning to his library, where newspapers, and literary journals, English and foreign, are found. These meetings are perfectly free from *gêne*, or ceremony of any sort. This is, I presume, the only establishment of the kind in England.[7]

Humphry Davy, at the time of Simond's visit, was under-secretary to the Society and gave reports of the previous meetings. The upper end of the room, Simond noted,

is decorated with a full-length portrait of Newton, whom the society is proud of having had for its first president. His signature was shewn to me in the register of members. I felt that an impulse of profound respect at the sight of it had made me bow unconsciously. The English do not say *Newton*, but *Sir Isaac Newton*. I cannot well express how much this *Monsieur le Chevalier* Newton shocks the ear of a foreigner.[8]

Banks evidently warmed to Ritchie, perhaps on discovering that he too was a passionate botanist, and with such eminent backing the young surgeon suddenly found himself within grasp of an opportunity which precisely fitted his ambition. He immediately resigned his Embassy post and returned to England.

In London Ritchie was interviewed, and his appointment confirmed, by Lord Bathurst, Secretary of State at the new War and Colonies Office. Bathurst ran his department from 14 Downing Street with a deputy and a few clerks, most of the works devolving on the secretary himself. He was highly professional and industrious, but the atmosphere of his office was friendly – clerks who arrived early to work were given a free breakfast as a reward before settling down to a hard day's work. He was a popular employer with a strong sense of humour, and he loved to entertain his clerks with stories. The advantage of such a small establishment was that Bathurst himself was in control of all transactions and could field questions on all subjects relevant to the department, of which Ritchie's expedition was one. Over finance, however, his hands were tied, this being the exclusive province of the Treasury, so that he was innocent of what was to prove the fatal underfunding of the projected Niger expedition.

A week before Haydon's dinner, Ritchie wrote to Garnett from London, having spent some time being briefed for his African adventure. 'You may probably have heard of my intention to take a trip to Africa,' he told his friend,

a project indeed which I have long meditated and the means for which have presented themselves at present in so singularly favourable a manner that I have had no hesitation in accepting the proposals which the government have made me. I return to Paris in the course of January, proceed to Marseilles or some other port of the Mediterranean from whence I shall sail for Malta where our Admiral of the Station (Sir C. Penrose) is to get me a conveyance to Tripoli. I shall be appointed Vice-Consul in Fezzan, a country in the interior dependent on the Bashaw of Tripoli – with directions to go where I see fit, as opportunities may offer themselves.

Ritchie's tone was a little defiant as he broke this news to Garnett:

I do not know what you and the rest of my Yorkshire friends will think of this undertaking of mine, but I know for my own part, that I have never been so happy in my life as since it has been finally determined on. The prospect which opens before me of my being enabled to devote the rest of my days to pursuits which I have always thought the most exalted and the most worthy to occupy the energies of man – and the possibility of my acting an important part in the events which may be preparing on behalf of the most abject and suffering part of our species give a buoyancy to my hopes, which the view of the dangers I am about to encounter cannot depress.

Ritchie was referring here to the plight of African slaves. His sympathy would have grown to some extent from his upbringing in the strictly Methodist atmosphere of his family, generated by the conversion of his aunt, Elizabeth Ritchie. She became one of John Wesley's closest friends, and travelled with him from a very young age on his journeys round the Methodist centres of England. Wesley was very fond of her, watched over her anxiously during a series of alarming illnesses with consumptive symptoms in her early years, and referred to her as 'Betsey' or 'my dear sister'. She was with him at the end of his life and nursed him through his last three days, and he left her his gold seal and other mementoes of their long friendship. Elizabeth Ritchie said that in his presence she 'enjoyed uninterrupted sunshine'. She shared the Methodist movement's active interest in the formation of a colony of freed slaves in Sierra Leone, about which Ritchie would have heard discussion, and particularly in the setting up of a factory to provide them with some employment. In the event the colony was not a success and had to be abandoned.

In spite of all his new preoccupations, in his December letter to Garnett Ritchie returned again to the question of Wordsworth: evidently Garnett had not responded well to his friend's panegyric on the poet, but Ritchie was not going to allow the subject to drop: 'I shall say nothing about Wordsworth at present, but when I see you, I will try to persuade you that he is really the greatest poet we have had (that I know of) since the day of Milton.' If Ritchie had by then had his invitation from Haydon to meet his hero face to face the next week, surely he would have told Garnett about it now; so it seems that his invitation to Lisson Grove must have been something of a last-minute affair.

There is a reference in the same letter to what might have been Ritchie's feelings towards the shadowy Eliza, when he says to Garnett, rather as an afterthought, 'I have no longer any questionings, such as our immortal bard alludes to, in his Lycidas:

> Were it not better done, as others use,
> To sport with Amaryllis in the shade,
> Or with the tangles of Neaera's hair?'

He ends his quotation there, but Milton's poem continues with the famous 'Fame is the spur' lines, ending in words that events were to prove chillingly apt:

> But the fair guerdon when we hope to find,
> And think to burst out into sudden blaze,
> Comes the blind Fury with th' abhorred shears
> And slits the thin-spun life.[9]

The letter finishes in a more affectionate manner than Ritchie customarily allowed himself, or perhaps just more excitedly:

> Adieu, et croyez moi, Toujours et surtout,
> Tout à vous, J. Ritchie

Keats referred to Ritchie in a letter to his brothers of 5 January 1818:

I forget whether I had written my last before my Sunday Evening at Haydon's – no I did not or I should have told you Tom of a young Man you met at Paris at Scott's of the name of Richer, I think – he is going to Fezan in Africa there to proceed if possible like Mungo Park – he was very polite to me and enquired very particularly after you.[10]

Ritchie had been introduced to Haydon by their mutual journalist friend John Scott, hence his presence at Haydon's party. At this time Keats was increasingly anxious about Tom's health, and also beginning to be uneasy about his own, and at the dinner his conversation with Ritchie would inevitably have touched on his brother's symptoms, Keats longing for reassurance, although aware that there was none to be had. Tom was already spitting blood, and the full implications of this would not have been lost upon the two young men with their medical knowledge, at a time when tuberculosis was the predominant scourge, particularly for the young between the ages of fifteen and twenty-five, and no treatment, even palliative, existed. In the eighteenth century the disease accounted for twenty per cent of all deaths, and by the early nineteenth century the percentage had risen dramatically and would continue to do so until towards the end of the century, when Louis Pasteur's work on the tubercle bacillus and on vaccination enabled the slow journey towards a tuberculosis-free world to begin.

Keats, just twenty-two, and Ritchie, a year or two older, were the youngest members of Haydon's party and had much in common. Both shared an intense determination to succeed in their chosen ways of life, while both had achieved medical qualifications, Ritchie as surgeon at the Lock Hospital, and Keats reaching the status of apothecary at Guy's, but deciding against sitting the examinations which would have qualified him as surgeon. Of Haydon's guests they were alone in having a scientific training, as against the classical background of the others. Both young men abandoned their projected medical careers soon after qualifying, in favour of something closer to

25. A sketch of Keats, 1816, by Benjamin Robert Haydon. After
the poet's death Haydon added the inscription: 'Keats was a spirit
that in passing over the Earth came within its attraction and
expired in fruitless struggles to make its dull inhabitants
comprehend the beauty of his soarings.'

their hearts. For Keats, this meant a life dedicated to poetry, which he saw as another healing art, the 'pouring of balm into the soul'.[11] Ritchie's decision was initially less specific. Like Keats he had continued to read and write poetry during his medical training, but his own verse was disappointingly stilted.

Having survived the horrendous experience of life as a house surgeon on the surgical wards of the Lock Hospital, Ritchie may well have felt that exploration could have nothing worse to offer. Both he, and Keats at Guy's and St Thomas's, had worked in conditions of unspeakable dirt, infection and stench. The senior surgeons operated in theatres packed with students, who shouted, 'Heads! Heads!' as those in the front row blocked their view; and the surgeons themselves scarcely had room for manoeuvre, sweating in their black coats and top hats – incredibly the surgical uniform of the time – in the fetid atmosphere. This scene of pandemonium was further aggravated by the screams of the wretched patient strapped down on the operating table. In those pre-anaesthetic days surgeons needed to work very fast, about fifteen minutes being considered the maximum time that a patient could survive the appalling pain and the shock to the nervous system. Many of the surgeons had inadequate knowledge of anatomy, and Keats was assigned as dresser to one of the worst of these, William Lucas, known as Butcher Lucas, who sliced at random through vital organs, leaving his young assistant to sew up the wounds and generally patch things together as best he could. But Keats was fortunate in being able to attend the lectures of the greatest surgeon of the day, the kind and brilliant Sir Astley Cooper. Cooper was a much-loved figure in the medical world, known for his sweetness of manner and courtesy to his patients. He always, and most unusually for the time, removed his top hat on entering the wards. Cooper took good care of his students, and he found lodgings for Keats with two others, one of

whom, Henry Stephens, later invented the eponymous blue/
black ink. At Guy's Keats was known for a certain remoteness,
as of a being set apart. For one thing, he dressed differently
from the other students, who wore buttoned collars and cra-
vats, whereas Keats kept to his open-necked shirts showing a
black ribbon tied round his neck in Byronic fashion. Stephens
later wrote of Keats's absolute devotion to poetry, 'the zenith
of all his aspirations', adding that he was inclined to walk and
talk in the company of the other medical students 'as one of
the Gods might be supposed to do when mingling with
mortals'.[12] He also remembered that Keats would scribble lines
of doggerel on the paper cover of his *Syllabus of Chemical
Lectures*. The only survivors are:

> Give me women, wine and snuff
> Until I cry out hold enough.
> You may do so sans objection
> Till ye day of resurrection
> For bless my beard they aye shall be
> My beloved Trinity.

Stephens later transcribed the lines, omitting 'women' from
the first, feeling it to be indelicate. He also copied out for
himself the whole of his fellow student's *Poems (1817)*.

When news of the battle of Waterloo reached London,
many of the younger surgeons, especially from the Lock
Hospital, rushed to embark for Belgium and the battlefield to
operate on the wounded, Astley Cooper himself going from
Guy's. Some good was to emerge from the horrors of the
battle, as surgeons were forced to operate at high speed under
tremendous pressure, struggling to repair the appalling injuries
of the wounded, with a consequent improvement in their
technique and knowledge of anatomy. Before returning to
London Cooper rescued twelve wounded war-horses, con-

sidered fit only for slaughter, and brought them back to his estate in Hertfordshire, where he worked on their injuries until they were fit to be turned out into the park. There they demonstrated that they had not forgotten their training. 'One morning,' Captain Gronow recounted in his *Reminiscences*, 'to his great delight, Cooper saw the noble animals form in line, charge, and then retreat, and afterwards gallop about, appearing greatly contented with the lot that had befallen them.'[13]

Astley Cooper insisted on his students at Guy's spending as much time as possible on the dissection of corpses. This necessitated his own involvement in the illicit and macabre trade of the bodysnatchers, or resurrection men, who procured bodies to order. They charged according to the state of the naked corpse: naked because to steal a clothed corpse constituted a felony, a naked one only a misdemeanour. Students were often expected to provide a corpse to dissect for themselves, and Cooper wrote of one young man, a hard-working student, who failed to pass his College of Surgeons examination in 1828 because of his ignorance of parts of the body, not having been able to equip himself in this way.[14] Cooper had his favourites among the resurrection men, on whom he knew he could rely. The authorities must have connived with his actions, recognizing their crucial role in the training of aspiring young surgeons – an impossible situation, and fraught with difficulties. The only bodies legally available for research were those of executed criminals, whose sentence included anatomizing. The bankrupt John Bellingham, a deranged Liverpool broker and Russia merchant who assassinated the prime minister Spencer Perceval in the lobby of the House of Commons in 1812, mistaking him for Lord Castlereagh, a member of the government against which he had a grudge, was one of these. But this supply was totally inadequate for the needs of the teaching hospitals and the private anatomy schools. Bodies could have been fairly easily obtained from

26. *The Royal College of Surgeons, Lincoln's Inn Fields,*
mid-nineteenth century. Sir Astley Cooper was the innovative
professor of comparative anatomy here from 1813. Among his
many surgical successes he was the first man to tie the abdominal
aorta in treating an aneurysm.

the poor houses and hospitals, but here a difficulty arose, the
poor having a rooted objection to the shame of their relations'
remains being included in the same category as murderers.
Some public-minded spirits left their bodies to hospitals in the
hope of lessening this prejudice, one of these being Jeremy
Bentham, over whose corpse the surgeon gave a grateful
oration before making the first incision. Another was a Mr
Boys, who left the extra proviso that his remains were subsequently to be reduced to 'essential salts' for the use of his
female friends 'to revive their drooping spirits'. One enter-
prising optimist wrote to Astley Cooper: 'Sir, I have been
informed you are in the habit of purchasing bodys and allowing
the person a sum weekly; knowing a poor woman that is

desirous of doing so, I have taken the liberty of calling to know the truth. I remain, your humble servant.' On the back of this missive Cooper wrote, 'The *truth* is that you deserve to be hanged for such an unfeeling offer. A.C.'[15]

The proliferation of private medical schools meant more people competing for bodies, and therefore prices rose, and gangs of resurrection men increased with the accelerating demand. At the beginning of each session – sessions ran from September to May – gang leaders visited the senior anatomy demonstrators and offered a guarantee of regular supplies in return for a fairly substantial down payment, and at the end of the session a finishing payment was also demanded. Astley Cooper recorded notes of such payments, listed later in the *Medical Times*: 'May 10 1827, paid Hollis, Vaughan and Llewellyn, finishing money £6. 6s. 0d. 1829 June 18, paid Murphy, Wildes and Naples, finishing money £6. 6s. 0d.' If a resurrectionist was caught and imprisoned, his customers were expected to help support his dependants during his absence, and Cooper is known to have spent large sums in this way. The gangs generally operated during the hours of darkness on moonless nights, helped by the cemetery custodians, who were often in their pay. If the custodians were caught and dismissed, they would usually join one of the gangs. The resurrectionists liked to work soon after a burial, before the ground had become too packed down. Paupers were generally buried several to a grave, which facilitated a gang's work. Sometimes new graves were guarded by armed friends, who took it in turn to watch all night for marauders; and sometimes mortsafes were used, frameworks of iron bars bolted down over the grave. Another trick of the trade was for a man and woman in deep mourning to visit a poorhouse and claim a body as that of a relative, and this ploy was usually successful. It was certainly a good deal less trouble than the dangerous tunnelling activities sometimes necessary in the burial grounds:

a gang would begin to dig some distance from the targeted new grave, so that the coffin could then be drawn out without disturbing the surface. By and large the bodysnatchers worked with great rapidity and success, as the diary of one of them, Joshua Naples, shows. Naples was an ex-sailor and had been at the battle of Cape St Vincent; later he became the grave-digger at Spa Fields, and finally resorted to the bodysnatcher's trade. The following are a few entries from his sixteen-page diary:

Thursday 12th. I went up to Brookes and Wilson, afterwards me, Bill and Daniel went to Bethnall Green, got 2. Jack, Ben went got 2 large and 1 large small back St Luke's, came home, afterwards met again and went to Bunhill Row got 6.

Saturday 21st. Went to St Thomas's sent 1 to Mr Taunton, 2 to Edinburgh, St Thomas's took 6 of the above this week, came home and stopt at home all night.

Tuesday 14th. At 1 a.m. got up, Ben, Bill and me went to St Luke's, 2 adults. Jack, Dan. Big Gates, 1 large and I small, took them to Bartholomew. Came home and went to St Thomas's, afterwards went to the other end of the town for orders. At home all night.

Sometimes things went wrong:

Friday 17th. Went and look out. Came home met at 11 except Dan. Went to the Hospital Crib and got 4, was stopt by the patrols, Butler, Horse and Cart were taken.

Joseph Henry Green, Keats's demonstrator at Guy's, who was a friend and executor of Coleridge's, was much involved with the trade. He was adamant about the crucial importance of dissection in a student's training, and risked a good deal to secure an adequate supply of bodies for the purpose. Even those involved in the trade found it horrifying. One of a gang,

Bill Harnett, eventually died at St Thomas's of tuberculosis, having first obtained Green's promise that he would not be anatomized. Southey wrote a ballad on the subject, *The Surgeon's Warning*, on a surgeon's dying fears that he might subsequently be served as he had served others:

> And my 'prentices will surely come
> > And carve me bone from bone,
> And I, who have rifled the dead man's grave,
> > Shall never rest in my own.
>
> Bury me in lead when I am dead,
> > My brethren, I entreat,
> And see the coffin weigh'd I beg,
> > Lest the plumber be a cheat.
>
> And let it be solder'd down
> > Strong as strong can be, I implore,
> And put it in a patent coffin
> > That I may rise no more . . .[16]

It was not until 1831 that an Act was at last passed through both Houses of Parliament which did much to remedy the macabre and ambivalent situation. The bodies of murderers were no longer to be available to the medical profession, but the bodies of all unknown or friendless dead from hospitals and workhouses were to be considered legal for use by the profession. As a result the trade of the resurrectionists, as many of the surgeons had predicted, became redundant. Art students also needed to learn anatomy, Haydon being particularly emphatic on dissection as a crucial condition in learning to draw accurately. He made arrangements for his students to work on bodies in the dissecting rooms of one of the anatomy theatres.

Wordsworth, in London at the time of Perceval's assassination, had planned to witness the execution of the murderer, scheduled to take place in Palace Yard at Westminster. Here he could have watched in safety from the roof of the Abbey, but at the last minute the grisly spectacle was switched to Newgate, and Wordsworth changed his mind: riots were expected, the event having added to the current threatening atmosphere of civil disturbance in the City.

It is strange to think of Keats and Ritchie, their minds preoccupied with poetic images, exposed to such horrors in their daily lives. Not that Keats was squeamish: in this context it is worth remembering his Isabella, who dug up her murdered lover's head in the forest and kept it planted in a pot of basil. However, their desire to extend their knowledge carried them through their experiences, and both made proficient pupils. Keats listened intently to Cooper's lectures, although occasionally his attention wandered a little: a lecture notebook still exists, decorated in the margins with his sketches of fruit and flowers. He was adept at blocking out extraneous impressions if he wished. Haydon was impressed at his friend's capacity to arrive at his lodgings straight from the operating table and at once immerse himself in readings and discussions of Shakespeare, but Keats felt that this facility could be dangerous. He later told Charles Brown that his last operation had been the opening of a man's temporal artery when he was deeply preoccupied with 'other matters', probably composition: 'I did it with the utmost nicety, but, reflecting on what passed through my mind at the time, my dexterity seemed a miracle, and I never took up the lancet again.'[17]

In December 1817 Ritchie was newly back from Paris, a city which for all Haydon's guests possessed great allure as the recent scene of cataclysmic events, tremendous triumphs and ultimate reversals, news of which had been followed with the closest attention from the English side of the Channel. When he had arrived at the British Embassy towards the end of 1815, only months after the battle of Waterloo, he found himself in a city experiencing a time of turmoil and change, with Napoleon's absolute rule suddenly shattered and the reinstatement of the old Bourbon monarchy unpopular and precarious. But Ritchie was not the only member of the dinner party to have this experience of Paris in a state of flux, the first of the group with such experience being Wordsworth, who was there during the Revolution. The bitterness of seeing his vision of Paris as the symbol of freedom shattered by the later excesses of the Terror had left him with a revulsion against all things French, but his first impressions had been of a very different nature.

Wordsworth had arrived in Paris in 1790 on the first anniversary of the storming of the Bastille, and the following year he was again drawn to France, stirred by the revolutionary fervour of the country. This time, after a brief visit to the capital, he went on to Orléans, where he met the young royalist Annette Vallon, a Catholic, with whom he fell in love. Early in 1792 Wordsworth followed Annette to her home at Blois, and it was here that he met Michel Beaupuy, a young captain with a passionate belief in the ideology of the Revolution. The two men spent many hours together, discussing political theory, and egalitarian concepts of liberty began to inflame Wordsworth's imagination. On Beaupuy's rejoining his regiment Wordsworth again returned to Paris, where he was horrified by the violence of the atmosphere, and haunted by the thought of the September massacres, by the unseen presence of the king and queen imprisoned in the Temple, around whose grim walls he walked, and by the sight of the guillotine in the Place de la Révolution. During this visit Robespierre was denounced and the climate of Paris became increasingly dangerous. In early December 1792 Wordsworth returned to England to try to raise funds for himself, Annette and their unborn child, but he was overtaken by events, firstly by the escalation of the Terror, and then, when France and England declared war, it became impossible for him to re-enter France. In mid-December his daughter by Annette, Caroline, was born, but her father was not to see her until she was nine years old. Wordsworth was traumatized by these experiences. On his return to England he tried to work but could not, and only a retreat to a farmhouse in Dorset, where Dorothy soothed and reassured him, saved his reason.

Napoleon was admired by many Englishmen at the time, including Hazlitt, whose hero he was. Haydon was reluctantly fascinated by him. These feelings were not shared by Wordsworth, who wrote to John Scott on 22 February 1816 of Napoleon as 'that audacious charlatan and remorseless desperado', and who always remained implacable in his hatred of the man. Nor was he among those who hurried to Paris as soon as it was possible after the emperor's removal. In 1814 his daughter Caroline became engaged to Jean-Baptiste Baudouin. Wordsworth himself does not seem to have made any move to meet the young couple, but Dorothy on his behalf was keen to be present at the wedding, at the urgent wish of both Annette and Caroline. Napoleon's return from Elba made her visit impossible, and it was then hoped that Caroline and Baudouin would visit England to see her father after Waterloo, but that plan did not materialize either, and in 1816 the pair were married without any English presence. Wordsworth made his daughter an allowance, and Mary Wordsworth always took an affectionate interest in her. Later Mary and Wordsworth did visit the Baudouins on two separate occasions.

Humphry Davy was in Paris on more than one occasion between 1813 and 1815, holding discussions with many of the city's scientific giants. In the spring of 1813 he seized the opportunity while collecting the Prix Napoléon he had been awarded by the French Institute to meet his fellow scientists in the French capital. The continuing war with France made it virtually impossible for an Englishman to obtain a passport, issued at that time not by the home authority but by the country to be visited, but Davy's fame made him *persona grata*, and passes were issued for himself, his new wife Jane, and, at the last moment, for the young Michael Faraday, his assistant, also acting as valet, Davy's own man having been so terrified at the idea of travelling to the dreaded enemy territory of France that he had refused to accompany the party. Lady Davy treated Faraday, destined in due course to rival and perhaps outshine her husband, as a servant, which Faraday endured good-naturedly, although understandably he did not like it. The Davys and Faraday visited the Louvre, where Davy was reported to have stalked rapidly through the galleries without glancing at the masterpieces surrounding him.[18] Davy's note-books of his tour, which was extended south to Naples, where he made detailed observations of Vesuvius in eruption, are filled with scientific notes interspersed with his poems, all neatly transcribed by the long-suffering Faraday.

Of the other diners, Haydon himself visited Paris in 1814, setting off in May within weeks of Napoleon's enforced with-drawal to Elba and the capitulation of Paris to contingents drawn from the allied armies of England, Prussia, Austria, Saxony and Russia. David Wilkie travelled with him, both men eager to take advantage of it being once more possible for English travellers to visit the city. The outskirts of Paris seemed forlorn and deserted, but as the two young men approached the centre Haydon's imagination was inflamed by the historic significance of what they were about to see: 'I was passionately affected. I had read everything from the first sitting of the National Convention to the dethronement of Napoleon, and was now plunging into the inextricable con-fusion of the rue St Honoré, shaken to my heart's core.'[19] The pair found themselves amid scenes of pandemonium. Like everyone else, they had intended to make straight for the Louvre, but after a brief initial visit they were seduced by the excitement of the streets, Haydon reflecting – wrongly, as events of the next year would show – that 'the great works will remain; the different tribes before us will separate in a few days, never again to meet in such a way';[20] and finding, among the jostling polyglot crowds, Bashkirs from Tartary more attractive than Raphael's *Transfiguration*. At the time this paint-ing was considered the crowning glory of the Louvre. It is now in the Vatican. Haydon recorded:

In the middle of the day the rue St Honoré was the most wonderful sight. Don Cossack chiefs loosely clothed and moving as their horses moved, with all the bendings of their bodies visible at every motion; the half-clothed savage Cossack horseman, his belt stuck full of pistols and watches and hatchets, crouched up on a little ragged-maned, dirty-looking, ill-bred, half-white pony; the Russian Imperial guardsman pinched in at the waist like a wasp, striding along like a giant, with an air of victory that made every Frenchman curse within his teeth as he passed him; the English officer, with his boyish face and broad shoulders; the heavy Austrian; the natty Prussian; and now and then a Bashkir Tartar, in the ancient Phrygian cap, with bow and arrows and chain-armour, gazing about from his horse in the midst of black-eyed grisettes, Jews, Turks and Christians from all countries in Europe and Asia. It was a pageant that kept one staring, musing and bewildered from morning till night.[21]

Haydon's first impression of the Louvre itself, the great object of his visit, was one of disappointment:

It is too long – it has too much the look as if one was looking in at the wrong end of a spy glass. From continually imagining what the *Transfiguration* must be, of course I formed a fancy very different from what it was. The consequence must always be what it was with me – the first glance made it look small and rather insignificant.[22]

Everyone seemed to be making for the Louvre, among them Henry Crabb Robinson, another English pilgrim, who arrived a little later than Haydon, towards the end of September 1814. He was excited to hear that the ubiquitous Mrs Siddons, whom he greatly admired, was in the building, and having tracked her down he followed as near as he could 'with decorum'. He found that 'there was something about her that disturbed me. So glorious a head ought not to have been covered with a small chip hat.'[23]

As Haydon continued his tour he became increasingly disenchanted with all he saw. He complained a good deal about the dirty condition of the city, the streets, the lodging houses, the people's clothes; after a while even the girls failed to please, and he longed for some 'wholesome English countrywoman' to hug. All the French women, he said ungallantly, had beards.

Haydon's account of the euphoric atmosphere of the city at that extraordinary time is full of impressions of the absent emperor. Eventually he was to paint more than forty studies of Napoleon musing on St Helena and, although he professed a proper horror of England's arch-enemy, with 'his folly, and his vice, his cruelty and tyranny', he was dazzled by the idea of the emperor's power and status as the undisputed heroic figure of the era. A year after Napoleon had crowned himself emperor in 1805, the young Ingres had painted his tremendous apotheosis of triumph, *Napoleon I on His Imperial Throne*, swathed in crimson and gold velvet and white ermine, crowned with gold laurel leaves and holding the gilded sceptre of Charles V in one hand and Charlemagne's hand of justice, symbol of monarchical power, in the other; a representation overwhelming in its impression of unassailable majesty.

Haydon would have applauded Ingres's hieratic stance as appropriate, and savoured the poignancy of hubris so soon brought low, but it is likely that by the time of his arrival in May 1814 the painting would have been removed and stored together with all other reminders of the emperor, only to be reinstated on Napoleon's return from Elba. Haydon's sense of history and occasion, his vivid awareness of living on the fringes of great events, is evident in his whole account of the visit. 'It might be said,' he reflected later, 'that when we arrived in Paris the ashes of Napoleon's last fire were hardly cool; the last candle by which he had read was hardly extinguished; the very book he had last read was to be seen turned down where he left it.'[24]

Haydon even characteristically daydreamed of parallels between himself and the great man. Once he tried on a hat that had belonged to the emperor and was gratified but not surprised to find it fitted him exactly. On a visit alone to Rambouillet, the royal hunting lodge – Wilkie, a timid traveller, having taken to his bed in an access of panic over the whole risky enterprise – he found himself in Napoleon's private closet:

Opposite the window was an arch, under which there was a most delicious sofa with pillows of the finest satin. On this luxurious couch he dreamed of conquered kings and great battles, and his imagination filled as he lay with future glories. It was impossible not to have profound associations with such a room. I stood, as it were, in his secret place.[25]

The Paris diaries of Wilkie and Haydon could hardly be more disparate. Whereas Haydon painted a scene of wild and colourful confusion, Wilkie calmly recorded their arrival in Paris amid troops of every nation as so quiet, that no one would suppose anything extraordinary had happened. While

22 *Rehearsing in the Green Room.* Sarah Siddons with her father Roger Kemble at Covent Garden, caricatured by T. Rowlandson. Haydon was overjoyed by the actress's public praise of his figure of Christ at the private view of *Christ's Entry into Jerusalem.*

23 George Clint's painting of Edmund Kean as Sir Giles Overreach in Massinger's *A New Way to Pay Old Debts.* Hazlitt admired his performance so much that he wrote, 'He was not at a single fault'– an opinion shared by Keats, who reviewed his Richard III a week before Haydon's dinner.

24 Apsley House, No. 1, London, bought by the Duke of Wellington from his brother in 1817. It made a splendid setting in which to display his trophies, including the magnificent dinner service decorated with his victories. This is a view from the park by T. Vivares, 1828.

26 *(Below)* Self-portrait of Edwin Landseer as a boy. Edwin had no formal education, as his father considered this to be harmful to artists. Instead he was sent out from a very early age to sketch in the fields then stretching from Marylebone to Hampstead.

25 *(Above)* William Bewick, Haydon's favourite pupil and the only one allowed to watch his master at work. 'I wish I could describe my feelings at receiving such friendship from this great man,' Bewick wrote to his brother.

27 *St James's in an Uproar, or the Quack Artist and His Assailants,* a caricature by J. Marks, 1819, mocking Haydon's exhibition of eight copies of Raphael cartoons and Elgin Marbles drawn by his pupils William Bewick and Thomas and Charles Landseer.

28 *Sir Humphry Davy Lecturing at the Surrey Institution*, a caricature by
T. Rowlandson and A.C. Pugin. Tickets for Davy's lectures reached the
black market, so popular were these occasions when his demonstrations
were apt to end with explosions as startling as fireworks.

29 *Entrance Hall of Charles Townley's Residence, 7 Park St, Westminster*,
watercolour by W. Chambers, *c.*1800. Townley, a great collector of
classical antiquities, was one of those connoisseurs who allowed artists
access to their collections.

30 'Part of the Allies Entering Paris 1814 – the Russian Contingent; Cossacks and Plunder', from *The Reminiscences and Recollections of Captain Gronow*. Haydon, visiting Paris that year, felt the Cossacks to be figures of glamour, but the journalist John Scott agreed with the message of this cartoon, saying that in Paris the word Cossack had come to mean rogue and thief.

31 Captain George Lyon, Joseph Ritchie's companion, dressed in exotic Eastern costume after his return from the ill-starred African expedition. Unlike his leader, who kept himself aloof, Lyon joined enthusiastically in the life of the community during the months they spent at Murzuk. Lithograph by R.J. Lane.

32 *View of Tripoli across the Harbour*, nineteenth-century engraving by Lacey. This was the scene Ritchie saw on his arrival in October 1818. He told Haydon, 'It was a day of exultation for me when I could realize what my imagination had fed on so long.'

33 *The Castle of Murzuk from Ritchie's Grave* from a drawing by Major Dixon Denham, who, with Dr Oudney and Captain Hugh Clapperton, followed in the footsteps of Ritchie and Lyon a year or so after Ritchie's tragic death.

34 Sir Astley Cooper, senior surgeon at Guy's Hospital during Keats's medical studies. Not only the most brilliant surgeon of his time, Cooper was also loved for his kindly temperament and for the unusual degree of respect he showed his patients.

35 The old operating theatre at St Thomas's Hospital, recently restored to its original state. Students fought for places in the small galleries, and heat and stench added to the horror of the screams of the unanaesthetized patients strapped down on the operating table.

36 An unfinished portrait of Charles and Mary Lamb in the last year of Charles's life, by Francis Stephen Cary, 1834. There is something a little disturbing about the placing of the two tiny figures with their intent gaze. The tools of their trade, quill pens and paper, lie on the table beside them.

37 The graves of Charles and Mary Lamb at Edmonton, by John Fulleylove. Charles died at Walden Cottage, Edmonton, in December 1834; Mary survived her brother until 1847.

38 *The Vale of Health, Hampstead, 1839*, by Henry A. Gillman. Leigh Hunt's cottage was here, among other attractive villas. Haydon was initially fond of Hunt, and visited him frequently in the Vale; but later he cooled towards him, disliking his aggressively anti-Christian stance.

39 A posthumous portrait of Keats reading in Wentworth Place, c.1822, by Joseph Severn. Keats lived here with Charles Brown for a few months from October 1819 to May 1820, during which time he wrote his great odes. In the other half of the house lived Mrs Brawne and her daughter, Keats's beloved Fanny.

40 St Mary's Church, Paddington Green, a watercolour by Lady Anna Maria Barrow, c.1849. Haydon's funeral took place here in the summer of 1846, attended by a huge crowd of mourners. His tomb bears the inscription, 'He devoted forty-two years to the improvement of the taste of the English People in high art and died broken hearted from pecuniary distresses.'

27. Sketch of David Wilkie, 1816, by Benjamin Robert Haydon. Wilkie looks startled, as if he had seen a ghost.

Wilkie contemplating a Rubens was slow to appreciate it and complained that some of the pictures appeared a little rubbed in parts, Haydon was a far more enthusiastic sightseer. Here is his reaction to the Correggios: 'Correggio gives me such sensations that I never think of him without having a musical harmonious strain undulate over my brain.'[26] When Wilkie had to return early to London, Haydon missed him:

My dear Wilkie set off for England this day; in spite of his heaviness of perception and total want of spirit, I feel low at his departure. Notwithstanding Paris was filled with all the nations of the earth, the greatest oddity in it was unquestionably David Wilkie. His horrible French, his strange, tottering, feeble pale look, his carrying about his prints to make bargains with printsellers, his resolute determination never to leave the restaurants till he got all his change right to a *centime*; his long disputes about *sous* and *demi-sous* with the *dame du comptoir*; whilst Madame tried to cheat him, and as she pressed her pretty fingers on his arm without making the least impression, her '*mais Monsieur*' and his Scotch '*mais Madame*', were worthy of Molière.[27]

Wilkie's practical plan to make useful contacts in Paris to sell his pictures during the visit is an example of his ordered nature, the opposite of his friend's, who continued throughout his life to miss opportunities and to antagonize the art establishment.

Keats himself never saw Paris, but his brothers George and Tom took a holiday there in the late summer of 1817, and on 10 September Keats wrote to his sister Fanny at her boarding school to tell her of a letter he had just received from them:

Like most Englishmen they feel a mighty preference for every thing English – the French meadows the trees the people the towns the churches the books the every thing – although they may be in themselves good; yet when put in comparison with our green island they all vanish like swallows in October. They have seen cathedrals, manuscripts, fountains, pictures, tragedy, comedy, with other things you may by chance meet in this country such as washerwomen, lamplighters, turnpikemen, fish kettles, dancing masters, kettle drums, sentry boxes, rocking horses etc.[28]

John Scott, who had witnessed the making of Haydon's life mask of Wordsworth, had lately handed over his editorship of the *Champion*, and was in Paris by himself in 1817, wretchedly unhappy over the death there the previous November of his little son Paul. It was through him that Ritchie first came to know of Keats. Tom Keats, who came to call, left a notebook with Scott in Paris into which he had copied his brother's early poems, and these would have been the first examples of the poet's work that Ritchie had seen.

Scott and his family had been in Paris a good deal since 1814, when Scott had written *A Visit to Paris*, an account of the city during Napoleon's absence on Elba. This had been a great success, Wordsworth being one of its admirers, and he now repeated the formula with *Paris Revisited in 1815*. The first book had lively descriptions of the bustle of the Paris streets, the diversity and ingenuity of the many side-shows, and the bizarre appearance, to English eyes, of the ladies' fashions. The second volume described French bitterness as looted works of art were being dismantled and restored to their rightful owner nations. Only a year earlier Haydon had decided to enjoy the excitement of the crowded streets rather than make the Louvre his first priority, feeling that the pictures would always be there to come back to. How wrong he had been. Tourists from all over Europe poured into the city to see the treasures in the Louvre before these were dispersed. Scott described the great gallery: 'Long blank spaces of dirty blue wall daily increased their size and number, and told how rapidly the monuments of the glory of France were disappearing.'[29] In spite of French rumours to the contrary, he thought that the porters did their work smoothly and quickly, and without damage, as they carried out priceless treasures under the inscription on the cornice of the great entrance which proclaimed *Les fruits de nos victoires!* Students gathered around the most important pictures, anxious to finish their copies before the workmen removed the originals. He went on:

Many young French girls were seen among these, perched up on small scaffolds, and calmly pursuing their labours in the midst of the throng and bustle. Our officers generally posted themselves close to these interesting artists, who seemed quite able to flirt with the foreign hussars, and copy a Holy Family at the same time.[30]

Scott wrote graphically to Haydon about the dismantling of the triumphal car on the top of the arch in the Place du

Carrousel in which Napoleon had planned to place a golden statue of himself, having already gilded the beautiful and ancient bronze horses taken from outside St Mark's in Venice: 'I saw the Horses go! I was most lucky in getting to the top of the Arch. I sat in the Car, I stood in the Car – I plundered the Car, and have brought with me a ram's horn from it – and with it I shall try to blow down the wall of the first Jericho at which I arrive.'[31] Scott singled out the Cossacks as the most badly behaved of the occupying military, and where Haydon had admired them as figures of glamour, he found that their reputation for trouble-making and stealing had led to 'Cossack' being used as the term for any military rowdyism in the city.

Lamb did not visit Paris at that time, but he did take Mary there later, in 1822. He thought it was 'a glorious picturesque city. London looks mean and new to it.' Always the gourmet, he enjoyed the new experience of eating frogs, 'the nicest little delicate things – rabbity-flavor'd – Imagine a Lilliputian rabbit – They fricassée them, but in my mind, drest seethed – plain, with parsley and butter, would have been the decision of Apicius.'[32] To John Clare, the Northamptonshire nature poet, he recommended that Mrs Clare should pick off the hindquarters: 'The fore quarters are not so good. She may let them hop off by themselves.'[33]

The Lambs' visit ended in disaster, as Mary suffered one of her attacks and had to be left behind when Charles could no longer postpone his return to his desk at East India House. Henry Crabb Robinson took care of her until she seemed fully recovered. Lamb left Mary a note of advice on Paris sightseeing:

Then you must walk along the borough side of the Seine, facing the Tuileries. There is a mile and a half of print-shops and bookstalls. If the latter were but English! Then there is a place where the Paris people put all the dead people, and bring them flowers and dolls, and gingerbread nuts, and sonnets, and such trifles; and that is all, I think worth seeing as sights except that the streets and shops of Paris are themselves the best sight.[34]

All these English visitors viewed Paris from their own characteristic angles. For Haydon it was a tremendous whirl of excitement, romance and emotion and, with his painter's eye, of visual stimulation; for Scott, as an experienced journalist, it offered a fascinating scene of political turmoil; while Lamb saw it chiefly as a prime source of his favourite occupations, bookstalls to browse through and ancient streets to wander. For Thomas Moore it presented a perfect new subject for satirical verse. He visited the capital in 1817 and on his return wrote *The Fudge Family in Paris*, a caricature in light verse of some of the English visitors who laid themselves open to ridicule with their gaucheries and absurdly outdated clothes. For all the travellers there was a sense of adventure and of the beginning of a new era, as the fabled city once more opened its gates to the world.

George and Tom Keats had been there at the same time as Moore, but they were far removed from his *Fudge Family* category. Their goal was to see absolutely everything of interest, provided Tom did not become too exhausted: tuberculosis was to kill him before the end of the following year. For the moment, however, he was enjoying himself, and John Scott proved the ideal guide for the two young men.

Scott was also seeing a good deal of Joseph Ritchie, whose gift of sympathetic understanding and quiet manner suited the bereaved father's mood. The two men had met each other through Thomas Hill, who was in Paris at the time. Hill, book collector and kind-hearted and amiable host, was described by a contemporary as 'the most innocent and ignorant of all the bibliomaniacs'.[35] He remained remarkably young-looking

28. *The Occupation of Paris, 1814*: 'English Visitors in the Palais Royal'. Parisians found English tourists great figures of fun. Captain Gronow noted that thousands of oddly dressed English flocked to Paris immediately after the war: 'Our countrymen and women having so long been excluded from French modes had adopted fashions of their own quite as remarkable and eccentric as those of the Parisians and much less graceful.'

to an advanced age, prompting the poet and banker Samuel Rogers's joke that he was one of the little Hills spoken of as skipping in the Psalms, and Leigh Hunt described him in his *Autobiography* as 'the jovial bachelor, plump and rosy as an abbot'.[36] He was a kind and uncomplicated man, and no doubt a comfort to Scott. An undated note from Scott to Hill includes a message for Ritchie: 'My best regards to Ritchie; in a day or two I should be glad to see him. My wife often mentions his name as one who takes a kind interest in our misfortune.'[37]

A year later Scott accepted the editorship of the new *London Magazine*, which he conducted with outstanding brilliance and success, Hazlitt's *Table Talk* and Lamb's Elia essays being among his famous inclusions. His career ended with tragic abruptness in 1821, when, within a day or two of Keats's death, he was fatally wounded in the last of the literary duels, fought over a critical article he had printed attacking John Gibson Lockhart's *Blackwood's Magazine*. Lockhart himself challenged him, but Scott refused to take this up; the affair escalated and eventually the duel did take place at Chalk Farm, then out in the fields and the traditional venue for such affairs, between Scott and Lockhart's deputy, Jonathan Christie. The duel was confused: in the first round Scott fired into the air, upon which the seconds should have declared the confrontation ended; this did not happen and Christie, having told his second he would then fire in the air, fired straight at Scott, and, whether by chance or not, hit the mark calculated to kill rather than wound.[38] Scott did not die for several days, and meanwhile Christie and his second, James Traill, and Scott's second, Peter Patmore, had to flee the country, their involvement in the duel leaving them open to prosecution for murder. In due course Christie and Traill were tried on a murder charge, but pronounced innocent.

Scott was thirty-seven at the time of his death and at the height of his powers: a great loss to the London literary world. Haydon, who had lately fallen out with his old friend, at first decided not to attend the funeral, but changed his mind at the last minute and followed the procession of hearse and mourners' carriages to St Martin-in-the-Fields:

As I squeezed by the coffin that contained the body of my former friend, with the long pall and black plumes trembling as the wind blew into the aisle, I shivered. All our conversations on death and Christianity and another world crowded into my mind, and when the four men took up the coffin, two at the head, and two at the foot, and staggered and reeled beneath its weight, my mind darted through the lid, and saw inwardly the pale corpse, still! stretched! silent! and cold!

As the coffin was taken down to the vault, the plumes were

taken off, and when they nodded to the followers against the light window, I thought them endowed with human features, as fates that bowed, as we walked in submission to their power!

I descended the steps into a dark chamber, and saw at a distance doors open and piles of black coffins to the ceiling, inside, each having a trembling light fixed to its side. The mourners crowded forward; I felt too much to move, and was hustled about, without one effort to resist before the room was half obscured by heads. I listened and heard the dry scraping of the cords, and then a dead jerk as if the body had settled in its place. Immediately after a mellow voice rose up inside like steam, reading the funeral service. Poor Scott! I took a last look of the coffin and walked away.[39]

7.   Tragedy in Africa

The prospect which opens before me of my being enabled to devote the rest of my days to pursuits which I have always thought the most exalted and the most worthy to occupy the energies of man – and the possibility of my acting an important part in the events which may be preparing on behalf of the most abject and suffering part of our species give a buoyancy to my hopes, which the view of the dangers I am about to encounter cannot depress.

Joseph Ritchie to Richard Garnett, 21 December 1817[1]

Haydon showed me a letter he had received from Tripoli – Ritchey was well and in good spirits, among camels, turbans, palm trees and sands – You may remember I promised to send him an Endymion which I did not – however he has one – you have one – one is in the wilds of America – the other is on a camel's back in the plains of Egypt.

John Keats to George and Georgiana Keats, 29 December 1818[2]

Soon after Haydon's dinner party Ritchie began in earnest to make preparations for his African adventure. Having taken a brief New Year holiday in order to say goodbye to his family in Yorkshire, and also to Richard Garnett, who had planned to meet him at Otley, he returned to London. Here he took leave of other friends, including John Scott's wife Caroline, the lively and attractive daughter of the printseller Paul

Colnaghi. She wrote to Haydon to tell him that she had been seeing Ritchie: 'Mr Ritchie took leave of us last night. You do not like to say goodbye I think, neither does Mr Ritchie, for he only said "good night" as usual.'³ Ritchie then returned to Paris, where he spent some months learning Arabic with an Egyptian acquaintance and continuing his studies in astronomy and the use of astronomical instruments at the Paris Observatory. He also read with close interest all the accounts available of his predecessors in Africa, some of which were still in manuscript form. He had already read Mungo Park's narrative of his first expedition, and followed this with the papers of the young German, Frederick Hornemann,⁴ and the Swiss J. Lewis Burckhardt, and then ranged back in time as far as the sixteenth-century historian of Moorish descent Leo Africanus. During this time he engaged a young assistant from the Jardin des Plantes called Dupont, who was to undertake the botanical side of the expedition. This proved to be a mistake: Dupont, having accepted a year's salary in advance on arrival in Tripoli, disappeared, Ritchie guessed at the instigation of the French consul. A more serious defection was that of Captain Frederick Marryat, at this time known as a distinguished naval officer rather than as the prolific and successful author, memorably of *Mr Midshipman Easy* and *Masterman Ready*, that he was later to become. A year or two younger than Ritchie, he had already seen service in the West Indies and elsewhere under Lord Cochrane, whose command was characterized by a buccaneering style of cliff-hanging adventure that would later provide the novelist with much of his material, and which exactly suited Marryat's own ebullient and daring nature. In 1815 his health had collapsed, but two years later he felt sufficiently restored to apply to join Ritchie's expedition, to which he would have contributed some much-needed experience. At the last minute, however, he withdrew, thanks to a misunderstanding with his naval superiors about a promotion to which he felt entitled, but would have forfeited if he had gone to Africa. His boisterous temperament might have made him a somewhat overwhelming partner for Ritchie, and his colourful and extrovert style might have grated upon his leader's reserved and fastidious nature; but he would certainly have been a source of comfort and encouragement when disaster struck the little party.

The mystery of the course of the river Niger, which had been one of the central focuses of government-financed African expeditions since the latter part of the eighteenth century, still remained unsolved when Ritchie was commissioned by the Colonial Office in 1817. There had been many theories down the centuries, from Herodotus' idea that the river was a tributary of the Nile, the sixteenth-century Leo Africanus' that it was a branch of the Senegal, and so on to Mungo Park, at the turn of the century, who thought it might be the northern branch of the Congo. Part of the problem's intractability stemmed from the river's bafflingly erratic course. It rose near the early reaches of the Gambia and then flowed to the north-east in the direction of that great magnet of all early African explorers, Timbuktu, with its fabled streets of gold. It then took a dive south until it broke up into a complex of waters forming its delta which finally debouched into the Bight of Benin, a termination not guessed at by Ritchie or his predecessors. Another barrier to any successful charting of the river's course was its great length – some 2,500 miles – in the course of which it traversed deserts, forests and, latterly, the disease-ridden swamps of southern Nigeria. It crossed as it went the boundaries of many countries known by a multiplicity of names, and with inhabitants with diverse languages, religions and ethnic origins. But the attempts continued, the most famous being those of Mungo Park, a protégé of Sir Joseph Banks.

Mungo Park was a Scotsman and, like Ritchie, a young

surgeon who abandoned medicine in favour of exploration. He wrote to Sir Joseph Banks in terms parallel with Ritchie's to Garnett a few years later, that 'A country surgeon is at best but a laborious employment; and I will gladly hang up the lancet and plaster ladle whenever I can obtain a more eligible situation.'[5] Park was commissioned in 1795 by the African Association to begin his search from the Gambia, and set off with a pitifully small train consisting of one negro servant, one boy and two asses. He endured great hardships, including imprisonment by suspicious Arab traders, from whom he was lucky to escape with the clothes he stood up in. These included his hat, in the crown of which were concealed the precious notes of his expedition, and a pocket compass he had managed to hide in the sand. He succeeded in attaining the upper reaches of the Niger, a moment he memorably recorded later: 'Looking forwards I saw with infinite pleasure the great object of my mission: the long sought for, majestic Niger, glittering in the morning sun, as broad as the Thames at Westminster, and flowing slowly to the eastward.'[6] Eventually he returned safely to Scotland and settled down to write an account of his expedition, *Travels in the Interior Districts of Africa*. His book was a tremendous success, running into three editions on its first appearance, and translated into most European languages; the Duchess of Devonshire even wrote a popular song about one of its more heartbreaking episodes. Park returned to Africa for a second time in 1805 with his brother-in-law, four carpenters, two sailors and a train of thirty soldiers complete with full uniforms, ludicrously unsuitable for the burning heat they were to encounter. His starting point was the same as on his first expedition, but at Pisania he took a course to the south, initially parallel to his earlier return journey. He did manage to reach the Niger, but at the expense of most of his company, who perished along the way. He himself was never seen again, and no word of his death reached England for a further five years. At last news came that he and his five surviving companions had been ambushed from both sides of the river at a rocky defile, forced to leap into the river and had all drowned.

The widely read story of Park's first heroic expedition gave a great impetus to public interest in African exploration throughout Europe, and to the general thirst for more information about the interior of the continent, vast tracts of which still remained so tantalizingly blank on the map of the world. Allied to this natural curiosity was another factor – the desire to seize further opportunities of extending commercial interests. And, as time went on, this became more urgent as it was realized that if British moves were not made quickly, other nations, and more particularly the French, would be first to what was thought to promise rich commercial pickings. In a speech to the African Association in 1799 Sir Joseph Banks had over-optimistically elaborated this point:

We have already by Mr Park's means opened a gate into the interior of Africa, into which it is easy for every nation to enter and to extend its commerce and discovery from the west to the eastern side of that immense continent . . . A detachment of five hundred chosen troops would soon make that road easy, and would build embarkations upon the Joliba [Niger] – if two hundred of these were to embark with field pieces they would be able to overcome the whole forces which Africa could bring against them.

Banks spoke of the value of the Moors' trading activities, mostly carried out with the towns situated on or near the river, which were said to produce a million pounds a year. This, he believed, was in the form of gold collected for the most part by the natives as gold dust near the mouths of the rivers:

If science should teach these ignorant savages, that the gold which is dust at the mouth of a river must be in the form of sand at the high part of the current, of gravel in a still more elevated station, or of pebbles when near the place from whence it was originally washed . . . is it not probable that the golden harvest they are already in the habit of gathering might be increased an hundred fold? As increased riches still increase the wants of the possessors, and as our manufactures are able to supply them, is not this prospect, of at once attaching to the country the whole of the interior trade now possessed by the Moors, with an incalculable further increase, worth some exertion and some expense to a trading nation? . . . it is easy to foretell that if this country delays much longer to possess themselves of the treasures laid open to them by the exertions of this Association, some rival nation will take possession of the banks of the Joliba, and assert by arms her right of prior possession, should we afterwards attempt to participate in the benefits of this new trade, or in the honour of exploring nations which are yet unknown to Europe.[7]

It seems extraordinary that Banks should have believed such evident fantasy. He also wrote privately to the prime minister, Lord Liverpool:

Should the experiment be made, I have little doubt that in a very few years a trading company might be established under immediate control of the government, who would take upon themselves the whole expense of the measure, would govern the negroes far more mildly and make them far more happy than they now are under the tyranny of their arbitrary princes, would become popular at home by converting them to the Christian religion by inculcating in their rough minds the mild morality which is engrafted on the tenets of our faith and by effecting the greatest practicable diminution of the slavery of mankind, upon the principles of natural justice and commercial benefit.[8]

Here another vexed question is raised: how to deal with that other major and far more profitable traffic than gold: slaves. Banks took a pragmatic view of the trade in slaves. In answer to an unnamed enquirer he gave as his opinion that if free men were available, they made better workers than did slaves, as the latter knew that it was impossible to improve their prospects and therefore had no incentive to work hard. But he resented those who thought it was a sin to employ slaves, as 'the Bible shows that Providence has tolerated slavery from the earliest times'; that many slaves are more comfortably settled than free men, 'as the Workhouses testify'; that if abolition was achieved, 'thousands of negroes who had been mustered in Africa would die of starvation; and those who oppose the trade from humanitarian motives should study the misery at home as shown by the Vagrant Laws'.[9] This blunt stance was still sympathetic to a strong element of society, though it would become less acceptable as the century went on.

Banks was suggesting a compromise course, 'the greatest practicable diminution' necessary to balance humanitarian considerations with those of commercial benefit; but meanwhile a group of influential and mainly wealthy men, predominantly Quakers, were agitating with startling success for the total suppression of the slave trade. Their particular focus was on the liberation of slaves in the East Indies and the discontinuance of the traffic from Africa. They were led in their endeavours by the persuasive advocacy of William Wilberforce and of Thomas Clarkson, both members of the Evangelical movement. Wilberforce was a friend of Pitt's, and secured his backing and that of the formidable lawyer Henry Brougham. By 1806 Wilberforce and Clarkson and their supporters had succeeded in achieving legislation abolishing the slave trade in the British Isles and dominions, although it was to take them nearly another thirty years before they attained their final triumph in the overall outlawing of slavery itself in British dominions. Their next success came in 1811, when, with the aid of Brougham's persuasive lobbying, the Felony Act was passed, which made involvement in the slave trade punishable by transportation. This proved an extremely effective measure, striking terror into the hearts of the traffickers. Lord Bathurst, Secretary of State for the Colonies, was one of those at the seat of power to be won over to the abolitionist side. His instructions to Ritchie on his African mission contained a humanitarian slant, readily acceptable to the young traveller, already himself dedicated to that end.

Despite the success of the abolitionists on the home front, and the efforts to intercept slave ships by British squadrons based on Sierra Leone, by the time Ritchie set off for Africa the slave trade still flourished throughout the continent, and there was a discouraging escalation in the number of black slaves taken to the West Indies, Cuba and Brazil. Traders took two main routes from the interior to the coast. One was that to West Africa, where the lethally unhealthy climate meant that the enemy to be faced by Europeans was predominantly disease, for the most part malaria and dysentery. The Gold Coast came to be known as the White Man's Grave not without reason, and consequently European traders preferred to wait on the coast for batches of slaves to be brought direct to their ships from the interior rather than try to penetrate up river themselves. The second route, that to be attempted by Ritchie, traversed the Sahara desert south from the Barbary coast, which stretched from the Straits of Gibraltar eastwards to the Gulf of Sirte in Libya. This area had earlier been notorious for the kidnapping raids of Muslim pirates on European ships sailing in the Mediterranean or along the east coast of Africa. In the seventeenth century as many as 25,000 white Christians, men and women, were held as slaves taken on these skirmishes. The Barbary ports were provinces of the

North-western
Africa

N

Tangier
Tunis
Gulf of Sirte
Tripoli
Mizda ·
Sokna ·
FEZZAN
Murzuk ·
Tasawa ·

AHAGGAR

S A H A R A   D E S E R T

TIBESTI

Timbuktu

Cape
Verde
SENEGAMBIA
R. Senegal
sania
R. Gambia
R. Niger
Segu

SIERRA
LEONE

ASHANTI
IVORY COAST
GOLD COAST
Volta
Benin
Bight of Benin

Busa
R. Niger

Kano ·

Lake Chad
BORNU

R. Benue

→ Mungo Park 1795–97
····· Mungo Park 1805
⟶ Ritchie and Lyon's journey to Murzuk 1819
--=-- Lyon's continuation after Ritchie's death and return journey

0 100 200 300 400 500 miles
0   500   1000 km

29. The routes taken by Joseph Ritchie and George Lyon; by Lyon
with John Belford the carpenter after Ritchie's death; and those
earlier ones of Mungo Park.

Ottoman empire and European countries found that the use
of diplomacy rather than force was the best method of trying
to deal with this nightmare situation. British consuls were
appointed for the purpose, frequently having to hand out large
sums in ransom for the more important of their enslaved
compatriots. By the early nineteenth century this piracy was
virtually extinguished, but the great slave-raiding caravans
from the north into the interior continued and increased, the
predators here being mainly the Arabs. For the miserable
slaves themselves the northern journey was worse than the
south-western, many died on the terrible trek across the
Sahara, and none arrived at the coast looking much more than
skeletons, before the cynical and shocking process of fattening
them up for the markets began.

There were insuperable difficulties in convincing the traders
that the British, for so long happy connivers in the acquisition
of slaves for the West Indian plantations, had suddenly, and
for no good reason that the slavers could see, begun to con-
demn, even to forbid, their manner of livelihood. The state
of slavery in Africa from the earliest times had formed an
endemic part of life, a situation that was to prove impervious
to change for a long time to come. In England, however,
anti-slavery attitudes were hardening. Wealthy possessors of
West Indian estates now began to be discreet about their West
Indian possessions, and demonstrations of support for the
humanitarian faction continued to grow. In August 1802
Wordsworth made a powerful contribution to the debate with
his fine sonnet to Toussaint L'Ouverture, a chief of the black
slaves freed by the decree of the French Convention in 1794,
who rose to become governor of St Domingo. He refused to
implement Napoleon's reimposition of slavery, was arrested
and sent to Paris, where he died in prison in April 1803, ten
months after his brave act of defiance:

Thou hast left behind
Powers that will work for thee; air, earth, and skies;
There's not a breathing of the common wind
That will forget thee; thou hast great allies;
Thy friends are exultations, agonies,
And love, and Man's unconquerable mind.

On a more mundane note, William and Dorothy Wordsworth, friends and in 1802 neighbours of the Clarksons, had
for a long time, in company with many others, refused to eat
the sugar produced at the expense of so much suffering. They
ate honey on their porridge and in their tea in place of the
tainted substance: a small gesture, perhaps, but indicative of the
growing atmosphere of support for abolition in the country. It
was calculated that a family of five renouncing sugar and rum
for twenty-one months would save the life of one slave; in
nineteen and a half years they would save a hundred.[10]

In spite of Sir Joseph Banks's astonishingly over-hopeful
remarks to the African Association about the trade in gold,
the reality in the interior of Africa was to prove disappointing,
small bags of gold dust being for the most part as much as could
be acquired. Herodotus had described the strange custom of
traders who, seeking gold, would put out piles of goods for
sale, and then withdraw. Later the natives would come and
put small heaps of gold dust beside the goods; if the piles were
considered too small, the traders ignored them and waited
until the gold dust was increased, removing the gold dust
when satisfied and leaving their own offerings. This same odd
transaction was still being deployed at the time of Ritchie's
expedition. The best gold deposits were to be found in the
forests of Ashanti, and areas to the south, hence the name of
the Gold Coast, the nearest accessible coastline. There were
old rumours, reported in the *Proceedings* of the African Association in 1792 as told by a Moor called Shabeni, of an area rich

SLAVE CARAVAN ON ITS WAY TO THE COAST.

30. Slave caravan on its way to the coast. Ritchie would have passed such wretched groups on his way south. Engraving from *Livingstone's Travels*, mid-nineteenth century.

in gold near the mysterious city of Housa. Here men went at night on camels whose legs and feet were covered to protect them against snakes. 'They take a bag of sand and mark with it the places that glitter with gold; in the morning they collect where marked, and carry it to refiners, who, for a small sum, separate the gold.'[11] But slaves, and such commodities as ivory, gum and palm oil, valued as an ingredient in the manufacture of soap, the demand for which increased with the nineteenth-century preoccupation with washing, were the staples of trade rather than the little leather bags of gold dust.

Against this background, in the early autumn of 1817 plans were under way for Ritchie's expedition. On 23 September Henry Goulburn, under-secretary at the Colonies Office, wrote to Sir John Barrow of the Admiralty to say that Lord Bathurst was anxious to proceed as fast as possible in the organization of Ritchie's projected journey from Tripoli to

Timbuktu. He would, he continued, instruct the consul-general in Tripoli, Colonel Warrington, to 'urge the Bashaw of Tripoli to fulfil his promise to do everything possible to procure a favourable issue' for Ritchie's mission.[12] On 13 October Sir Joseph Banks wrote to his friend Sir Charles Blagden about the project, saying that Bathurst had asked his advice on a suitable candidate to lead the mission, and that he had recommended Ritchie. By now Ritchie had received verbal instructions about his task, but it was not until 1 February 1818, a month after Haydon's dinner, that he received his formal commission from Bathurst, a long document which opened: 'His Majesty's Government having determined to establish a Vice-Consulship at Fezzan, with a view to the successful prosecution of the discoveries now attempting in the interior of Africa, I have the satisfaction to acquaint you that you have been selected to fill that situation.'[13] The content of the letter of instruction was necessarily vague, though not to quite the extent of Banks's Polonius-like instructions to Burckhardt in 1809: 'Whatever you resolve upon, let neither rashness nor timid caution influence your conduct. The one might lose us the harvest of your labours, the other might make you lose those opportunities which you might have employed to best effect.'[14] Ritchie was to make himself known to the British vice-consul on arrival in Tripoli; then to proceed as soon as practicable southwards to Murzuk, the principal town of the Fezzan, where he was to spend some time in collecting information relevant to his projected journey south in the direction of Timbuktu. He was to send home detailed information of a general nature about the physical and political state of the interior; and, more specifically, to find out as much as possible about the course of the river Niger. A further task, not listed in this formal document, was to gather information about the extent and state of the traffic in slaves, Bathurst's own particular interest as a convinced sponsor of abolition.

31. The most picturesque object in a valley close to Murzuk was
the old village of Tasawa. From Heinrich Barth's *Travels and
Discoveries in North and Central Africa*, 1857–8.

There was an element of urgency in most of the communications Ritchie was to receive from his employers, largely
attributable to an increasing anxiety that the French might
pre-empt the British plans. This fear had been sharpened by a
report from Sir Charles Stuart in Paris at the beginning of
December 1817 of a rumoured expedition to the interior of
Africa then under consideration by the French government.
Partly for this reason, Bathurst emphasized to Ritchie the
importance of not allowing anyone in Tripoli, and even more
in Murzuk, to become aware of his precise brief or of any new
information he was able to gather.

For the time being, however, while he was still waiting in
Paris, Ritchie's one anxiety was to get under way on his
journey as soon as practicable, but it was not until 6 September
1818 that he was able to set off from Marseilles en route to

Malta. His brother accompanied him as far as Marseilles, and on 29 September Ritchie wrote to Garnett, regretting that his friend had not been able to be with them too. He had found his fellow travellers on board tiresome, or worse: 'The greatest brute and rascal we have amongst us was a hero of the ci-devant Imperial Guard, except the Captain's son who was one of the most impudent thieves I ever met with, and had his fingers everywhere.' To satisfy his need for privacy and silence he took his mattress up on deck and, covering himself with his greatcoat, curled up in the ship's jolly boat in the stern, and 'took up my lodging there'. He ended this last surviving letter to his friend: 'Having brought up the affairs of the expedition to our safe arrival at Malta – and it being near twelve – and being moreover at the bottom of the sheet – I shall say good night and joy be wi' ye a'n to you and all my friends in your part of the world.' Garnett later endorsed this letter 'ob. Dec. 1819'.

At Valetta there was another delay, as Admiral Sir Charles Penrose advised the young explorer not to sail in a merchant vessel but to wait for a ship of war, so that his arrival at Tripoli should make a sufficiently imposing impression on its Bashaw. About now, and probably during the imposed wait in Malta, Ritchie wrote a poem which later enjoyed some success, partly no doubt because of the author's tragic end. It first appeared in the *Monthly Magazine* in June 1820, seven months after his death; was printed again in the *London Magazine* the following year under the title 'Albion'; and in 1828 was included as 'A Farewell to England' in Alaric Watt's *Poetical Album*, next to Coleridge's 'The Exchange'. Here is one of the six stanzas:

> Strong in thy strength I go, and wheresoe'er
> My steps may wander, may I ne'er forget
> All that I owe to thee; and O may ne'er
> My frailties tempt me to abjure that debt!

> And what, if far from thee my star must set,
> Hast thou not hearts that shall with sadness hear
> The tale, and some fair cheeks that shall be wet,
> And some bright eyes, in which the swelling tear
> Shall start for him who sleeps in Afric's desarts drear.

Ritchie would have been pleased, probably astonished, to find himself appearing in John Scott's prestigious *London Magazine* in company with Lamb in his Elia guise and just before the appearance there of De Quincey's *Confessions of an English Opium Eater*. The poem did not appear under Scott's aegis, his fatal duel having taken place two months earlier, although as a friend of Ritchie's it is likely that he would have already selected it for inclusion.

On 12 October 1818 Ritchie at last set foot on African soil, and a fortnight later he wrote to Haydon an ebullient letter full of his first impressions:

It was a day of exultation for me when I could realize what my imagination had fed on so long. The spying glass was many and many a time up to my eye as we coasted along in making the harbour. It would have done your heart good to have seen the group by the seashore to the eastward of the port as we entered – the camels laden with the produce of the country were coming into the town – Arab tents were pitched under the date trees – and their masters strolling about or lying down near them – horsemen were exercising their steeds – and a whole crowd of turban'd heads were watching our vessel come into the port.

Colonel Warrington, the consul, came out to meet Ritchie with his boat, escorted him ashore and walked him through the narrow streets to his town house. Ritchie was delighted with all the exotic scenes through which they passed:

32. 'Two musicians dancing' from *Travels in Northern Africa* by Denham, Clapperton and Oudney, 1828.

Camels were lying down at every street corner and I saw on every side negro slaves with their fantastic ornaments. It was a season in which they hold one of the Mohammedan feasts, and the next day a number of black slaves (or rather servants) came before the door of the Consular House to dance the dances of their own country. Some writer says that Africa, alluding to negro Africa of course, every evening forms one immense ball-room, so attached are they to this kind of diversion . . . I never saw an amusement entered into with greater spirit, or one from which everybody concerned seemed to derive more enjoyment.

He told Haydon that he had already visited the ruins of Leptis Magna. He wished that Haydon had been with him on the expedition 'without wishing you to run the gauntlet of all the hair-breadth escapes which I intend to brave', partly for the luxury of having somebody with whom to quote Wordsworth and Shakespeare. He had come on one man with whom he could share his literary thoughts, 'a Scotch doctor, a very worthy man, whom I contrive to bore a little occasionally in this way when I am full to bursting':

Pray tell Keats that *Endymion* has arrived this far on his way to the desert, and when you are sitting over your Christmas fare will be jogging (in all probability) on a camel's back 'over those African sands immeasurable'. To return to our Libida journey, you should have seen our tent and our dinner party – all the varieties of costume from Moorish burnooshes to English shooting jackets stretched on the ground and fingering the dishes with as much good will as if it had been a dinner on which Vuy or Beauvilliers had exhausted his gastronomic science.

He was fascinated by his first experience of the desert:

– a monotonous succession of hillocks of sand, strikingly resembling a rough sea turned by magic from water into an impalpable sand, without the slightest trace of any kind of vegetation; and peopled here by black beetles and small lizards which leave their foot-marks wherever they crawl until the next gust of wind effaces them.

'As for the ruins of Leptis,' he continued, 'we will talk them over the next time we meet at the tea table.' A poignant remark in view of subsequent events.

In a few weeks I shall turn my back on Tripoli and then farewell to congresses, reviews, exhibitions, new poems, parliamentary debates and in short to the *quid quid agunt homines*[15] of European life for a long time. If any of them penetrate to me across my almost impracticable deserts they must come 'like Angel visits few and far between', and last year's 'news' will soon be to me the same thing that the damp smoking folio which has just reached your breakfast table from the Strand is to you. Then I shall have bright suns, and clear skies and a new and more magnificent face of nature before me wherever I go – and if the good providence of God go with us

      In after times they'll hear us tell

      What in the anterior parts befel.

    Kind remembrances to Mrs Scott and all friends.

Yours ever,

J. Ritchie[16]

The letter's relaxed and intimate tone suggests a warm relationship with Haydon. And it is good to hear Ritchie in so happy and excited a mood in this last known of his private letters.

Hanmer Warrington, British consul-general in the Regency of Tripoli, was a colourful character, capable of great warmth and also of outrageous and infuriating behaviour, which, over a long period of years, drove his superiors at the Colonies Office to the brink of despair. He was usually in financial difficulties, stemming, he said, from an inheritance of £60,000 which was disputed in the courts. 'As from that

circumstance I date my financial ruin,' he told the Colonies
Office, 'as the Chancery Court plunged me . . . into that awful
abyss from which I have never been able to extricate myself':[17]
a remark reminiscent of many of Haydon's on the subject of
debt. In spite of his proclaimed penniless situation, Warrington
had arrived to take up his post in Tripoli in 1814 accompanied
by his wife, five children, a governess and three servants.
He soon became a close confidant of the Bashaw, Yusuf
Karamanli, the absolute ruler of Tripoli, who now retained
only a tenuous relationship with the Ottoman empire to which
Tripoli had earlier belonged. He was willing to favour the
British, largely because of Nelson's achievement in having
driven Napoleon out of Egypt. Warrington's consequent
special position irritated the other consuls, who resented his
patronizing them, and even more his interference in their
work. There is an inimitable remark of his at the end of a
complaining letter to the Colonies Office over a disagreement
with one of them: 'I am an Englishman (thank God). He is
not.'

Warrington used his influence with the Bashaw to coax
him to send the Prince Regent the gift of a small temple from
the ruins of Leptis Magna, which was erected by James Wyatt
on the shores of Virginia Water, where it still remains. Many
other looted gifts of Tripolitan antiquities followed, viewed
by Warrington as a means of ingratiating himself with Lord
Bathurst rather than of generosity on the part of the Bashaw.
Bathurst, however, punctiliously passed everything that
reached London straight on to the British Museum. These
depradations were carried out at the height of the Elgin
Marbles controversy, but they escaped the limelight of disapproval cast over that affair.

Ritchie became fond of Warrington in spite of his faults
and his sudden violent rages, and grateful to him for encouragement and help. Warrington for his part immediately took

to Ritchie, writing to Sir Charles Penrose at Valetta soon after his arrival that he found him 'a gentleman with those prepossessing manners which is the best passport, particularly so, when on further acquaintance we find disposition and principle in full union with such address'.[18] Warrington accompanied Ritchie to his first audience with the Bashaw, who, on the evidence of an unascribed letter to Goulburn at the Colonies Office, was an unsavoury character:

I return the papers of Mr Ritchie which appear to me more valuable and interesting than any I have yet seen — if however his success depends upon any agency of the Bashaw of Tripoli, it is desperate, as from my own personal knowledge of that man, so far back as 1793, a greater villain never infested the Earth; he was then Prince Josef, third son of the Bashaw and he ascended the throne by stabbing his eldest brother and expelling the second.[19]

On Warrington's advice not to meet the Bashaw empty-handed, Ritchie took with him presents on his own behalf as distinct from those from the Prince Regent. He wrote about this in his letter to Bathurst announcing his arrival in Tripoli,[20] listing the presents as a double-barrelled fowling piece, a bale of cloth, a gold snuff-box, some fine gunpowder and a large kaleidoscope. This last item was the 1816 brainchild of the Scottish scientist Sir David Brewster, whose special interest was in optics. Brewster took out a patent, and kaleidoscopes were first launched on the market in 1817, when an astonishing 200,000 were sold on the streets of London and Paris during the first three months.[21] Wordsworth's little son John was among those bewitched by the device.

Ritchie's audience with the Bashaw was only a qualified success. The latter reluctantly agreed to guarantee the expedition's safety, but only so far as his jurisdiction reached, namely to Murzuk in the Fezzan, and no further. After that, he declared, he had no influence at all, rather the reverse. Ritchie, who had been given to understand quite otherwise, was dismayed, and took against the Bashaw in spite of Warrington's encouragement to trust him. He wrote to Bathurst that the Bashaw insisted that no mission of his would be respected in any part of the Sudan as his only friend in the interior, the King of Bornu, was dead and the country at present in a state of anarchy and confusion. He added that when he asked for permission to accompany Mohammed el Mukni, the Bey of Fezzan, in his predatory excursions against different tribes, as a means of penetrating further south, the Bashaw attempted to discourage the plan, but on Ritchie's persisting agreed to give him every protection and facility, although this was still to be limited to the Bashaw's own dominions.[22]

Mohammed el Mukni had arrived in Tripoli a few weeks earlier, bringing with him a considerable number of slaves collected on one of his notorious raids. Ritchie – misguidedly as events turned out – liked him, thought him a fine soldier-like man, and felt confidence in his judgement. He intended to journey south under the protection of el Mukni's projected expedition against the Bashaw of Waday together with a considerable force of men. This was unlikely to set off for a further six months, to Ritchie's anxiety, as the inadequate funds of the little group were already in an alarmingly low state. A month later he wrote again to Bathurst to report progress, giving a more realistic account of the activities of el Mukni:

In conversations which I have had with negroes from Bornou and other parts of Soudan, I have been uniformly told that the bad understanding existing at present between Tripoli and those countries, originates in the predatory excursions made by the Bey of Fezzan into unprotected districts for the purpose of carrying off slaves which have been as extensive and successful as to render his name the terror of those regions.

But he still felt that the projected journey with el Mukni would give him a great opportunity of learning much more about the nature of these raids and the general state of the slave traffic in the interior: 'It might probably be practicable to open a certain road into the interior by Great Britain becoming a mediator between the Bashaw of Tripoli and the persecuted inhabitants of Soudan, and to advance under the safeguard of such a route into the very centre of Africa.' He added with astonishing naivety that 'some pecuniary indemnity for the abandonment of this lucrative system of robbery would probably be expected by the Bashaw from the British government, as it at present constitutes one of the principal branches of his revenue'.[23]

Bathurst felt uneasy about Ritchie's selected escort. He agreed that el Mukni's expedition presented a good opportunity of penetrating further south than Ritchie would have been able to achieve on his own. But he warned the young man to be alert to the Bey's underlying purpose, which he feared was a further extension of the slave raids.

In the event, el Mukni's foray was dropped, to everyone's relief, and it was not until March 1819 that Ritchie, with Marryat's replacement, a young naval officer called George Lyon, and Belford, a carpenter from the naval base in Malta, finally set out in his train for the Fezzan. All three were, on el Mukni's advice, disguised as Arabs, wearing robes and shaving their heads, though not their beards. The recommended costume was quite a complicated affair: turbans, for instance, were not to be green, which indicated descent from the Prophet, nor blue, which was reserved for Jews. They also assumed Arab names – Ritchie's, not very inventively, was Yusuf el Ritchie – and learnt Muslim forms of prayer. It was crucial to their safety to conceal that they were Christians. They were mounted on horses, and had hired a number of camels to carry their considerable baggage.

Ritchie was happy that the long delay was at last at an end and that they were on the road, although the ebullient excitement of his first arrival in Tripoli was now moderated. He had a clearer idea of the difficulties ahead of him, and was in a constant state of apprehension, never to be relieved, about money. Quite how all the little group's allowance had been eaten up during the winter months of waiting is not clear, but as they set off they were already practically penniless, and Ritchie's appeals for added funds from London to reinforce their inadequate government allowance remained un-answered. His appointment as British vice-consul in Fezzan, it was hoped, would assure him some standing on his arrival in Murzuk, against which he might borrow money.

The caravan passed Roman ruins, this having been the Roman route to the interior; and, horrifically, many pitiful skeletons of slaves who had not survived the northward jour-ney to Tripoli. After his experiences at the Lock Hospital, Ritchie would scarcely have been squeamish, but he was appalled at the evidence of inhumanity he saw. Some of the slaves were obtained in the course of barter (seven yards of red cloth rated seven handsome black women); but the trade largely depended on the great raids of el Mukni and other traders, facilitated by the connivance of bordering states.

The Bey proved a congenial travelling companion on the ninety days' journey to Murzuk, and generously shared his food with Ritchie's little group. The British travellers suffered intense thirst, one of the worst of their trials, and dry and splitting skin; and they endured sandstorms that filled ears, eyes, nostrils and worst of all throats with rasping grit, which was drawn down into their lungs at each breath. The nights were bitterly cold, but none the less welcomed by the Europeans after the roasting heat of the days. Belford and Lyon were both tough and accustomed to rough conditions, but for Ritchie, unacclimatized and unused to strenuous exercise, the journey was a nightmare. The caravan consisted of 200 men and their camels, a number of freed slaves hoping to return to their homes, el Mukni's two wives in curtained litters, and his little son and attendants, all dressed in brilliant silks. Ritchie, very slim and fair, cut a conspicuous figure in spite of his disguise. It was soon common knowledge that he was a surgeon, and he was constantly sought out for help. Lyon, gregarious and party-loving, amused himself by joining in the caravan's evening junketings. On one occasion he coaxed the beautiful fat wife of the Bey's factotum to unveil herself and dance for him, revealing her legs and arms, an unthinkable licence. On Ritchie's entering the tent, however, his dignified presence made her hurriedly veil herself again and vanish.

Murzuk, when achieved, was something of a disappointment: a city of mud huts surrounding the Bey's castle. There was no sign of the luxuriant oasis of Ritchie's imagination, only a thin array of palm trees and pathetic attempts at little gardens, the watering of which proved a heavy burden for the owners, buckets of water having to be hauled up from the wells outside the walls. These shallow wells were a breeding place for mosquitoes and the three British travellers soon fell ill with fevers, most likely predominantly malarial. No connection had yet been made between mosquitoes and fever, and treatment would not include quinine for some twenty years to come, so they were without any protection from the disease. The climate was reputed to be one of the worst in Africa, with temperatures rising as high as 130 degrees Fahrenheit for as much as six months at a stretch.

The inhabitants of Murzuk were of an unattractive appearance, and the Bey's fifty wives had understandably been selected from a different and more handsome tribe. The far more striking Tuaregs, tall and dignified, the men being remarkable for their custom of wearing veils across their faces, had appeared from time to time during the trek. They then dominated the central Sahara, but because of the Bey's presence, they left the caravan unmolested.

Ritchie and his companions were accommodated within the castle precincts in a large house which offered the privacy for which Ritchie longed. For a time all went fairly well: el Mukni remained affable and the town's inhabitants proved friendly. Ritchie wrote several long letters to Warrington, addressing him in what for the time was the intimate form 'My dear Colonel' and ending 'Yours ever'. On 8 August he wrote of a planned report to Lord Bathurst which he would send via Warrington for forwarding on to London, in which he would set out his views in detail on the possibility of reducing or even eliminating the slave trade, but that at present he felt too ill for the task. He added tantalizingly, 'I should have much to say to you if I could have the gratification of saying what I am unwilling to commit to paper.'[24]

From London Bathurst wrote thanking Ritchie for two dispatches, expressing his satisfaction at their contents and adding some complimentary remarks about Ritchie's conduct of his mission. He then turned to the question of the slave trade:

The expectation which you hold out as to the possibility of inducing the nations of the interior of Africa to abandon the traffic in slaves, is by no means the least interesting or important part of your communication. I have already had occasion to give you the necessary instruction for your guidance on this subject; and I have, therefore, only further to assure you that the abolition of the trade in the northern part of Africa is an object which His Majesty's Government have so much at heart, that if its continuance should in any case depend upon its being looked to as a source of revenue, you may consider yourself at liberty, if other proposals should fail of effect, to offer on the part of the Prince Regent a pecuniary compensation to a limited extent, as the price of its utter and effectual abolition.[25]

Some instructions about the arrangement of funding in such an eventuality followed, but no mention of actual amounts. It seems strange that Ritchie should have been given *carte blanche* in such a matter; and even stranger that Bathurst should have thought such a scheme remotely likely of achievement.

Ritchie and Belford now succumbed to violent attacks of fever. Ritchie never really recovered from his bout, and Belford was left permanently deaf. Lyon also fell sick from time to time during the next months both with fever and also attacks of dysentery, but his general state of health was such that he could more easily throw off illness and continue to collect information, a task which he found highly enjoyable, both about the Fezzan and also the surrounding countries, which the party hoped to traverse on their way to Timbuktu. But increasingly the main problem for the three men was that of money: there was so little left that they were faced with the likelihood of starvation. Lyon was puzzled that Ritchie would not allow him in this emergency to try and sell some of the camel loads of goods they had brought with them. Ritchie thought that to do so would lower them in the eyes of the people, but Lyon wondered wryly why that should seem preferable to starving to death. For six weeks, as Lyon recorded in his memoir of the expedition, they were without animal food, and lived for the most part on tiny portions of corn and dates.

As soon as their penury became obvious, el Mukni's attitude changed. He refused to lend them money or to give any other kind of help, and it became evident that he hoped that they would soon die. Lyon began to suspect that he might even have plans to murder them, and one night Ritchie was woken by a man climbing about on their roof and peering down through an opening, who moved away only when Lyon shouted at him. Whenever Ritchie was sufficiently well he helped the town's sick, who came to him in increasing numbers demanding medicines; and he even tended the Bey through a sharp illness, without any thanks or reward, or change in the latter's hostile attitude. When Ritchie was too ill Lyon took on the task of dispenser, but gave remedies designed to deter further requests from even the most persistent patient.

To Lyon's anxiety, Ritchie's attacks of fever became more frequent, and were accompanied by delirium. He was unable to take anything but water, though he craved for milk, which his companions were unable to procure for him. The Bey had fifty goats, but, as Lyon reported, 'he made so many excuses and difficulties about affording us any, that we were obliged to give up all hopes of gratifying him'.[26] Lyon, as he described in his memoir, was near to despair:

My situation was now such as to create the most gloomy apprehensions; for I reflected that, if my two companions were to die, which there was every reason to apprehend, I had no money with which to bury them, or to support myself; and must in that case have actually perished from want, in a land of comparative plenty. My naturally sanguine mind, however, and above all, my firm reliance in that Power which had so mercifully protected me on so many trying occasions, prevented my giving way to despondency; and, Belford beginning soon to rally a little, we united, and took turns in nursing and attending on our poor companion. At this time, having no servant, we performed for Mr Ritchie and for ourselves the most menial offices, Mr Ritchie being wholly unable to assist himself.[27]

Towards the end of the summer Ritchie improved a little, but Lyon remarked on the worrying depression evidently resulting from his long illness, saying that 'he almost constantly remained secluded in his own apartment, silent, unoccupied, and averse to every kind of society'.[28]

A large caravan of Arabs now arrived from Bornu, bringing 1,400 slaves with them. Lyon watched the arrival and was horrified at the state of the wretched captives, whose grotesquely swollen feet contrasted with their skeletal bodies. All, even small children, were forced to carry heavy burdens. On arrival care was taken to arrange the women's hair as prettily as possible, and the men were shaved, so as to present a more appetizing appearance. The Tibboo tribe, who brought slaves from Bornu, never made the journey across the Sahara, Lyon noted, but preferred to exchange them for horses. 'A fine horse will, in the Negro country, sell for ten or fifteen Negresses; each of which, at the Barbary ports, is worth from eighty to a hundred and fifty dollars.'[29]

During October Ritchie seemed a little improved, and Lyon took this opportunity to take part in various entertainments in the town, where he had become well known and liked. His memoir is full of enthusiastic descriptions of these, and of the songs and dances he watched or with which he joined in. He translated one Arab song full of charm, sung to him by a young man in a low, monotonous voice 'though far from disagreeable':

Here I am, well mounted, on a horse whose ears are like pens, who runs like an antelope, and knows none but his master. My new red cap becomes me well; my sword is sharp, my pistols well cleaned, and my belt shines in the sun. As the heart of a pigeon beats when she finds she is robbed of her young, so will my love's heart beat when she sees me. She will not allow the dog to bark and she will leave the tent as if in search of wood. Should her kinsmen see her with me, she shall not fall under their displeasure. I will lift her on my horse, and fly with her; for my steed has ears like pens, he runs like an antelope, and knows none but his master. My new *tagaia* becomes me well; my sword is sharp, my pistols clean, and my belt shines in the sun.[30]

Early in November Ritchie once more became alarmingly ill, and Lyon's jollities in the town had to be abandoned. He looked after his leader as best he could, and was distressed when, during a lucid interval, Ritchie asked if any of the further allowance of money they hoped for from London had arrived, and he was compelled to say it had not. Ritchie meanwhile was existing on a mixture of vinegar and water only. On the 17th he seemed sufficiently recovered to get up and be dressed, and Belford and Lyon lifted him on to the mat in the centre of the room, where there was a little more air, for which he was grateful. He then asked for coffee, which Lyon felt anxiously would not be good for him, but Ritchie was so insistent that he felt obliged to give in. Ritchie spent the night on his bed, which the other two had made up on the mat, and Lyon lay beside him. The next morning Ritchie looked at his tongue in the glass and was alarmed by its blackness, until he remembered he had drunk strong coffee. Otherwise, he told Lyon, it would have suggested the onset of a bilious fever, most likely to prove fatal. On the 20th Belford managed to get a chicken with which he made some broth, which Ritchie liked and which seemed to revive him, and after a while he lay down to sleep. Lyon placed his bed at the entrance to the room, and kept watch over his friend, who was having some difficulty with his breathing; but Lyon had often noticed this before when he was unwell (and this tends to suggest that his constitutional weakness may have been asthma or some other pulmonary complaint) and so he was not particularly alarmed. About an hour later, however, Belford looked in and exclaimed loudly, 'He is dying!' When Lyon examined Ritchie he seemed to be sleeping peacefully, but a little later his breathing suddenly stopped, and Lyon found that he had died in the same position as that in which he had fallen asleep.

'And now, for the first time in all our distresses,' wrote Lyon, 'my hopes did indeed fail me':

Belford, as well as he was able, hastened to form a rough coffin out of our chests; and a sad and painful task it was. The washers of the dead came to us to perform their melancholy office, and Mr Ritchie's body was washed, perfumed, and rubbed with camphor; and I procured some white linen, with which the grave-clothes were made. During our preparations for the burial, the women, who are always hired to cry at the death of persons whose friends are able to pay them, proposed to perform that disgusting office in our house; but I would not allow it, and very unceremoniously shut the door against them. While I was out of sight, either our servant or some of our officious visitors stole several of our effects, and I clearly saw that we were now considered as lawful plunder. The coffin being completed, I hired men to carry it with ropes, but one of them having suddenly gone away, poor Belford was obliged to take his place; when, attended by our small party of Mamelukes, we proceeded at a quick pace to the grave, at about ten o'clock. The clay below the sand was white, which was considered as a good omen; and Belford and myself threw the first earth into the grave. During the night we had, unknown to the people, read our Protestant burial service over the body; and now publicly recited the first chapter of the Koran, which the most serious Christian would consider as a beautiful and applicable prayer on such an occasion.[31]

With a painful irony, one hour after the funeral a courier arrived from Tripoli with the news that an allowance of a further £1,000 had been made by the government towards the expenses of the expedition.

For a few days the two survivors were too overwhelmed to take any significant action, but eventually they forced themselves to go upstairs to Ritchie's sitting room, where they found only a few papers, an unfinished journal and some letters. Then, in a phrase calculated to cast gloom into a biographer's heart, Lyon recorded that 'in Belford's presence [I] burnt all which were private'.[32] Both men were astonished by the absence of records, and although Lyon generously ascribed this to Ritchie's repeated episodes of illness, and to his sufferings from the heat, it still seems strange that nothing was found. Bathurst's repeated injunctions to Ritchie about the importance of secrecy were probably one reason for this. He had insisted that nothing should be committed to paper or spoken of that might militate against the mission's progress, and particularly nothing in relation to attempts to mitigate the traffic in slaves. Another factor to be considered is that Ritchie, at least from Tripoli, and initially from Murzuk, wrote long and detailed accounts directly to Bathurst about the current state of the expedition. Lyon said, however, that although he frequently suggested that Ritchie should dictate his journal to him, in order to save the effort of writing, his leader always refused. He concluded, and it does seem possible, that Ritchie was always waiting for a favourable time to set the contents of his unusually retentive memory down on paper, and that that day had never come.

Another disconcerting discovery made by Lyon concerned the contents of the chests of merchandise which Ritchie had refused to have opened or sold. These turned out to contain, among other things, about 600 pounds of lead, one camel-load of corks for preserving insects on, and two loads of brown paper for preparing plants: no doubt these had been destined for Sir Joseph Banks, but none had been used. Lyon left all these things in comparative safety in Murzuk, but took with him on his departure five hundredweight of books and two chests of instruments. The general opinion afterwards was that Ritchie had not understood how his mission should be equipped, or had been wrongly advised by the authorities. Bafflingly, none of Lyon's discoveries seem to accord with the nature of the Ritchie who had always been so meticulous, and who had written such efficient and realistic letters to his superiors.

Lyon's subsequent adventures, as recounted in his memoirs, do not belong to this story, but make lively reading, enhanced with his own brilliantly coloured paintings of scenes of desert travel. He and Belford did manage to travel a little further south, but lack of funds – it was not possible to obtain the extra allowance without returning to Tripoli to claim it in person – drove them north again, and they arrived in Tripoli on 25 March 1820, exactly one year after they had set out, Lyon shouting out 'God Save the King' and 'Rule Britannia' at the top of his voice on first catching sight of the sea.

Partly because of his failure to leave records of his mission, and of Lyon's widely read account of his depressions and habit of withdrawal from his companions, amplified and distorted in a review of Lyon's book in the *Quarterly Review*, Ritchie's suitability to lead an expedition of such rigour began to be questioned. But his desire for solitude seems understandable in one so finely tuned, travelling in such tryingly close quarters with two men of quite different temperaments from his own. In addition, his instructions from Bathurst had emphasized that he must always demonstrate his position of absolute authority over his companions, making a certain degree of distancing a necessity. On 28 December 1819, two years to the day after Haydon's Immortal Dinner, Warrington wrote to Bathurst in the most affectionate terms of his young friend:

My Lord, Seldom if ever has it fallen to my lot to communicate so sad and distressing news as the death of poor Ritchie. As a public character his whole conduct since I have had the honour to know him entitled him to my warmest approbation and highest admiration. As a private one I am deprived of that friendship I valued as much as that of any human being. Although our acquaintance was but of short duration, still his talents and prepossessing and most engaging disposition were so conspicuous that it was impossible not to feel more than a common degree of friendship towards him, and the most lively interest on every point relating to his welfare.

Warrington went on to reassure Bathurst of continuing possibilities for the expedition:

Your Lordship must not attribute my gloom to any despondency in the success of the undertaking. The great object is most assuredly to be accomplished from this quarter, and I am proud to add that Ritchie's opinion confirms my sentiments that it is that infernal traffic for the barter of human flesh that shuts the avenue to all communications, and making use of his own words 'if that were done away with the road from Fezzan to Guinea would be as open as that from London to Edinburgh'.[33]

Ritchie's early letters to Garnett had shown a young man of talent and ambition, with a desire to excel, initially in a literary way of life, and subsequently in a noble dedication to work for the amelioration of the lot of slaves, a far cry from the depressive figure of Lyon's account. The warmth of Warrington's words reinforces the impression of his gift for friendship and his devotion to the hard task he had taken upon himself. When he came to Haydon's dinner he seemed set for a glorious future, a worthy member of that distinguished company. His remains a story of brilliant promise tragically cut off and of noble aspirations left unfulfilled. The Venerable Bede's image of man's life as the passage of a bird provides a metaphoric precursor of Ritchie's own experience of a goal striven for and briefly achieved, but at once followed by tragedy. An unknown nobleman, urging the cause of Christianity upon King Edwin of Northumbria, is putting his case:

The present life of man, O King, in comparison with that time that is unknown to us, seems to me like the swift flight of a sparrow through the room in which you sit at supper in wintertime round the fire while the wind howls and the snow drifts outside. The bird passes swiftly in at one door and out at the other, feeling for the moment the warmth and shelter of your hall; but it flies from winter back into winter, and in a flash disappears from our sight. Such is our life here, and if anyone can tell us with certainty what lies beyond it, we shall do wisely to follow his teaching.[34]

8.   Patrons and a Comptroller of Stamps

There is no describing this scene adequately. There was not the restraint of refined company, nor the vulgar freedom of low, but a frank, natural license, such as one sees in an act of Shakespeare, every man expressing his natural emotions without fear. Into this company, a little heated with wine, a Comptroller of the Stamp Office walked, frilled, dressed, and official, with a due awe of the powers above him and a due contempt for those beneath him. His astonishment at finding where he was come cannot be conceived, and in the midst of his mild namby pamby opinions, Lamb's address deadened his views. When they separated, Wordsworth softened his feelings, but Lamb kept saying in the painting room, 'Who is that fellow? Let me go and hold the candle once more to his face –

My son John
Went to bed with his breeches on –

and these were the last words of C. Lamb. The door was closed upon him.

Benjamin Robert Haydon, *Diary*[1]

In the terms of Bede's parable, the time of outer darkness still lay in the future for Ritchie as he threw himself into the heady excitement of Haydon's party, enjoying to the full his brief interlude in the brilliant light of the occasion. After the high tone and noble poetry of the first part of the proceedings came a relaxation of tension, an element of farce developing with the arrival on the scene of John Kingston, a comptroller of stamps. This pompous but evidently well-intentioned man was seized upon by Lamb, appropriately enough with Twelfth Night only a few days off, and translated into a Malvolio-like buffoon for the remainder of the evening, for similar reasons that the original Malvolio was tormented: a rising of anarchical feelings, among the younger members of the dinner at least, versus what they saw as the oppressive control of authority, personified by the comptroller. Haydon, in his autobiography, explained the presence of this incongruous guest:

In the morning of this delightful day a gentleman, a perfect stranger, had called on me. He said he knew my friends, had an enthusiasm for Wordsworth, and begged I would procure him the happiness of an introduction. He told me he was a Comptroller of Stamps, and often had correspondence with the poet. I thought it a liberty; but still, as he seemed a gentleman, I told him he might come. When we retired to tea we found the Comptroller. In introducing him to Wordsworth I forgot to say who he was.[2]

The comptroller was, in fact, Wordsworth's immediate superior at the Stamp Office. In 1813, in order to augment his income, the poet had accepted a minor civil service appointment, procured for him by the interest of Lord Lonsdale, as Distributor of Stamps for Westmorland and part of Cumberland. The position carried no salary, but was expected to realize about £400 a year. His friends thought of it as something of a sinecure, but in fact it took up a good deal of his time in an unrewarding and niggling manner. Also the reward proved much smaller than had been anticipated, although at least he was provided with a clerk who usefully doubled as gardener. Wordsworth had never before met John Kingston, the comptroller, and his presence made him noticeably uncomfortable. Haydon said:

The moment he was introduced he let Wordsworth know *who* he officially was. This was an exquisite touch of human nature. Though Wordsworth of course would not have suffered him to speak indecently or impiously without reproof, yet he had a visible effect on Wordsworth. I felt pain at the slavery of office. The Comptroller was a very mild and nice fellow but rather weak and very fond of talking.[3]

Kingston, anxious to make the right impression on Wordsworth, began a series of ridiculously inappropriate remarks. Haydon said that after a little time he looked down, looked up, and said to Wordsworth, 'Don't you think, sir, Milton was a great genius?'

Keats looked at me, Wordsworth looked at the Comptroller. Lamb, who was dozing by the fire, turned round and said, 'Pray, sir, did you say Milton was a great genius?' 'No, sir, I asked Mr Wordsworth if he were not.' 'Why then, sir, I say, hiccup, you are – you are a silly fellow.' This operated like thunder! The Comptroller knew nothing of his previous tipsiness and looked at him like a man bewildered. The venerable anxiety of Wordsworth to prevent the Comptroller being angry, and his expostulations with Lamb, who had sunk back again into his doze, as insensible to the confusion he had produced as a being above it; the astonishment of Landseer the engraver,[4] who was totally deaf, and with his hand to his ear and his eye was trying to catch the meaning of the gestures he saw; and the agonizing attempts of Keats, Ritchie and I to suppress our laughter; and the smiling struggle of the Comptroller to take all in good part, without losing his dignity, made up a story of comic expressions totally unrivalled in Nature. 'Charles, my dear Charles,' said Wordsworth; but Lamb, perfectly innocent of the confusion he had created, was off again by the fire. After an awful pause the Comptroller said, 'Don't you think Newton a great genius?' I could stand it no longer. Keats put his head into my books. Ritchie squeezed in a laugh. Lamb got up, and, taking a candle, said, 'Sir, will you allow me to look at your phrenological development?' He then turned his back on the poor man, and at every question of the Comptroller he chaunted:

> Diddle diddle dumkins, my son John
> Went to bed with his breeches on.[5]

Before Monkhouse and Ritchie had bundled him away into the next room so that he could do no further damage to the comptroller's *amour propre*, Lamb had begged to have another look 'at that gentleman's organs'. Phrenology, or cerebral physiology, as it was otherwise called, was one of the many peripheral crazes of the time, much discussed in the post-Waterloo years, and believed in by Haydon, who accepted the idea that characteristics such as 'moral feelings' could be deduced by examination of an individual's cranial bones. This theory was first initiated by the German physicist Franz-Joseph Gall. Gall's work was suppressed as being against religion, but was continued by his follower Johann Spurzheim, who became a popular lecturer on the subject in England. While enthusiastically following the new science of Humphry Davy, Haydon was not alone in casting backward glances at the greyer area of such pseudo-science as phrenology: a combination not entirely unlike Newton's juggling with science and alchemy. Spurzheim divided the whole scalp into thirty-five areas representing two major divisions: feelings – propensities, impulses, emotions and so on, each one carefully named and allocated to a specific area – and intellectual faculties, further divided into perceptive faculties and reflective faculties. Much influenced by Spurzheim, George Combe, the Scottish lawyer, also became a fervent believer in the theory. In 1833 Combe married Mrs Siddons's daughter Cecilia, having first examined her head: 'finding that the anterior lobe was large; her Benevolence, Conscientiousness,

Firmness, Self-esteem, and Love of Approbation were amply developed; whilst her Veneration and Wonder were equally moderate with his own'.[6] The marriage was a perfectly happy one.

Haydon records two occasions when he went to listen to Spurzheim lecturing in London, one in 1815 and another in 1817. During the first his attention was diverted from the lecturer, as he recorded in his diary with a typical Haydonian gloss:

April 8. There is nothing like the sight of a lovely woman! Nothing so subdues one, so controls one; I feel the influence of her eyes if they wander down my form just like electrical air from a point. I sat by one this morning at a lecture of Spurzheim's, and without one atom of appetite or passion felt an affectionate desire to put her sweet arm round my neck and nestle my own cheek on her lovely bosom – with pure heartfelt softness. She looked so gentle, so delicate, so soft, so yielding, that one's manly feelings of protection were roused, and one's gentle emotions of tenderness were excited.[7]

Haydon evidently struck up an acquaintance with the lecturer, as there is a letter of 1815 to him from Spurzheim, accompanying a copy of the cast of the face of Voltaire – a great treasure for the painter, who was already at work on *Christ's Entry into Jerusalem*. Haydon collected plaster casts, which he could use both as models and to decipher the characters of his sitters. He also exercised his phrenological skills on drawings of the heads of Socrates and Canning, focusing in particular on their parietal bones, in which comparison Socrates came out the winner for virtuous qualities, against Canning's whose lines indicated, Haydon said, 'self-confidence but absence of veneration, like Godwin'.[8]

Not everyone shared Haydon's phrenological enthusiasm: Hazlitt remained sceptical, and was delighted when Spurzheim pronounced Coleridge to be lacking in 'ideality',[9] a faculty listed under 'Superior Sentiments', and translated into French as '*poésie*'. Gall had pinpointed ideality's precise location on the skull, having noticed it in the busts of poets, it being, he thought, that part touched by the poet's hand during composition. From Wordsworth's phrenological development Haydon diagnosed the poet as being 'without constructiveness while imagination is as big as an egg'.

The only person in the room acquainted with John Kingston that evening seems to have been Keats, who had met him dining with Horace Smith the previous week, when he had wished himself in the company of the bohemian Kean rather than such precious and brittle society as that of the Smiths. After that experience he was no doubt delighted to watch Kingston's present discomfiture. He described the scene to his brothers a few days later, saying that Lamb 'got tipsey and blew up Kingston – proceeding so far as to take the candle across the room hold it to his face and show us wh–a–at–sor–fello he–waas'.[10]

Kingston himself was bewildered by the bizarre treatment he received at Lamb's hands, and unable to understand what he could have done to deserve such a reception; and in any case it must have been alarming to find himself in the somewhat overexcited company which now confronted him, having come prepared for a calm and dignified discussion on poetry with the revered Wordsworth. To find himself inappropriately overdressed in formal evening clothes complete with frilled shirt put the finishing touches to his embarrassment. Kingston had joined the civil service after Cambridge, and although at the time of Haydon's dinner he was still a comptroller of stamps, a year later he was promoted to become one of the seven Commissioners of Stamp Duties, a senior position he held until 1827. He was accustomed to being received with that certain degree of deference he felt to be appropriate to his professional status.

From Haydon's account Kingston would seem to have been an unexceptional man, although somewhat garrulous and obtuse, and Lamb's reaction to his presence would have stemmed less from personal dislike than from distress at the marked change in Wordsworth's demeanour once he had realized Kingston's identity. Lamb wrote later to Mary Wordsworth about his feeling of 'inexplicable moral antipathies and distances' between himself and the comptroller, from whom he had 'so strangely recoiled':

I think I had an instinct that he was the head of an office. I hate all such people – accountants, deputy accountants. The dear abstract notion of the East India Company, as long as she is unseen, is pretty, rather poetical; but as she makes herself manifest by the persons of such beasts, I loathe and detest her as the scarlet what-do-you-call-her of Babylon.[11]

He then revealed his particular grudge of the moment against the Company, which may have added a dash of vicarious vitriol to his treatment of Kingston:

I thought, after abridging us of all our red-letter days,[12] they had done their worst; but I was deceived in the length to which heads of offices, those true liberty-haters, can go. They are the tyrants; not Ferdinand, nor Nero. By a decree passed this week, they have abridged us of the immemorially-observed custom of going at one o'clock of a Saturday, the little shadow of a holiday left us. Dear W.W., be thankful for liberty.[13]

Here, perhaps, by exaggerating a little his own loss of freedom, he sought to comfort Wordsworth, who had not in fact shown himself to be in any need of comforting, by implicitly emphasizing the lightness of the poet's burden as compared with his own. But Haydon, as well as Lamb, was upset by what he saw as Wordsworth's uneasy reaction to Kingston:

I felt pain that such a poet as Wordsworth should be under the supervisorship of such a being as this Comptroller. The people of England have a horror of office, an instinct against it. They are right. A man's liberty is gone the moment he becomes official; he is the slave of superiors, and makes others slaves to him.[14]

Leigh Hunt also resented the ambivalence of Wordsworth's position, though his feeling was specifically political: that the revered Wordsworth should accept employment from a government despised by the radical young. In 1815 he had written in his *Examiner* that 'Mr Southey and Mr Wordsworth have both accepted office under government of such a nature as absolutely ties up their independence': Southey's sin here being that he had accepted the appointment to the Laureate-ship. Hazlitt, also in the *Examiner*, without mentioning Wordsworth or Southey by name, indicted

poets who do not like to be left out when laurels are to be given away at court – or places under government are to be disposed of – in romantic situations in the country. They are happy to be reconciled on the first opportunity to prince and people, and to exchange their principles for a pension.[15]

Shelley too had voiced his outrage at the sight of Wordsworth the government employee in his sonnet of reproach at what he saw as the poet's apostasy from his early radical stance:

> In honoured poverty thy voice did weave
> Songs consecrate to truth and liberty, –
> Deserting these, thou leavest me to grieve,
> Thus having been, that thou shouldst cease to be.[16]

This feeling of outrage and loss persisted, to be echoed as late
as 1845 by Robert Browning in his poem 'The Lost Leader',
written in protest against Wordsworth, when he, in his turn,
became Poet Laureate.

> Just for a handful of silver he left us,
>   Just for a riband to stick in his coat . . .
> We that had loved him so, followed him, honoured him,
>   Lived in his mild and magnificent eye,
> Learned his great language, caught his clear accents,
>   Made him our pattern to live and to die! . . .
>
> Life's night begins: let him never come back to us!
>   There would be doubt, hesitation and pain,
> Forced praise on our part – the glimmer of twilight,
>   Never glad confident morning again! . . .

Robert Southey made perhaps the most sensible remark on
the whole matter to Shelley, in another context, saying that
the real difference between him and the younger man was
that he was the elder by twenty years.

For Keats, watching the Lisson Grove encounter between
Kingston and Wordsworth, a process of disillusionment with
Wordsworth the social animal began, but always as distinct
from Wordsworth the poet. A few days later, when he went
to call on the Wordsworths at their Mortimer Street lodgings,
he was kept waiting while the older man dressed himself in
formal evening clothes, knee breeches, frilled shirt and silk
stockings and with a stiff collar, ready to dine with Kingston.
This struck Keats as another indication of subservience to
authority. And on a visit to the Wordsworths in the New
Year Keats was surprised when Mary Wordsworth put a
restraining hand on his arm as he was about to speak, saying,
'Mr Wordsworth is never interrupted.' But none of these

minor irritations affected his reverence for Wordsworth the poet.

Whereas the younger men, such as Keats and Shelley, felt disappointed anger at Wordsworth's attempt to increase his income at the hands of a Tory government, for his nearer contemporaries Haydon and Lamb the feeling was more one of protective sadness; and among his older and less idealistic Westmorland friends there was rejoicing that a little of the financial burden of supporting his family had been lifted, by however small an amount.

Wordsworth had obtained his Stamp Office appointment by means of patronage and influence, that of Lord Lonsdale and to a lesser degree of Samuel Rogers, who had furthered Lonsdale's recommendation, and this served to compound the poet's radical friends' disapproval of what they viewed as a shameful transaction. But, with the exception of Monkhouse, a successful City merchant who was himself something of a patron of artists and writers, Haydon and his guests were all in varying degrees indebted to interest or to patrons in a society where advance as an artist or writer so often depended upon attracting the notice of one of these benevolent and influential men, most of whom, because society was still small and tightly knit, were known to each other. Even Lamb was indebted to the benevolence of the East India Company for turning a blind eye to his exploitation of its time, allowing him to use some of his working day for the development of his inimitable essays. Keats was indebted firstly to Charles Cowden Clarke, who had a crucial enabling role in launching the young poet on his career, both by introducing him to many of the great writers of the past, and in reading them with him; and also in his happy introduction of Keats to Leigh Hunt at the precise moment when the young man needed the stimulus of the society of Hunt and of his circle, and the benefit of being a member of that prestigious group in the establishment of his

33. Sketches by Benjamin Robert Haydon of Sir George Beaumont on first seeing the painter's *Solomon* hung in the gallery of his house in Grosvenor Square, *c.*1815. Haydon was delighted by his patron's reaction: 'this said more than all praise'.

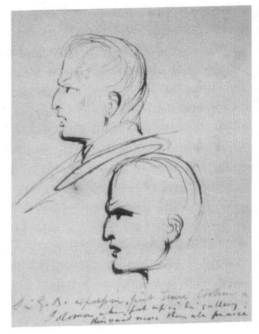

early reputation. Although later Keats's enthusiasm for Hunt waned, nothing can take away the importance of the latter's predominantly benign influence at this early stage.

But Wordsworth and Haydon both enjoyed the patronage of great connoisseurs of the arts, who were to prove the last of their kind. Wordsworth benefited from the patronage and, unusually for the time, the real friendship of both Lord Lonsdale and Sir George Beaumont. Haydon, arriving as a penniless aspiring art student from Devonshire, had the good fortune to become the friend of David Wilkie, who, already himself under the wing of Lord Mulgrave and Sir George Beaumont, helped him to broach their magic circle, first by singing his friend's praises and then by arranging introductions to his patrons.

The Beaumonts were a devoted couple of great gaiety and charm; rich, handsome and generous, both of them possessed the attractive gift of being able to make their social inferiors feel their equals. Sir George was himself a landscape painter of some ability, and in an age of patronage he was perhaps the most notable of them all for the good he did to young artists in directing them and launching them on their careers, tirelessly promoting them in any way he could. His habit of writing them letters of detailed instructions, rather than suggestions, for their work in progress could prove an embarrassment when they disagreed with his views, but this was a small price to pay for his support. Most importantly, at a time when there were only occasional public exhibitions of art, so that for the most part access to the great painters of the past was unsatisfactorily limited to monochrome etchings of their work, Sir George was generous in encouraging artists to study his own considerable collection of old masters, both in his house in Grosvenor Square and at Coleorton, his Leicestershire estate. He was not the only collector to make his pictures available to artists: others included his friends and fellow patrons of the arts Lord Mulgrave, Sir John Leicester, Lord Stafford and Lord Egremont, who kept open house for artists and writers at Petworth. And, perhaps most important of all, these generous men hung the pictures they had commissioned in their great houses, so ensuring that they were seen by the maximum number of patrons likely to produce further commissions for paintings.

Some patrons even allowed their precious pictures to be taken away to copy. Haydon spent much time studying colour and technique in this manner, and seemed to take it for granted that he should be allowed access to private collections. William Bewick remembered later in his life an occasion when he had visited Sir John Leicester's gallery:

I remember I was there in company with Mr Leigh Hunt, Keats and Haydon, the Landseers, and others. Mr Haydon had asked permission to take this party; and Sir John gave orders that when he and his party came he should be informed. He and Lady Leicester and their friends came in to see those remarkable men, and we all were introduced (a very unusual thing on such occasions). Lady Leicester was beautiful, there was a full-length portrait of her by Sir Thomas Lawrence.

Beautiful, but not very observant: 'Looking at me she asked Mr Haydon if all his pupils had black hair (the Landseers have all flaxen polls).'[17]

Beaumont's own collection, the central passion of his life, contained fine works by English watercolourists, and was also notable for two Rembrandts, Rubens's *The Château de Steen*, and, his greatest treasures, four Claudes, one of which he loved so much that it always travelled with him when he moved between London and Leicestershire. But his greatest gift to posterity was his enabling role in the foundation of the National Gallery, a project that had always been his dream. Towards the end of his life this became a reality with the bequest of the collection of the banker Angerstein, to which two years later Beaumont added his own treasures, only stipulating that he might keep back his most precious Claude on loan until his death.

Haydon was initially much petted and encouraged by the Beaumonts, and Lady Beaumont pleased him by saying he had 'an antique head'. Sir George was friendly, expressing a real and kindly concern in his progress. Before long he was invited to dine in their London house. He arrived in a state of euphoria. The Beaumonts had earlier visited his studio and admired his canvas, *Joseph and Mary Resting on the Road to Egypt*, displayed on the easel. This was Haydon's first large-scale work, painted as a trial run before he began his first commission from Lord Mulgrave to paint *The Assassination of Dentatus*. Haydon described every detail of the occasion to his parents 'how Lady Beaumont looked – what *she* had on – how tall Sir George was – how he looked – what *he* had on – what Lady Beaumont said – what Sir George said – what David Wilkie did not say, and what he ought to have said'.[18] This was a great coup for Haydon, and to crown it all he was now to dine at their London house:

The awful day came, when a youth from the country, who had never in his life dined at any table higher than a country parson's, was to make his debut at a party in high life. 'God only knows how I shall go into the room,' thought I: 'I will keep behind Wilkie; at any rate I am a match for him, and I will *not* drink Lady Beaumont's health in porter.'

Wilkie called – I had been shaving until my chin was half skinned – washing until I was quite in a heat – and dressing and redressing until my back ached again – brushing my hair – looking behind me in the glass – putting the glass on the floor and then opening the door – bowing and talking to myself and wishing that my mother could see me! I was ready and away we drove, I in a cold perspiration. We reached the house, the door opened, and we marched through a line of servants who bawled out our names from the entrance. In went Wilkie and in went I, and in five minutes was much more at ease than I ever had been in my life, sitting on an ottoman talking to Lady Beaumont. Dance the architect and several others followed, and after some little chatting in the gallery dinner was served. Davy took Lady Beaumont, the rest followed as they pleased, and I was placed within one of her Ladyship. The dinner went off well with me, for I felt quite at ease; everyone seemed to be kind. At dessert Lady Beaumont, leaning forward, said: 'When do you begin Lord Mulgrave's picture, Mr Haydon?' Immediately all eyes were fixed upon Mr Haydon who was going to paint a picture for Lord Mulgrave. I was the new man of the night! 'Who is he?' was asked. Nobody knew, and that was more delightful still.[19]

34. Sir George Beaumont's house at Coleorton, Leicestershire, where he and Lady Beaumont were generous hosts to artists and poets, including Wordsworth, Haydon and Wilkie.

Soon afterwards Haydon and Wilkie were invited to stay at Coleorton. Haydon's account of the visit shows how delightful the relationship between patron and artist could be at its best:

Sir George painted, and Lady Beaumont drew, and Wilkie and I made our respective studies for our own purposes. At lunch we assembled and chatted over what we had been doing, and at dinner we all brought down our respective sketches and cut up each other in great good humour.

We dined with the Claude and Rembrandt before us, breakfasted with the Rubens landscape, and did nothing, morning, noon or night, but think of painting, talk of painting, dream of painting, and wake to paint again.

On the way up to bed all lingered on the stairs and studied the effect of candlelight upon each other. They wondered how the shadows could be reproduced to look as sharp as they were in reality:

Sometimes Sir George made Wilkie stand with the light in a proper direction, and he and I studied the colour; sometimes he held the candle himself and made Wilkie join me; at another time he would say: 'Stop where you are. Come here, Wilkie. Asphaltum thinly glazed over on a cool preparation I *think* would do it.' And Davy and I would suggest something else. We then unwillingly separated for the night, and rose with the lark to go at it again, all of us feeling as jealous as if we were artists struggling for fame.[20]

Wilkie's nature was more flexible than his friend's – where Haydon focused rigidly on Raphael and Michelangelo as his exclusive examples of genius, Wilkie could see worth in a wider spectrum, insisting that although the rose might be the most beautiful of flowers, the daisy too had its own loveliness, and he could accommodate himself happily to the whims of his patron, whose friendship he retained for the rest of his life. But the Coleorton idyll came to an end for Haydon when Sir George suggested that he should paint him a scene from *Macbeth*. Haydon understood that the arrangement was for a lifesize representation, but when Beaumont saw the considerable canvas he was dismayed and denied having suggested such a large picture, which, he said, would be difficult for him to accommodate. At this stage all could easily have been put right, but Haydon chose instead to take offence, refused to paint something on a smaller scale, disregarded the advice of his friends to give in to the wishes of his influential patron, fired off angry letters to Beaumont, and generally behaved against his own interests with a foolish recklessness. Lord Mulgrave, another of Haydon's benefactors, intervened at dinner on one occasion, 'in the kindest manner' saying, 'Haydon, if you consent to oblige Sir George, you will please us all.'

I looked at Sir George across the table, but his face expressed rigid indifference. Lady Beaumont chattered away to Lady Mulgrave. Wilkie and Jackson cast down their eyes and said nothing. Had Sir George expressed the slightest wish, after such a pointed desire from Lord Mulgrave, had he looked towards me, I had been vanquished; but no, not a word, and not a word from me. Lord Mulgrave, apparently astonished at the whole affair, changed the conversation. At leaving, Lord Mulgrave shook me kindly by the hand and whispered, 'Yield,' looking more than he whispered.[21]

But Haydon would not give way, and eventually Beaumont, coldly displeased, stopped answering the painter's letters and the relationship lapsed for a considerable time. Eventually, although Haydon gave the impression that this was not the case, Beaumont did buy the picture.

In this sorry story, so typical of Haydon's fatal lack of common sense, the likelihood would seem to be that the fault lay entirely with the painter, were it not for another strange instance of perversity on Beaumont's part. This was his inexplicable and implacable persecution of Turner, whom he began to revile in a most damaging manner over a number of years beginning in 1803, to such an extent that Turner's ability to earn his living was greatly endangered as clients, influenced by Beaumont's powerful voice, stopped buying his paintings, until eventually his health began to suffer.

Poor Haydon confided to his diary that he did have faults over his handling of the *Macbeth* affair. 'Why did I not yield?' he asked himself, and decided that the reason was that his will had not been curbed in youth. If only it had been, he concluded sadly, 'the same power might have been put forth with more discretion, and I should have been less harassed by the world'.[22] Unfortunately for him he never learnt to benefit from past experience. The rift with Beaumont continued for some years, but at last, in the spring of 1818, soon after his Immortal Dinner, Haydon's diary has an entry about a reconciliation:

April 9. After nine years' banishment for daring to resist the wishes of my early employers Lord Mulgrave and Sir G. Beaumont as to painting large pictures, I was again last night admitted to the old family party. Lord Mulgrave, Lord Normanby [his eldest son], Sir G. and Lady Beaumont, Lady Mulgrave, Augustus, and General Phipps and Mrs Phipps. Nine years! It has made a hole in our lives, they all drank wine with me, which was symptomatic of concession to my views. What I have gone through in that nine years! Lord Mulgrave was much older, but full of good-humoured pleasant fun as usual; Lord Normanby was then a boy, was now a fine young nobleman just returned from the Continent, having his own establishment, and leaving us for a ball in his own carriage. It made me muse the whole evening. Nine years more one of us will have taken his flight.[23]

Haydon's relationship with another patron, Lord Egremont, had also nearly foundered, this time partly because of the strange behaviour at Petworth with his bedclothes described earlier. Lord Egremont was one of the greatest of the early nineteenth-century patrons of the arts. Many artists benefited from being allowed to work at Petworth. Turner painted many of his finest canvases there, having a special room, the Old Library, reserved for his own exclusive use. He liked to lock himself in while he worked, and even his host had to give the signal of a double knock before being granted access. Egremont cherished his artists, and cared for them when they were in distress. Haydon was among those who had cause for gratitude, Egremont sending him £200, a substantial sum, on an occasion when he was threatened with bankruptcy and imprisonment. He also bought Haydon's *Alexander Taming Bucephalus*, and later commissioned him to paint his *Eucles*.

Rossi, Haydon's landlord at Lisson Grove, also enjoyed Egremont's patronage, executing several sculptures for Petworth. His career was a generally successful one but, like his lodger, Rossi was a bad manager of his money, and he died in poverty.

Egremont spent a considerable proportion of his great wealth on charitable objects. According to Haydon,

Lord Egremont is represented by the people of the country as a plain man, rather shy, odd, and whimsical; which is saying a great deal in a country where this disposition is common enough to escape observation. He suffers the peasants of his village to play bowls and cricket on the lawn before the house.[24]

Egremont gave an annual fête at Petworth for some 6,000 poor people, said to have been the gayest of spectacles, and always enjoyed by the host as much as anyone else. This exemplary character, not surprisingly, was much loved. But he never married, though he was surrounded by crowds of illegitimate children (one estimate – that of Lady Spencer – put their number at forty-three) and their various disgruntled mothers, constantly worrying the patriarch with their squabbles.

Haydon loved Mulgrave – his 'dear Lord Mulgrave' – and for a long time there were no disagreements to mar this relationship. Haydon dined with him frequently and the atmosphere was relaxed and congenial, perhaps partly because Mulgrave was a much busier man than Beaumont, reaching high government office and consequently having less time to notice or imagine slights. Haydon spent many happy evenings with him at the Admiralty when he was First Lord. Haydon thought Mulgrave was 'a fine character, manly, perfectly bred, and as noble an example of his order as I ever knew. He had high notions of art, a great respect for talent, and believed Englishmen as capable of becoming great artists as any people

that had ever existed. His treatment of me was nobly generous.'[25] Haydon told an anecdote that demonstrates the relaxed
atmosphere permitted by Mulgrave to his young protégés:

The dramatist George Colman, the younger (whose father Lord
Mulgrave particularly liked), sometimes made one of the circle, and
one night, just before joining the ladies, we were loitering about
the picture of Lord Mulgrave's brother blocked up in the ice, in the
Arctic expedition in which Nelson sailed as a middy. Lord Mulgrave,
holding the lamp, said: 'What is that my brother has got hold of? Is
it a boat-hook?' 'No, my Lord!' said Colman, in his half-throttled,
witty voice, 'it's the North Pole!'[26]

In 1816 this mutually happy relationship received a jolt when
Haydon published his virulent letter of attack on Payne Knight
at the height of the Elgin Marbles affair:

Lord Mulgrave, always regarding me, had at the very moment the
letter appeared laid a plan before the directors of the Institution to
send me out to Italy. It would have been done, but the moment
the letter appeared he sent for a friend. 'What the devil is Haydon
about?' 'Upon my word I don't know, my lord.' 'Here have I been
planning to get him a handsome income for three years and send
him to Italy, and out comes this indiscreet and abominable letter.'[27]

This missed opportunity, which might well have transformed
Haydon's life, makes painful reading, coming, as it did, at the
very juncture in his life when it would have been of greatest
benefit to him, and before he was tied by a wife and children.
But at the time he was too flown with the notoriety achieved
by his letter to pay much attention to what he had lost,
ascribing it to his customary bad luck rather than to his fatal
passion for having the last word on paper. Sir George Beaumont had warned him against this in 1815:

As your sincere well-wisher, I earnestly request you to abstain from writing, except upon broad and general subjects chiefly allusive to your art. If any severe or unjust remarks are made upon you or your works, paint them down. You can. But if you retort in words action will produce re-action, and your whole remaining life be one scene of pernicious contention. Your mind, which should be 'a mansion for all lovely thoughts', will be for ever disturbed by anger and sarcastic movements, and never in a state to enable you to sit down to your easel with that composed dignity your 'high calling' demands.[28]

This kind and eminently sensible appeal did not prevent Haydon from continuing his mistaken course. Four years later Beaumont returned to the charge:

I confess I am sorry you have answered your opponents. Depend on it they will think you wounded and redouble their attacks; your peace will be disturbed, and your time consumed in this unprofitable and detestable warfare. Abjure your pen, seize your pencil, exert the powers with which Nature has so amply supplied you, and *paint them into the earth!*[29]

Haydon himself knew this was true, that for an artist to indulge in contentious writing destroyed that tranquillity of mind so crucial for the fruitful pursuit of his work. Nevertheless, he was unable to relinquish the delicious hobby of dashing off another broadside at the Academy or whatever part of the establishment was his target of the day, aided by his unfortunate facility of composition.

Wordsworth and Beaumont had come to know one another when the latter rented part of Greta Hall at Keswick in the summer of 1803, not realizing that Coleridge was already established in the other half. The Beaumonts had already met Coleridge in London and had not taken to him, finding him garrulous and irritating, and were dismayed to find themselves such close neighbours, but they soon fell under his spell. Soon after they arrived at Greta Hall, and although Wordsworth and Beaumont were still the merest acquaintances, Beaumont gave Coleridge the deeds of a nearby parcel of land, Applethwaite, for him to present as a gift to Wordsworth. Wordsworth was startled and embarrassed by this unexpected and lavish generosity, and was at a loss as to how to respond. Beaumont, with the most delicate tact, insisted that his idea was primarily to benefit Coleridge, hoping that if the Wordsworths moved to Applethwaite the two poets could resume the fruitful creative partnership of their earlier West Country days. After an awkward gap of several weeks, during which he found himself quite unable to frame a reply, Wordsworth wrote to Beaumont explaining that he would accept the land only as its steward, that it was unlikely that he would ever be able to build himself a house on it, partly because he lacked the funds, and partly because Coleridge was shortly to leave Greta Hall, but expressing his gratitude and appreciation as best he could for this exquisite piece of patronage. Beaumont replied in a tone which set the complexion of their coming relationship – one in which each could admire and learn from the other. In answer to Wordsworth he now wrote of the pleasure it would give him to think that 'the sweet place with its rocks, its banks, and mountain stream are in the possession of such a mind as yours'.[30] Wordsworth never did live at Applethwaite, but the incident initiated one of the happiest friendships of his life, into which, in spite of the Beaumonts' continuing kindnesses, no feeling of an uneasy burden of indebtedness on the poet's side was allowed to obtrude. Their friendship was further sealed by the affection which soon developed between Dorothy Wordsworth and Lady Beaumont, on the face of it an incongruous pair.

A few years later, when Dove Cottage had become too

cramped to contain the growing family, Beaumont lent the Wordsworths a farmhouse at Coleorton, where they spent the winter while waiting to be able to move into a larger house at Grasmere. During this time Wordsworth made an appearance in the uncharacteristic guise of landscape architect, creating a highly romantic winter garden to give pleasure to Lady Beaumont, designed, he said, to give a feeling of 'shelter and seclusion' in surroundings of calm shades of green, so that 'the whole would be still, unvaried, and cloistral, soothing but not stirring the mind, or tempting it out of itself'. The mossy floor would be scattered with primroses and other wild flowers, and, in a little glade, 'there should be a basin of water inhabited by two gold or silver fish . . . these little creatures to be the "genii" of the pool and of the place'.[31]

For their part the Beaumonts felt themselves honoured by the poet's friendship. Lady Beaumont was always his great advocate, to such an extent that Beaumont told her people would think she was paid to sing the poet's praises, and Dorothy Wordsworth was sometimes made uneasy by her excessive outbursts, feeling they might well end up being counter-productive.

It was the Beaumonts who introduced Wordsworth to Lord Lonsdale. The Earl of Lonsdale, as William Lowther, had inherited his cousin's vast estates and wealth in 1802, together with the title of Viscount Lowther of Whitehaven. As there was no direct heir to the title the earldom had died out, but in 1807 Lowther was made Earl of Lonsdale 'of the second creation'. In politics Lonsdale was a staunch supporter of Pitt, and was invited to be one of the chief mourners at the great man's funeral. He held office under several administrations, but politics were not his first concern, this remaining the care of his vast northern empire and his role in local government. Lonsdale was already a large landowner when he inherited Lowther and its vast territory of about 100,000 acres, and it

35. *Lowther Castle and Park, Westmorland,* engraved by T. Allom.
The terrace of Lord Lonsdale's enormous crenellated mansion
stretched for nearly a mile.

was said that he could cross England from coast to coast
without ever stepping off his own land. A part of his great
wealth – his income was in excess of £200,000 – derived
from the working of the rich seams of coal lying beneath his
property. Lonsdale's favourite sport was hunting, and the
breeding of fox hounds was one of his greatest interests. He
founded the Cottesmore Hunt in Leicestershire, and many of
today's hounds descend from the strain he bred. He was Master
of the Cottesmore for fifty years and was so devoted to his
hounds that in the summer months he had them all trotted
back across country to be with him at Lowther, a journey
which took nearly a month.[32].

As he was in the happy position of being able to carry out
any project on which he set his heart, soon after he inherited
Lonsdale he set about the reconstruction of the dilapidated
Lowther, and with the aid of the young architect Robert
Smirke he created an extravaganza of Gothic crenellations and

towers on a huge scale: the terrace was nearly a mile long and the interior of the central part of the house was like a vast draughty cathedral. Upstairs there were more than a hundred bedrooms linked by a maze of icy passages, but guests commented on the luxury and comfort provided by an army of indoor servants. The new building, which took eight years to complete, was renamed Lowther Castle. Smirke lived there for most of the building period, being treated with great kindness by the earl, who, during an illness of the architect's, visited his young employee several times each day in his room to watch over his recovery.

Wordsworth's father had been the previous earl's steward and right-hand man in all his legal, business and political affairs, and on his death the earl had refused to pay the Wordsworth family the then substantial sum of nearly £5,000 owed by him to their father. This first Lonsdale was a politically ambitious man of violent temper, universally disliked and known as the Bad Earl. His treatment of the young Wordsworths, who by his action were left virtually penniless, had a harsh effect on their upbringing, the orphaned children being split between various relations and faced with uncertain futures. Fortunately the Lord Lonsdale of Wordsworth's adult years was of a very different calibre, and one of his first acts on inheriting was to clear his predecessor's debt. He was already an admirer of the poet's work, and when Wordsworth applied to him for help in obtaining a paid position with which to augment his small income he immediately offered to pay him an annuity of £100. Wordsworth at first refused this, but, on an assurance that Lonsdale would soon be able to procure him the government appointment of the Stamp Distributorship for Westmorland and part of Cumberland, he accepted the money until such time as the position fell vacant.

The earl was tactful in his approaches to Wordsworth, and they enjoyed an increasingly warm and happy relationship, so that in 1814 Wordsworth felt it natural to dedicate *The Excursion* to him. The endearing detail that Lonsdale had lent Wordsworth his boots to wear on top of the coach that brought the latter to London in the winter of 1817 was a typical example of his benefactor's thoughtful and intimate kindnesses. For his part Wordsworth became increasingly fond of Lonsdale whom he greatly admired. The friendship between the Wordsworth and the Lonsdale families developed happily over the years, and Wordsworth, with Mary or Dorothy, paid annual visits to Lowther Castle. The poet also became very fond of Lady Lonsdale, an affection shared with the politician and diarist Thomas Creevey, who said that 'dear Lady Lonsdale is the girl for my money'.[33] There does not seem to have been any element of condescension in Lonsdale's attitude to the poet, who was seventeen years his senior, and he was grateful to Wordsworth for his help over the elections that took place in June 1818, when the great lawyer and radical reformer Brougham stood against Lonsdale's two sons, Lord Lowther and Colonel Henry Lowther, an unprecedented move in what for generations had been unopposed family seats.

It was at about the time of Haydon's dinner, when he was still in London, that Wordsworth first got wind of Brougham's intention through Tom Monkhouse, and he wrote immediately to Lonsdale, offering his services in any way that would be useful. Wordsworth's politics had by now shifted firmly in the Tory direction. His enthusiastic involvement in the Lonsdale political interest came as a shock to Keats that coming summer when, during his northern walking tour with his friend Charles Brown, he called at Rydal Mount, the Wordsworths' home just outside Grasmere, in the hope of seeing him, but was told that he and the family were out electioneering for the Tory faction. A few days earlier Keats had written to tell his brother Tom that he had asked a waiter at

an inn where he would find Wordsworth, and heard the news
of his allegiance to the Lowther interest. 'What think you of
that – Wordsworth versus Brougham!! Sad – sad – sad – and
yet the family has been his friend always. What can we say?'[34]
The two poets never met again.

For Charles and Mary Lamb, 1817 had proved a relatively
untroubled year. There is only one recorded instance of Mary
suffering an attack of madness, although this does not necessarily mean there were no others. But they were never free of
the heavy shadow over their lives, and in the circumstances it
is hardly surprising that Lamb often drank too much. Mary
worried about this, as she knew how dangerous drink was to
one of so precariously balanced a temperament. She admon-
ished him as much as she could without upsetting him. Sometimes she succeeded in stopping him for a few months, and
then there would be a relapse. In 1812 Lamb had written
'Confessions of a Drunkard',[35] in which he spoke with painful
frankness of the humiliations of his condition and his vain
attempts at reform, but when this was later reprinted as an Elia
essay he appended an afterthought, 'Elia on his Confessions of
a Drunkard', in which he partly recanted on the extreme
nature of his addiction. However badly he behaved, his friends
always rallied to his defence, protecting him as far as they
could, and regarding him with affectionate pity rather than
irritation or disgust. His habit of falling asleep after dinner, as
at Haydon's party, was described in such a manner by Thomas
De Quincey:

In regard to wine Lamb and myself had the same habit – perhaps it
rose to the dignity of a principle – viz., to take a great deal *during*
dinner – none *after* it. Consequently, as Miss Lamb (who drank only
water) retired almost with the dinner itself, nothing remained for
men of our principles, the rigour of which we had illustrated by
taking rather too much of old port before the cloth was drawn,

except talking; amoebaean colloquy, or, in Dr Johnson's phrase, a dialogue of 'brisk reciprocation'. But this was impossible: over Lamb, at this period of his life, there passed regularly, after taking wine, a brief eclipse of sleep. It descended upon him as softly as a shadow. In a gross person, laden with superfluous flesh, and sleeping heavily, this would have been disagreeable; but in Lamb, thin even to meagreness, spare and wiry as an Arab of the desert, or as Thomas Aquinas, wasted by scholastic vigils, the affection of sleep seemed rather a network of aerial gossamer than of earthly cobweb – more like a golden haze falling upon him gently from the heavens than a cloud exhaling upwards from the flesh. Motionless in his chair as a bust, breathing so gently as scarcely to seem certainly alive, he presented the image of repose midway between life and death, like the repose of sculpture; and, to one who knew his history, a repose affectingly contrasting with the calamities and internal storms of his life.

De Quincey's account goes on to show that Lamb's 'Diddle diddle dumpkins' recital at Haydon's dinner was not entirely a mockery of the comptroller, but also a regular incantation with which to bridge his passage back from sleep:

On awaking from his brief slumber, Lamb sat for some time in profound silence, and then, with the most startling rapidity – sang out – 'Diddle, diddle, dumpkins'. I could not help laughing aloud at the extreme energy of this sudden communication, contrasted with the deep silence that went before and followed. Lamb smilingly begged to know what I was laughing at, and with a look of as much surprise as if it were I that had done something unaccountable, and not himself. I told him (as was the truth) that there had suddenly occurred to me the possibility of my being in some future period or other called on to give an account of this very evening before some literary committee. The committee might say to me – (supposing the case that I outlived him) – 'You dined with Mr Lamb in

January, 1822; now, can you remember any remark or memorable observation which that celebrated man made before or after dinner?'

I as *Respondent*. 'Oh yes, I can.'

Com. 'What was it?'

Resp. 'Diddle, diddle, dumpkins.'[36]

On the night of Haydon's party the person who took charge of the drunken Lamb was Tom Monkhouse. It was typical of this kind, self-effacing man, that it was he who removed Lamb at the moment when his antics were becoming a threat to the party's equilibrium, and took him back to Russell Street, a great distance out of his own way home to Queen Anne Street. Monkhouse was the silent host, according to Thomas Moore, at another dinner party a few years later. Moore wrote in his diary of 4 April 1823:

Dined at Mr Monkhouse's (a gentleman I had never seen before), on Wordsworth's invitation, who lives there whenever he comes to town. A singular party: Coleridge, Rogers, Wordsworth and wife, Charles Lamb and his sister (the poor woman who went mad with him in the diligence on the way to Paris), and a Mr Robinson, one of the *minora sidera* of this constellation of the Lakes, the host himself, a Maecenas of the school, contributing nothing but good dinners and silence.[37]

Monkhouse himself wrote to his sister-in-law Miss Horrocks about the evening:

The party went off in the most delightful way – being as Rogers pronounced it – the *most brilliant thing* this season – It wanted nothing to make it complete – but Sir George & Lady Beaumont who were quite distressed that they were so engaged that they could not come. He is the most perfect gentleman in England – a perfect pattern – she a good creature – sensible tho' oddish – Jane enjoyed the evening vastly. Coleridge was most eloquent and C. Lamb most witty – but perfectly *steady*. Lord Lowther was asked – but was obliged to leave Town yesterday . . .[38]

The host, touchingly pleased with the success of his party, and so proud of his wife, who was recovering from an illness, only lived two more years, dying of tuberculosis. He was a universal favourite, a sweet-tempered and generous man. One small instance of his kindness came in the autumn of 1817 when he arranged for the portrait painter Richard Carruthers to paint not only Wordsworth but also himself, a helpful boost for the young artist.

Carruthers's depiction of Wordsworth was successful, the poet choosing to wear a frilled white evening shirt for the sittings, and Dorothy thought the result 'charming'. Sara Hutchinson disagreed: initially she felt the face to be 'too fat and the expression unnatural, but this was not the artist's fault for William himself sat, as Joanna Hutchinson told him, in "a perpetual smirk" '.[39] It lacks the impression of confidence and power of Haydon's portrait of a few months later, known in the Wordsworth family as 'The Brigand'; and is certainly not as impressive as his later *Wordsworth on Helvellyn* nor of his lovely drawing of the poet, the preliminary sketch for his portrait in *Christ's Entry into Jerusalem*.

The Lambs' friends were increasingly anxious about the strain under which the pair were forced to live. Present opinion of Mary's condition is that she was probably a manic depressive: her symptoms certainly seem to have been compatible with such a diagnosis. Just before an attack Charles would be warned of its approach by a significant hyperactivity, when Mary's speech would become more and more rapid and tense, and she would move around incessantly and without any evident purpose. All too soon this would escalate into mania: her speech would grow louder and louder, an aspect of her

condition Charles found peculiarly distressing in one customarily so quiet and gentle, and her behaviour would become
violent with threatening gestures, at which point it would be
necessary to get her as soon as possible to the asylum. A
letter from Lamb to the Clarksons of August 1810 graphically
demonstrates the humiliations of such a situation. Thomas
Clarkson was the great reformer and anti-slavery activist, and
Charles and Mary had been visiting him and his wife near
Bury St Edmunds when one of Mary's attacks began. Her
brother was forced to hurry her back to London by public
coach, a risky undertaking.

You will wish to know how we performed our journey. My sister
was tolerably quiet until we got to Chelmsford, when she began to
be very bad indeed, as your friends William Knight and his family
can tell you when you see them. What I should have done without
their kindness, I don't know, but among other acts of great attention,
they provided me with a waistcoat to confine her arms, by the help
of which we went through the rest of our journey. But sadly tired
and considerably depressed she was before we arrived at Hoxton.
We got there about half past eight, and now 'tis all over. I have
great satisfaction that she is among people who have been used to
her. In all probability a few months or even weeks will restore her
(her last illness confined her ten weeks) but if she does recover I
shall be very careful how I take her so far from home again.

That 'if she does recover' emphasizes the miserable uncertainties of the position. Lamb added a request which he may
well have felt to be the last straw: 'She tells me something
about having given away one of my coats to your servant. It
is a new one, and perhaps may be of small use to him. If
you get it me again, I shall be very willing to give him a
compensation.'[40]
    Once the violent part of an attack was past, Mary had to

suffer what was for her perhaps the worst part of her illness, extreme depression. During this process she would experience delusions and even hallucinations, feel anxious and sleepless and endure nightmares. At these times her mind would sometimes roam over the past. Lamb's biographer Thomas Noon Talfourd describes such an episode when elation rather than depression possessed her:

Her ramblings often sparkled with brilliant description and shattered beauty. She would fancy herself in the days of Queen Anne or George the First, and describe the brocaded dames and courtly manners as though she had been bred among them, in the best style of the old comedy. It was all broken and disjointed, so that the hearer could remember little of her discourse; but the fragments were like the jewelled speeches of Congreve, only shaken from their setting. There was sometimes even a vein of crazy logic running through them, associating things essentially most dissimilar, but connecting them by verbal association in strange order.[41]

Over the years Mary's periods of violence became longer and more alarming, and occurred at more frequent intervals. Eventually Charles decided to settle her permanently in the house of a Mr and Mrs Walden at Edmonton, who were accustomed to looking after the mentally disturbed; and, as he felt that the constant shifts from home to the asylum were an added distress for her, he himself moved in with her. Lamb stipulated that he and Mary should be the sole inmates, a proviso whose cost must have weighed heavily on him. In Mary's by now frequent attacks of frenzy her voice would rise into shrieks only too clearly audible through the thin walls of the villa, turning Lamb's life into a nightmare from which he was never to escape. To the outside world, however, he presented his usual face, and few knew anything of his difficulties and heartache. Manic depression is genetically passed

'Kids a-cock-horse'!

Mrs Gilpin riding to Edmonton.

36. A caricature of Mary Lamb attempting to climb a stile on one of her rambles with her brother, by the Lambs' friend, the poet, novelist and humorous writer Thomas Hood, a regular attender at their Wednesday evenings. Hood is best remembered now for his poems 'The Song of the Shirt' and 'The Bridge of Sighs'. He shows Mary in her long-outdated bonnet, which she never abandoned. When indoors she always wore a similarly old-fashioned mob cap.

down through generations, and Lamb, having suffered one episode of insanity himself in his youth, was never free from the additional fear that he might lose his own reason and be unable to care any longer for his sister. Happily he was spared this final horror. It is painful to think that, had Mary been alive today, her condition would have been ameliorated by drugs, possibly entirely cured.[42]

Had Lamb not acted so swiftly in removing Mary to a private mental home after her first disastrous attack, she would undoubtedly have been confined to Bedlam. The Bethlehem Royal Hospital, always known as Bedlam or Bethlem, had originally been at Bishopsgate, but towards the end of the

37. *Bethlehem Royal Hospital* (Bedlam), built in the grand manner in the 1670s, when John Evelyn compared it to the Tuileries, but reduced to appalling squalor by the early nineteenth century. Shortly after Haydon's dinner the inmates were moved to a new building at Lambeth.

seventeenth century a new and grand building was erected at Moorfields, complete with Cibber's statues of Madness and Melancholy guarding over the entrance. Here visitors were allowed in to stare at the wretched inmates, who were chained in cells in galleries, like animals at a zoo. This dreadful spectacle became one of the sights of London, and warders made a good income from allowing access to hordes of onlookers who goaded and provoked the lunatics in order to drive them to further excesses of frenzy, until in 1770 it was decided, rather late in the day, that this was not in the patients' best interests. Their lot did then begin to improve, and some of the ignorant and cruel measures formerly used to keep them docile were discontinued. But conditions were still horrific, with dirt and stench paramount, and a continuous shattering noise over all as the patients roared, screamed and wailed. Many poor people, unlike Mary Lamb, did not have relations willing or able to pay the fees of private institutions. One such unfortunate was Mary Turner, mother of the painter. Turner and his father seem to have taken no part in her incarceration or stood as bond holders, nor was any move made to allow her special treatment, and neither is known to have visited her or indeed done anything towards her welfare. Turner at the time was already successful, and had just acquired grand premises in Harley Street, so financial need cannot have been the reason for this neglect. Mrs Turner died two and a half years after her committal. In partial mitigation only, it has to be said that she had tormented her husband and son for a long time with violent outbursts of bad temper and rage.

By the early nineteenth century attitudes to madness were becoming more liberal, partly because of the shadow cast and the pity engendered by the illness of the popular George III. His disease, porphyria, is now controllable. Many 'eccentric' people were kept privately in the community, both such harmless individuals as Betsey Trotwood's Mr Dick in *David Copperfield*, but many, too, who posed more of a threat to those around them. In 1800 the Moorfields building was finally proclaimed unsafe, and by 1815 patients were moved to a splendid new hospital at Lambeth, the central block of which is now the Imperial War Museum. But this was all too late for poor Mary Turner.[43]

Although Lamb hardly ever allowed himself to talk about his tormenting worries over Mary – or wished to do so, his nature being of such a reserved kind – he did write two letters within a few days of each other in February 1834, the last year of his life, when he was feeling particularly low, which poignantly outline the nature of his burden. The first was to Maria Fryer, a school friend of his ward Emma Isola, who had evidently written to him anxiously about the situation:

In one word, be less uneasy about me; I bear my privations very well; I am not in the depths of desolation, as heretofore. Your admonitions are not lost upon me. Your kindness has sunk into my heart. Have faith in me! It is no new thing for me to be left to my sister. When she is not violent, her rambling chat is better to me than the sense and sanity of this world. Her heart is obscured, not buried; it breaks out occasionally; and one can discern a strong mind struggling with the billows that have gone over it. I could be nowhere happier than under the same roof with her. Her memory is unnaturally strong; and from ages past, if we may so call the earliest records of our poor life, she fetches thousands of names and things that never would have dawned upon me again, and thousands from the ten years she lived before me. What took place from early girlhood to her coming of age, principally lives again (every important thing, and every trifle) in her brain, with the vividness of real presence. For twelve hours incessantly she will pour out without intermission all her past life, forgetting nothing, pouring out name after name to the Waldens, as a dream; sense and nonsense; truths and errors huddled together; a medley between inspiration and possession. What things we are! I know you will bear with me, talking of these things. It seems to ease me, for I have nobody to tell these things to now.[44]

And the following week he allowed himself one despairing remark at the end of a letter to Wordsworth: 'Poor Mary is ill again, after a short lucid interval of four or five months. In short, I may call her half dead to me.'[45]

Haydon's guests who were invited to arrive at Lisson Grove after dinner on 28 December were regaled with little cakes or biscuits and tea, or, if they preferred, brandy or some other spirit mixed with hot water. The more substantial supper, to which Kingston was asked to stay as a sop to his damaged equilibrium, took place towards the end of the evening. For this the company probably returned to sit around the painting-room table. And it was now that Keats, as he told his brothers in his letter of 5 January, 'astonished Kingston at supper with a pertinacity in favour of drinking – keeping my two glasses at work in a knowing way'.[46]

The whole company combined to sooth the comptroller and restore his self-esteem, and by the end of the evening, as Haydon said, 'being a good-natured man, we parted all in good humour, and no ill effects followed'.[47] His departure and that of Monkhouse with the blissfully befuddled Lamb began the breaking up of the party. Coats and cloaks were put on, and the guests went out into the night air, which after a day of slow cold thaw was now beginning to freeze again, and set off on their different ways home. Keats, well muffled against the cold, arrived back safely at Well Walk through the frosty air and under bright starlight, which helped to make his long uphill trudge more pleasant than it might otherwise have been: there were long uninhabited stretches to cross on the way back up to Hampstead after leaving the houses behind, where pickpockets were inclined to lurk in wait for returning diners on dark nights. He seems not to have suffered any harm on this occasion from his prolonged exposure to the freezing air.

Haydon, left alone among the debris, could settle down to write his account of the evening in his diary while it was still fresh in his mind. He had been delighted with Wordsworth's good-humoured mood, the poet appearing in all the radiant charm of his best self, relaxed, happy to laugh with the company and to shine in his noble recitation, in a manner which reinforced his host's veneration and affection. There were to be occasional rocky times ahead in their relationship, passionate on Haydon's side, largely unremarked by Wordsworth. But by the end of Haydon's life they were to recapture much of the intimacy of that glorious evening.

For his part Wordsworth was fond of Haydon, and took his vagaries with equanimity. Frederic Haydon, in his memoir of his father, said that two years before his death in 1850 Wordsworth had spoken warmly of the painter:

'Your father,' he said, 'was a fine, frank, generous nature, a capital talker, and well-informed. He is the first painter in his grand style of art that England or any other country has produced since the days of Titian. He may be disregarded and scorned now by the ignorant and malevolent, but posterity will do him justice. There are things in his works that have never been surpassed, they will be the textbook of art hereafter.'[48]

How pleased Haydon would have been.

When he had finished writing the account of his Immortal Dinner, Haydon concluded his entry for 28 December 1817 with a justifiably complacent flourish:

There was something interesting in seeing Wordsworth sitting, and Keats and Lamb, and my picture of Christ's Entry towering up behind them, occasionally brightened by the gleams of flame that sparkled from the fire, and hearing the voice of Wordsworth repeating Milton with an intonation like the funeral bell of St Paul's and the music of Handel mingled, and then Lamb's wit came sparkling in between, and Keats's rich fancy of satyrs and fauns and doves and white clouds, wound up the stream of conversation. I never passed a more delightful day, and I am convinced that nothing in Boswell is equal to what came out from these Poets. Indeed there was no such poets in his time. It was an evening worthy of the Elizabethan age, and will long flash upon

> 'that inward eye
> Which is the bliss of solitude.'[49]

Hail and farewell!

Epilogue

Ah! my dear old friend, you and I shall never see such days again!
The peaches are not so big now as they were in our days.

Benjamin Robert Haydon to William Wordsworth,
16 October 1842[1]

Stretch me no longer on this rough world.[2]

Haydon's final diary entry, 22 June 1846[3]

On New Year's Eve, three days after his party, Haydon completed his diary for 1817 with his customary survey of the past year. On the whole he felt that things had gone well for him, his life had been easier, happier and more tranquil.

My health has become better in consequence. I have better habits of study, and I hope in God all will go on well. I still remain ignorant, nearly so, of the anatomy of the horse. I do not know enough of perspective, but in power of painting, I am visibly improved, and dash about with more fearless experiment than I ever did before.

He then turned his attention to the progress of *Christ's Entry into Jerusalem*. He felt anxious about the challenge facing him to achieve the perfect head of Christ, 'the great test of my genius', and for this purpose he enlisted the help of God, in a long paragraph of special pleading, ending: 'Grant I may produce a great, grand, and original head, one that may affect all hearts, and dispose all feelings to adore and love and worship, from the depths of my soul, I pray thee grant this, I humbly and awfully pray thee, grant it. Amen, with all my being.' Feeling that he had done his best in that direction, he returned to his review: his satisfactory new lodgings, 'a nice comfortable house'; his pupils' progress; his especial pride in the achievements of his star pupil Bewick; and his hopes that his crusade about the central importance of High Art should prevail with the public. 'It is now fourteen years since I first began to think as a Man,' he mused:

Today I thought as seriously as I did at that time. It is now a similar era. I was then approaching youth, I am now a man. I pray God to bless my resolutions, whatever they be, and grant that I may deserve to be so protected and blessed during the ensuing year as I have been during this. Amen in gratitude.
Finis – 1/4 past eleven at night. Lisson Grove.[4]

Eighteen seventeen was probably one of the best years of his life. Ahead lay other good things, a happy marriage, children, a number of triumphs, some successful paintings, many friends. But setbacks, nearly always caused by his temperamental incapacity to remain solvent, or by his fatal tendency to indulge in quarrels over what he imagined to be insults, gradually outweighed his successes, destroyed his confidence and wore him down. On several occasions he was imprisoned for debt, leaving a distraught and penniless wife to manage as best she could with children to feed and bailiffs in the house. The natural ebullience of his temperament, one of his most attractive traits, which for so long had carried him through crisis after crisis, began to abandon him, and he felt increasingly that he was always discriminated against through no fault of his own.

From time to time he returned to his diary entry for the Immortal Dinner to add footnotes. The first two recorded the deaths of the youngest members of the party, who shared the same fate of dying just as they approached full maturity and of being buried in lonely isolation far from their friends: 'Since writing this, poor Ritchie is dead! He died on this route, 1819. Lamb's feeling was prophetic.'

Four years later the entry was for the death of Keats: 'Keats too is gone! How one ought to treasure such evenings, when life gives us so few of them. 1823, Nov.'

Keats had died at the age of twenty-five two years earlier, on the evening of 23 February 1821, in an apartment in the house at the foot of the Spanish Steps in Rome, where he spent the last weeks of his life. It was three weeks before the news reached England in a letter from his devoted friend Joseph Severn, who had nursed him to the end, to Keats's friend Charles Brown in Hampstead. The funeral had to take place without delay, due to the infectious nature of Keats's disease, and he was buried in the Protestant cemetery under a daisy-studded turf. The grave is now surrounded with wild strawberry plants whose leaves make a brilliant emerald carpet in the early Roman summer and, as he wished, the gravestone bears the message 'Here lies one whose name was writ in water'.

On 11 February 1824, Haydon recorded in his diary that he had been looking into *Endymion*: 'Dear Keats! I remember his repeating to me that exquisite ode to Pan, just after he had conceived it, in a low, half chaunting, trembling tone. What a true genius he was . . . I was to have made a drawing of him, and my neglect really gave him a pang as it now does me.'[5] And in his *Autobiography* he elaborated on memories of his young friend:

In fireside conversation he was weak and inconsistent, but he was in his glory in the fields. The humming of a bee, the sight of a flower, the glitter of the sun, seemed to make his nature tremble; then his eyes flashed, his cheek glowed, his mouth quivered. He was the most unselfish of human creatures: unadapted to this world, he cared not for himself, and put himself to any inconvenience for the sake of his friends. He was haughty and had a fierce hatred of rank; but he had a kind gentle heart, and would have shared his fortune with any man who wanted it. His classical knowledge was inconsiderable, but he could feel the beauties of the classical writers.[6]

He went on to complain about what he considered to be Keats's dissipated behaviour towards the end of his London life. Haydon's disapproving tone was most likely coloured by Keats having refused to lend him money, which he had bitterly resented. A happier memory of the two together dates back to a month or two after the Immortal Dinner, when Keats, Haydon and Bewick dined together, Keats bringing a friend with him – 'a noodle' according to Haydon.

After dinner to his horror when he expected we should all be discussing Milton and Raphael etc., we burst into the most boister- ous merriment. We had all been working dreadfully hard the whole week. I proposed to strike up a concert. Keats was the bassoon, Bewick the flagellet, and I was the organ and so on. We went on imitating the sounds of these instruments till we were ready to burst with laughing. Then I took a piano forte and they something else, and so we went, while the wiseacre sat by without saying a word, blushing and sipping his wine as if we meant to insult him.[7]

The next annotation to Haydon's diary entry was the final one: 'Lamb is gone too! Monkhouse, the other friend, is gone. Wordsworth and I alone remain of the party. If the Comptroller lives I know not. Jany. 24, 1837.' Monkhouse had died of tuberculosis in 1825; Lamb survived until 1834, when he died after a fall on 27 December, six months after the death of Coleridge. He was nearly sixty. Mary, so often despaired of, lived until she was eighty-two.

In June 1842 Haydon wrote of 'dear Wordsworth' sitting for his portrait:

Wordsworth sat and looked venerable, but I was tired with the heat and very heavy, and he had an inflamed lid and could only sit in one light, a light I detest, for it hurts my eyes. I made a successful sketch . . . We talked of our merry dinner with C. Lamb and John Keats. He then fell asleep, and so did I nearly, it was so hot; but I suppose we are getting dozy.[8]

In October Haydon wrote to Wordsworth in a mood of happily complacent reminiscence, tracing once more, after a quarter of a century, the events of the Immortal Dinner:

In the words of our dear departed friend, Charles Lamb, 'You good-for-nothing old Lake Poet', what has become of you? Do you remember his saying that at my table in 1819,[9] with 'Jerusalem' towering behind us in the painting room, and Keats and your friend Monkhouse of the party? Do you remember Lamb voting me absent, and then making a speech descanting on my excellent port, and proposing a vote of thanks? Do you remember his then voting me present? – I had never left my chair – and informing me of what had been done during my retirement, and hoping I was duly sensible of the honour? Do you remember the Commissioner (of Stamps and Taxes) who asked you if you did not think Milton a great genius, and Lamb getting up and asking leave with a candle to examine his phrenological development? Do you remember poor dear Lamb, whenever the Commissioner was equally profound, saying: 'My son John went to bed with his breeches on', to the dismay of the learned man? Do you remember you and I and Monkhouse getting Lamb out of the room by force, and putting on his greatcoat, he reiterating his earnest desire to examine the

Commissioner's skull? And don't you remember Keats proposing 'Confusion to the memory of Newton' and upon your insisting on an explanation before you drank it, his saying: 'Because he destroyed the poetry of the rainbow by reducing it to a prism.' Ah! my dear old friend, you and I shall never see such days again! The peaches are not so big now as they were in our days.[10]

The following year he suffered a severe blow when his cartoons were not selected in the competition for the adornment of the new Houses of Parliament. He had tried to prepare his mind for this eventuality, but when it came he was shattered, most of all in his vanity. Twenty thousand people and more visited the exhibition of the fortunate winning competitors every day for two months, and there were valuable premiums of up to £300 to be had for the artists.

Four years later, in the oppressive heat of June 1846 when temperatures reached 96 degrees Fahrenheit in the shade, theatres were empty, typhus outbreaks occurred and many died of heatstroke, Haydon found himself in an impasse of debt and despair. The heat prevented him sleeping at night; he saw no way out of his problems; the energy which in the old days would probably have seen him through had now left him; he was sixty and felt older. In the spring he had taken a room in the Egyptian Hall for an exhibition of his work. Nothing about this exhibition went well, and it opened at Easter to resounding silence. In the adjacent Great Room, where years before he had enjoyed the triumphant reception of *Christ's Entry into Jerusalem*, there was a rival attraction: the showman Barnum was exhibiting a thirty-one-inch dwarf, General Tom Thumb, and all London poured in to see the curiosity. While Haydon's daily takings never rose above a pound, Barnum was making a fortune. This was a humiliation difficult to bear, and in May poor Haydon closed his exhibition at a loss of more than £100. During the following weeks the pressure of debts increased. He could not think where to turn, how to raise funds to save himself and his family, and meanwhile the abnormally fierce June heatwave was driving him towards madness.

The climax came towards the end of the month. On Saturday 20 June Haydon wrote a single sentence in his diary: 'O God bless us all through the evils of this day. Amen.' The next day, Sunday 21st, he wrote: 'Slept horribly. Prayed in sorrow and got up in agitation.' In the afternoon he walked up to Hampstead. His son Frank went with him part of the way, and Haydon confided to him that he had been contemplating suicide. Frank, alarmed, told his mother on his return that he thought a doctor should be called, but Mary laughed at the idea, feeling sure that her husband would never abandon her in such a way. By bedtime Haydon seemed normal, although the household could hear him walking about in his room most of the night, during which time he must have been trying to make up his mind what to do. Early on Monday morning he went out and bought one of a pair of pistols, had his breakfast alone, and wrote farewell letters to his wife and children. During the morning Mary came up to his painting room, and found the door locked. This was quite usual, and she was still not worried. Haydon then emerged and kissed her fondly, and she set out on a visit which he had asked her to make to a friend. Later his daughter came up to the painting room and finding the door unlocked went in to comfort her father. At first she could not see him, and then, crossing the room, she found him on the floor. She thought perhaps he was lying down to get a particular angle on his picture, which he sometimes did, and walking quietly towards him so as not to interrupt him, she slipped in a great pool of his blood.

Haydon had failed to kill himself with his pistol – his wife and daughter had heard the shot, but thought it came from troops on exercise in the park – and he had then staggered across the room and slit his throat from side to side with his razor. The horror was increased by its contrast to the neatness of the surroundings, his clothes clean and tidy, letters to his wife and children, and his will placed neatly on his writing table, an early portrait of his wife placed on an easel beside the table, and his diary open at the last entry, in which the only indication of his desperate state was the uncharacteristic misquotation from his beloved *Lear*.

God forgive me. Amen.

Finis

of

B. R. HAYDON

'Stretch me no longer on this rough world.'

Lear

End of Twenty-sixth Volume

That night the heatwave, which had undoubtedly contributed to his suicide, ended with a tremendous thunderstorm and torrential rain, which created havoc throughout the country.

The coroner's verdict on Haydon was that he had killed himself while of unsound mind, but his friends did not believe this to be the case. Bewick was particularly emphatic on the point: 'never was there a greater mistake'. Haydon left a letter to the prime minister, Sir Robert Peel, written during his last hours: 'June 22nd. Life is insupportable. Accept my gratitude for *always* feeling for me in adversity. I hope I have earned for my dearest wife security from want. God bless you.' This seems to indicate that his suicide was deliberately intended as a means of raising money for his widow and children, and, if so, his sad ruse was successful. Peel, who had been kind to him on several occasions in the past, gave £100 and Lady Peel contributed an annual sum of £25. The committee formed to raise subscriptions received £400 on the first day, and Mary was granted a civil-list pension of £50 a year.

Haydon was buried in the New Churchyard of St Mary's on Paddington Green, near the grave of Mrs Siddons, and a huge crowd followed the coffin. St Mary's was a popular choice for artists – Nollekens was buried there – and Rossi executed a fine memorial tomb near the church. Hogarth's runaway marriage took place there, and there John Donne preached his first sermon. Haydon had earlier written out his own epitaph, but it was considered far too long, and perhaps too controversial, and was not used.

Here

Lieth the Body

of

Benjamin Robert Haydon,

An English Historical Painter, who, in a struggle to make the People, the Legislature, the Nobility, and the Sovereign of England give due dignity and rank to the highest Art, which had ever languished, and, until the Government interferes, ever will languish in England, fell a Victim to his ardour and his love of country; an evidence that to seek the benefit of your Country by telling the Truth to Power, is a crime that can only be expiated by the ruin and destruction of the Man who is so patriotic and so imprudent.

He was born at Plymouth, 26th January, 1786, and died on the —, believing in Christ as the Mediator and Advocate of Mankind:–
'What various ills the Painter's life assail,
Pride, Envy, Want, the Patron, and the Jail.'
This I wish written upon my tombstone when my day comes.
B. R. Haydon.

Wordsworth, the eldest member of Haydon's Immortal Dinner, lived on until 1850, surviving all the others, full of vigour until the last few days, eighty years old, tranquil and full of honours.

Notes

Abbreviations

Autobiography: Elwin, Malcolm (ed.), *The Autobiography and Journals of Benjamin Robert Haydon* (London, 1950)

Correspondence and Table-Talk: Haydon, Frederic Wordsworth (ed.), *Benjamin Robert Haydon: Correspondence and Table-Talk*, 2 vols (London, 1876)

Diary: Pope, W. B. (ed.), *The Diary of Benjamin Robert Haydon*, 2 vols (Cambridge, Mass., 1960)

Letters of Charles Lamb: Rhys, Ernest (ed.), *The Letters of Charles Lamb*, 2 vols (New York, 1926)

Letters of John Keats: Gittings, Robert (ed.), *The Letters of John Keats* (London, 1970)

1. The Host

1   *Autobiography*, p. 316
2   George, Eric, *The Life and Death of Benjamin Robert Haydon 1786–1846* (London, 1948), p. 61
3   *Autobiography*, p. 51
4   In May 1823 Haydon was imprisoned for debt in the King's Bench Prison and his pictures, including *Christ's Entry into Jerusalem*, were seized and sold.
5   *Autobiography*, pp. 416–17
6   ibid., p. 418

7 An anecdote told by Lord Egremont and quoted in Eric
   George's *Life and Death of Benjamin Robert Haydon*, p. 184

8 *Letters of Charles Lamb*, to Haydon, March 1827, vol. 2, pp.
   166–7

9 *Diary*, vol. 2, pp. 22–3

10 George, Eric, *Life and Death of Benjamin Robert Haydon*, p. 126

11 Horace, *Odes*, Book 3, I, i. '*odi profanum vulgus*' (I hate the
   common crowd)

12 *Diary*, vol. 2, pp. 348–51

13 ibid., vol. 1, p. 37

14 ibid., pp. 423–4

15 ibid., vol. 2, p. 5

16 ibid., vol. 1, p. 212

17 *Autobiography*, p. 249

18 ibid., p. 250

19 ibid.

20 De Selincourt, Ernest (ed.), *The Letters of William and Dorothy
   Wordsworth: The Middle Years* (London, 1937), William Wordsworth to John Scott, 22 February 1816, vol. 2, p. 709

21 *Correspondence and Table-Talk*, vol. 1, p. 288

22 *Autobiography*, pp. 256–7

23 ibid., p. 256

24 Woof, Robert, *The Wordsworth Circle* (Grasmere, 1979), p. 8

25 *Autobiography*, p. 123

26 ibid., p. 124

27 ibid., p. 358

28 *Diary*, vol. 1, p. 450

29 *Autobiography*, p. 246

30 *Correspondence and Table-Talk*, vol. 2, p. 46

31 *Diary*, vol. 1, p. 29

32 ibid., p. 483

33 *Autobiography*, p. 282

34 ibid.

35   ibid., p. 283

36   Summerson, John, *Georgian London* (London, 1946), pp. 223–5

37   John O'London (ed.),*London Stories* (London, 1911)

38   *Diary*, vol. 2, p. 21

39   *Correspondence and Table-Talk*, Haydon to Miss Mitford, 6 December 1825, vol. 2, p. 101

40   *Diary*, vol. 2, p. 1

41   ibid., p. 121

42   ibid., p. 170

43   ibid., p. 131

44   ibid., p. 145

45   ibid., p. 131

46   ibid., p. 132

47   ibid.

48   ibid., p. 137

49   ibid., p. 138

50   ibid., pp. 144–5

2. Crossing London

1   *Correspondence and Table-Talk*, vol. 2, p. 30

2   Coburn, Kathleen (ed.), *The Letters of Sara Hutchinson* (London, 1954), to Tom Monkhouse, 24 November 1815, p. 89

3   Burton, Mary E. (ed.), *The Letters of Mary Wordsworth 1800–1855* (Clarendon Press, 1958), pp. 32–3

4   Landseer, Thomas (ed.), *Life and Letters of William Bewick (Artist)* (London, 1871), vol. 2, p. 25

5   'The Londoner', *Morning Post*, February 1802

6   Coburn (ed.), *Letters of Sara Hutchinson*, to Dorothy Wordsworth (Dora), 4 January 1818, p. 113

7   *Autobiography*, p. 47

8   Wright, David (ed.), *Thomas De Quincey: Recollections of the Lakes and the Lake Poets* (London, 1988), p. 135

9   Morley, Edith J. (ed.), *Henry Crabb Robinson on Books and Their Writers* (London, 1938), vol. 1

10 Simond, Louis, *Journal of a Tour and Residence in Great Britain during the Years 1810 and 1811* (Edinburgh, 1817), vol. 2, p. 339

11 *Correspondence and Table-Talk*, vol. 2, p. 32

12 *Diary*, vol. 2, pp. 147–8

13 Morley (ed.), *Henry Crabb Robinson on Books and Their Writers*, vol. 1, p. 214

14 Morley, Edith J. (ed.), *The Correspondence of Henry Crabb Robinson with the Wordsworth Circle* (London, 1927), Catherine Clarkson to Henry Crabb Robinson, 15 January 1818, vol. 1, p. 94

15 Hill, Alan (ed.), *A Selection of the Letters of William Wordsworth* (London, 1984), to John Payne Collier, December 1817 or January 1818, dated 'Wednesday', p. 199

16 *Letters of Charles Lamb*, to William Wordsworth, April 1815, vol. 1, p. 239

17 ibid., 30 January 1801, vol. 1, p. 178

18 ibid., to Thomas Manning, 24 September 1802, vol. 1, p. 201

19 Wordsworth, William, *The Prelude* (1805), Book VII, ll. 658–60 and 691–4

20 De Selincourt, Ernest (ed.), *The Letters of William and Dorothy Wordsworth: The Middle Years* (London, 1937), William Wordsworth to Sir George Beaumont, 8 April 1808, vol. 1, p. 186

21 *Letters of Charles Lamb*, to Dorothy Wordsworth, 21 November 1817, vol. 1, p. 370

22 Weinreb, Ben and Hibbert, Christopher (eds), *The London Encyclopaedia* (London, 1983), pp. 208–9

23 *Letters of Charles Lamb*, to William Wordsworth, 14 August 1814, vol. 1, pp. 315–16

24 ibid., to Samuel Taylor Coleridge, 27 May 1796, vol. 1, p. 2

25 ibid., 10 June 1796, vol. 1, p. 16

26 Cecil, David, *A Portrait of Charles Lamb* (London, 1983), p. 77

27 *Letters of Charles Lamb*, to Coleridge, 3 October 1796, vol. 1, p. 34

28 ibid., to Sara Hutchinson, 19 October 1815, vol. 1, p. 344

29 *Letters of John Keats*, to Charles Cowden Clarke, 9 October 1816, p. 1

30 ibid., 31 October 1816, p. 2

31 *Diary*, vol. 2, p. 107

32 *Letters of John Keats*, to Haydon, 19 November 1816, p. 2

33 *Correspondence and Table-Talk*, Haydon to Wordsworth, 11 May 1817, vol. 2, p. 2

34 De Selincourt (ed.), *Letters of William and Dorothy Wordsworth*, William Wordsworth to Haydon, 20 January 1817, vol. 3, p. 360

35 Clarke, Charles and Mary Cowden, *Recollections of Writers* (1878), ed. Robert Gittings (London, 1969), p. 130

36 ibid.

37 *Correspondence and Table-Talk*, Haydon to Keats, 11 May 1817, vol. 2, p. 2

38 *Letters of John Keats*, to Haydon, 10/11 May 1817, pp. 12–15

39 Keats, John, 'You say you love; but with a voice' (?1817), first published in *The Times Literary Supplement*, 16 April 1914

40 *Letters of John Keats*, to George and Tom Keats, 5 January 1818, p. 44

41 ibid., to Fanny Keats, 10 September 1817, p. 20

42 ibid., to Haydon, 10 January 1818, p. 48

43 Rollins, Hyder E. (ed.), *The Keats Circle: Letters and Papers 1816–1878* (Cambridge, Mass., 1948), Haydon to Edward Moxon, 29 November 1845, vol. 1, pp. 143–5

44 *Letters of John Keats*, to George and Tom Keats, 21, 27(?) December 1817, p. 43

45 ibid., 5 January 1818, p. 45

46 ibid.

3. *The Guests Assemble*

1   *Autobiography*, pp. 316–17

2   *Diary*, vol. 2, p. 303

3   Landseer, Thomas (ed.), *Life and Letters of William Bewick (Artist)* (London, 1871), vol. 1, pp. 118–19

4   Hazlitt, William, 'My First Acquaintance with Poets' (*Liberal*, 1823), in Blythe, Ronald (ed.), *William Hazlitt: Selected Writings* (London, 1982), pp. 58–9

5   Hazlitt, William, 'On the Living Poets' (1818), reprinted in *The Spirit of the Age*, 1825

6   De Quincey is quoting from Wordsworth's 'Elegiac Stanzas', written in 1806 after his brother John Wordsworth's death from drowning.

7   De Quincey, Thomas, 'William Wordsworth', in *Selections Grave and Gay from the Writings of Thomas De Quincey* (Edinburgh, 1854)

8   Chasles, Philarète, 'Le Dernier Humoriste Anglais', *Revue des Deux Mondes*, 1842

9   Hazlitt, William, 'On the Conversation of Authors', *Plain Speaker*, September 1820

10   *Autobiography*, p. 296

11   *Letters of Charles Lamb*, to William Wordsworth, 6 April 1825, vol. 2, p. 114

12   Hazlitt, 'My First Acquaintance with Poets'

13   Landseer (ed.), *Life and Letters of William Bewick*, vol. 1, p. 73

14   *Letters of Charles Lamb*, to Joseph Hume, 29 December 1807, vol. 1, p. 271

15   *Letters of John Keats*, to George and Georgiana Keats, journal letter begun 14 February 1819, p. 215

16   *Diary*, vol. 2, p. 317

17   Lamb, Charles, 'A Dissertation on Roast Pig', *London Magazine*, 1821

18 Lamb, Charles, 'Grace before Meat', *London Magazine*, 1822

19 *Letters of Charles Lamb*, to Charles Chambers, 1 September 1817, vol. 1, p. 364

20 Simond, Louis, *Journal of a Tour and Residence in Great Britain during the Years 1810 and 1811* (Edinburgh, 1817), vol. 1, pp. 57, 58n, 58, 59

21 ibid., p. 62

22 *Letters of John Keats*, to George and Tom Keats, 5 January 1818, p. 47

23 Simond, *Journal of a Tour*, vol. 2, p. 62

24 Southey, Robert, *Letters from England by Don Manuel Alvarez Espriella* (London, 1807), vol. 1, p. 88

25 ibid., p. 89

26 ibid., p. 90

27 Raymond, John (ed.), *The Reminiscences and Recollections of Captain Gronow 1810–1860* (London, 1964), p. 46

28 ibid., p. 46

29 Johnson, Paul, *The Birth of the Modern: World Society 1815–1830* (London, 1991), p. 758

30 *Diary*, vol. 3, 14 June 1828

31 *Autobiography*, pp. 316–17

32 De Selincourt, Ernest (ed.), *The Letters of William and Dorothy Wordsworth* (London, 1937), Dorothy Wordsworth to Catherine Clarkson, 12 November 1810, vol. 1, p. 406

33 *Diary*, vol. 2, p. 147

34 ibid., p. 464

35 Hazlitt, 'My First Acquaintance with Poets'

36 Howitt, William, *Homes and Haunts of the Most Eminent British Poets*, 1847

37 This piece of verse is from an early Alfoxden manuscript. Wordsworth included the last six lines in 1817 in the second part of his 'Ode to Lycoris', ll. 42–51.

38 Woof, Pamela (ed.), *Dorothy Wordsworth: The Grasmere Journals* (Oxford, 1991), 4 May 1802, p. 96

39 Hazlitt, William, 'Mr Wordsworth', *On the Living Poets* (1818),
    in Blythe (ed.), *Hazlitt: Selected Writings*, p. 226

4. Christ's Entry into Jerusalem

1   *Diary*, vol. 2, p. 64
2   ibid., p. 319
3   *Correspondence and Table-Talk*, vol. 1, p. 269
4   *Autobiography*, p. 239
5   George, Eric, *The Life and Death of Benjamin Robert Haydon*
    (London, 1948), p. 106
6   *Autobiography*, p. 298
7   Brown, David Blayney, Woof, Robert and Hebron, Stephen
    (eds), *Benjamin Robert Haydon 1786–1846: Painter and Writer,
    Friend of Wordsworth and Keats* (Grasmere, 1996), p. 129
8   Now at the Royal Albert Museum, Exeter.
9   *Diary*, vol. 2, p. 73
10 Landseer, Thomas (ed.), *Life and Letters of William Bewick (Artist)*
    (London, 1871), vol. 2, pp. 61–2
11 Hazlitt, William, 'My First Acquaintance with Poets' (*Liberal*,
    1823), in Blythe, Ronald (ed.), *William Hazlitt: Selected Writings*
    (Harmondsworth, 1982), p. 59
12 The poem was printed in the *Champion* in Latin on 7 May 1820,
    and in Lamb's free translation on 14 May 1820
13 *Correspondence and Table-Talk*, vol. 2, p. 22
14 ibid., pp. 24–5
15 *Letters of John Keats*, to Benjamin Bailey, 8 October 1817, p. 26
16 Fox, Celina, *London World City, 1800–1840* (New Haven,
    Conn., and London, 1992), p. 116
17 *Autobiography*, p. 330
18 ibid.
19 ibid., p. 331
20 ibid., p. 332

21 ibid., p. 339

22 ibid., p. 333

23 Morley, Edith J. (ed.), *Henry Crabb Robinson on Books and Their Writers* (London, 1938), vol. 1, pp. 239–40

24 Sir Thomas Lawrence, then president of the Royal Academy.

25 *Diary*, vol. 2, pp. 310–11

26 Lockhart, John Gibson, *Blackwood's Magazine* (1820), in George (ed.), *The Life and Death of Haydon* (London, 1948), pp. 133–4

27 The Ilyssus was one of the Elgin statues from which Haydon made drawings and took moulds.

28 *Diary*, vol. 2, p. 415, n. 8

29 This now hangs in St Mary's Seminary, Ohio.

30 *Autobiography*, p. 487

31 ibid., p. 515

32 *Diary*, vol. 2, p. 64

33 *Autobiography*, p. 291

34 ibid.

35 Cummings, Frederick, 'B. R. Haydon and His School', *Journal of the Warburg & Courtauld Institutes* (1963), vol. 26

36 Thornbury, Walter, *The Life and Correspondence of J. M. W. Turner RA* (1862; rev. London, 1897), p. 269. For most other references to Turner I am indebted to James Hamilton's *Turner: A Life* (London, 1997)

37 *Autobiography*, p. 620

38 George, *Life and Death of Haydon*, p. 107

39 Landseer (ed.), *Life and Letters of William Bewick*, vol. 1, p. 24

40 *Autobiography*, p. 292

41 Landseer (ed.), *Life and Letters of William Bewick*, vol. 1, p. 40

42 ibid., vol. 2, p. 168

43 *Autobiography*, p. 363

44 ibid., p. 300

45 Landseer (ed.), *Life and Letters of William Bewick*, vol. 1, p. 42

46 *Autobiography*, p. 292

47 ibid., p. 293

48 St Clair, William, *Lord Elgin and the Marbles* (Oxford, 1998), p. 23

49 Cook, B. F., *The Elgin Marbles* (London, 1997), p. 73

50 St Clair, *Lord Elgin and the Marbles*, p. 164

51 *Autobiography*, p. 244

52 ibid., p. 77

53 This figure is now thought to be Dionysos.

54 *Autobiography*, pp. 77–8

55 ibid., pp. 78–9

56 ibid., p. 80

57 De Selincourt, Ernest (ed.), *The Letters of William and Dorothy Wordsworth: The Middle Years* (London, 1937), William Wordsworth to Haydon, 21 December 1815, vol. 2, p. 685

58 Simond, Louis, *Journal of a Tour and Residence in Great Britain during the Years 1810 and 1811* (Edinburgh, 1817), vol. 2, pp. 194–5

59 *Autobiography*, p. 266

60 ibid., p. 273

61 ibid.

62 Sharp, William, *The Life and Letters of Joseph Severn* (London, 1892)

63 *Autobiography*, pp. 273, 281

5. *The Mystery of the Rainbow*

1 *Diary*, vol. 2, p. 173

2 ibid., p. 61

3 Wordsworth, William, *The Excursion* (1800), II, ll. 484–6

4 Blake, William, *Notebooks* (c.1802–4), in *William Blake: Selected Poems*, ed. P. H. Butler, (London, 1982), pp. 126–7

5 *Letters of John Keats*, to George and Tom Keats, 21 February 1818, p. 69

6 ibid., to Charles Brown, c. June 1820, p. 382

7 Keats, John, *Lamia* (1820), II, ll. 229–37

8 *Diary*, vol. 2, p. 172

9 ibid., p. 173

10 ibid., p. 55

11 Besterman, Theodore, *Voltaire* (London, 1969), p. 236

12 Voltaire, 'On Descartes and Newton', letter 14 (1733), in *Voltaire: Letters on England*, Tancock, Leonard (ed. and trans.) (London, 1980), p. 70

13 *Diary*, vol. 2, p. 263

14 Keynes, John Maynard, 'Newton the Man', in the Royal Society's *Newton Tercentenary Celebrations*, quoted from Michael White's *Isaac Newton: The Last Sorcerer* (London, 1998), p. 3

15 Wordsworth, William, *The Prelude* (1805), III, ll. 58–63

16 Hazlitt, William, 'On Poetry in General', *Lectures on the English Poets* (London, 1818)

17 Wordsworth, William, 'Among all lovely things my Love had been', composed in April 1802 and published in 1807, ll. 17–20

18 Garlich, Kenneth, Macintyre, Angus and Cave, Kathryn (eds), *The Diary of Joseph Farington*, quoted in James Hamilton's *Turner: A Life* (London, 1997), p. 132

19 Quoted in Knight, David, *Humphry Davy: Science and Power* (Cambridge, 1992), p. 38

20 Knight, *Humphry Davy*, title page

21 Humphry Davy notebook 13d, quoted in Knight, *Humphry Davy*, p. 36

22 Treneer, A., *The Mercurial Chemist: A Life of Sir Humphry Davy* (London, 1963), p. 95

23 Simond, Louis, *Journal of a Tour and Residence in Great Britain during the Years 1810 and 1811* (Edinburgh, 1817), vol. 1, p. 43

24 ibid., vol. 2, pp. 196–7

25 *Autobiography*, pp. 49–50

26 De Selincourt, Ernest (ed.), *The Letters of William and Dorothy Wordsworth: The Middle Years* (London, 1937), William Wordsworth to Sir John Stoddart, 23 July 1831, vol. 2, p. 415

27 Masson, David (ed.), *The Collected Writings of Thomas De Quincey* (Edinburgh, 1890), vol. 3, pp. 13–14

28 *Letters of Charles Lamb*, to George Dyer, December 1830, vol. 2, pp. 288–9

29 Mary Shelley's introduction to her novel *Frankenstein or The Modern Prometheus*, for the revised edition of 1831.

30 Hamilton, James, *Turner and the Scientists* (London, 1998), p. 10

31 Lloyd, Mary, *Sunny Memories* (London, 1880), vol. 2, pp. 22–3

32 Hamilton, *Turner: A Life*, p. 222

33 Woof, Robert and Hebron, Stephen, *John Keats* (Grasmere, 1995), p. 148

34 Brown, Eluned (ed.), *The London Theatre 1811–1866: Selections from the Diary of Henry Crabb Robinson* (London, 1966), pp. 56, 57

35 Keats, John, 'Mr Kean', *Champion*, 21 December 1817

36 *Letters of John Keats*, to George and Tom Keats, January 1818, p. 43

37 Southey, Robert, *Letters from England by Don Manuel Alvarez Espriella* (London, 1807), vol. 1, p. 187

38 Brown (ed.), *The London Theatre 1811–1866*, p. 48

39 *Diary*, vol. 1, p. 22

40 ibid., pp. 22, 23

41 ibid., vol. 2, p. 268

42 ibid., vol. 1, p. 397

43 ibid., vol. 2, p. 124

44 Lamb, Charles, 'My First Play', *London Magazine*, 1821

45 *Letters of Charles Lamb*, to William Wordsworth, 11 December 1806, vol. 1, p. 266

46 Lucas, E. V., *The Life of Charles Lamb* (London, 1907), p. 581

47 *Letters of Charles Lamb*, to Mary Wordsworth, 18 February 1818, vol. 1, p. 372

48 ibid., 20 July 1819, vol. 1, pp. 388–9. Lamb's proposal, Fanny's reply and Lamb's rejoinder were all written on the same day.

6. Medicine and Poets

1   *Diary*, vol. 2, p. 173

2   From a letter written by Joseph Ritchie to Richard Garnett from Paris, 1817, first published by the late David Garnett in *New Statesman and Nation*, 10 June 1933

3   Ritchie to Garnett, 26 November 1811

4   Ritchie to Garnett from Paris, 1817

5   Raymond, John (ed.), *The Reminiscences and Recollections of Captain Gronow . . . 1810–1860* (London, 1964), p. 358

6   From an unpublished and undated letter from Alexander von Humboldt to Ritchie, now in the possession of the Wellcome Trust

7   Simond, Louis, *Journal of a Tour and Residence in Great Britain during the Years 1810 and 1811* (Edinburgh, 1817), vol. 1, p. 39

8   ibid., pp. 39–40

9   Milton, John, *Lycidas*, I (1638), 64, ll. 67–76

10   *Letters of John Keats*, to George and Tom Keats, 5 January 1818, p. 45

11   Keats, John, 'The Fall of Hyperion: A Dream' (1818), ll. 198–202

12   Rollins, Hyder E. (ed.), *The Keats Circle: Letters and Papers 1816–1878* (Cambridge, Mass., 1948), Henry Stephens to G. F. Mathew, 1847, vol. 2, pp. 206–7

13   ibid., p. 88

14   Information about the resurrectionists in this chapter is from James Blake Bailey, librarian of the Royal College of Surgeons, *The Diary of a Resurrectionist 1811–1812* (London, 1896)

15   Cooper, Bransby Blake, *The Life of Sir Astley Cooper, Bart., Interspersed with Sketches from His Note-Books of Distinguished Contemporary Characters* (London, 1843), vol. 1, p. 398

16   Southey, Robert, *The Surgeon's Warning* (1798) in *The Poetical Works of Robert Southey* (London, 1880), pp. 457–8

17 Rollins (ed.), *The Keats Circle*, vol. 2, p. 56

18 Knight, David, *Humphry Davy: Science and Power* (Cambridge, 1992), p. 99

19 *Autobiography*, p. 208

20 ibid., p. 211

21 ibid., p. 212

22 *Diary*, vol. 1, p. 357

23 Sadler, Thomas (ed.), *Diary, Reminiscences and Correspondence of Henry Crabb Robinson* (London, 1869), vol. 1, pp. 47–8

24 *Autobiography*, p. 211

25 *Diary*, vol. 1, pp. 368–9

26 ibid., p. 358

27 *Autobiography*, p. 228

28 *Letters of John Keats*, to Fanny Keats, 10 September 1817, p. 19

29 Scott, John, *Paris Revisited in 1815* (London, 1816), p. 333

30 ibid., p. 336

31 O'Leary, Patrick, *Regency Editor: Life of John Scott* (Aberdeen, 1983), p. 71

32 *Letters of Charles Lamb*, to Baron Field, 22 September 1822, vol. 2, p. 26. Marcus Apicius, a first-century Roman nobleman and gourmet, wrote the world's first known book of recipes, *Of Culinary Matters*

33 ibid., to John Clare from India House, 31 August 1822, vol. 2, p. 22

34 ibid., fragment of a letter to Mary Lamb, September 1822, vol. 2, p. 22

35 Remark by John Gibson Lockhart quoted in the *Dictionary of National Biography*

36 Hunt, Leigh, *Autobiography* (London, 1860), p. 177

37 O'Leary, *Regency Editor*, p. 92

38 ibid., p. 170

39 *Diary*, vol. 2, pp. 313–14

7. *Tragedy in Africa*

1   From an unpublished letter dated 21 December 1817 from
    Ritchie to Garnett, in the possession of the estate of the late
    David Garnett.

2   *Letters of John Keats*, to George and Georgiana Keats, 21
    December 1818, p. 185

3   O'Leary, Patrick, *Regency Editor: Life of John Scott* (Aberdeen,
    1983), p. 92

4   Ritchie was later able to send back word from Murzuk of
    Hornemann's death from dysentery near the Gold Coast, his
    fate having previously been unknown.

5   Dawson, Warren R. (ed.), *The Banks Letters: A Calendar of the
    Manuscript Correspondence of Sir Joseph Banks* (London, 1958),
    Mungo Park to Sir Joseph Banks, Peebles, 13 October 1801,
    p. 648

6   Park, Mungo, *Travels in the Interior Districts of Africa* (1799), quoted
    in Howard, C. (ed.), *West African Explorers* (London, 1951), p. 122

7   Hallett, Robin (ed.), *Records of the African Association 1788–1831*
    (London, 1964), pp. 168–9

8   Dawson (ed.), *The Banks Letters*, p. 364

9   ibid.

10 Johnson, Paul, *The Birth of the Modern: World Society 1815–1830*
    (London, 1991), p. 325

11 From Beaufoy's *Conclusions*, quoted in Hallett's *Records of the
    African Association*, p. 116

12 Dawson (ed.), *The Banks Letters*, p. 364

13 Foreign Office papers in the Public Record Office, F.O. 76/
    13, p. 13

14 Hallett (ed.), *Records of the African Association*, p. 221

15 A quotation from Juvenal, loosely translated as 'whatever people
    do'.

16 Ritchie to Haydon, 30 October 1818 (letter in the possession
    of the Houghton Library, Harvard University)

17 Public Record Office. F.O.76/20b. Information about Hanmer Warrington in this chapter is from E. W. Bovill's essay 'Colonel Warrington', in *Geographical Journal*, vol. 131, 2, June 1965

18 PRO C.O.2/9/162, Warrington to Charles Penrose, 24 October 1818

19 ibid., C.O.2/9/215, unknown correspondent to Henry Goulburn, 15 July 1819

20 ibid., C.O.2/9/16–18, Ritchie to Bathurst, 28 October 1818

21 Johnson, *Birth of the Modern*, p. 454

22 PRO C.O.2/9/16–18, Ritchie to Bathurst, 28 October 1818

23 PRO C.O.2/9/22, Ritchie to Bathurst, *c.* November 1818

24 PRO F.O.76.13, Ritchie to Warrington, 8 August 1819

25 PRO F.O.8/7.45, Bathurst to Ritchie, 10 August 1819

26 Lyon, Captain George R.N., *A Narrative of Travels in Northern Africa in the Years 1818, 19 and 20* (London, 1821), p. 103

27 ibid., p. 101

28 ibid., p. 120

29 ibid., p. 121

30 ibid., p. 174

31 ibid., p. 192

32 ibid., p. 195

33 PRO F.O.8/7.45, Warrington to Bathurst, 28 December 1819

34 The Venerable Bede, *Ecclesiastical History of the English Nation*, AD 731, taken from Ralph Arnold's *A Social History of England from 55 BC to AD 1215* (London, 1967), p. 147

8. *Patrons and a Comptroller of Stamps*

1 *Diary*, vol. 2, pp. 175–6

2 *Autobiography*, p. 317

3 *Diary*, vol. 2, p. 174

4 John Landseer was one of Haydon's after-dinner guests.

5 *Autobiography*, p. 318

6   Gibbon, Charles, *Life of George Combe* (London, 1878), vol. 1,
    p. 298

7   *Diary*, vol. 1, p. 419

8   Haydon, B. R., *Lectures on Painting and Design* (London, 1844),
    p. 64

9   Jones, Stanley, *Hazlitt: A Life* (Oxford, 1991), p. 187

10 *Letters of John Keats*, to George and Tom Keats, 5 January 1818,
    vol. 2, p. 45

11 *Letters of Charles Lamb*, to Mary Wordsworth, 18 February 1818,
    vol. 1, p. 376

12 Red-letter days were saints' days or church festivals indicated
    in the ecclesiastical calendar by red letters, and often observed
    as holidays.

13 *Letters of Charles Lamb*, to Wordsworth from East India House,
    at the end of a letter to Mary Wordsworth, 18 January 1818,
    vol. 1, p. 374

14 *Diary*, vol. 2, pp. 196–7

15 Howe, P. (ed.), *William Hazlitt: Collected Works*, vol. 7 (London,
    1930–34), p. 143

16 Shelley, Percy Bysshe, 'To Wordsworth' (1816), ll. 11–14

17 Landseer, Thomas (ed.), *Life and Letters of William Bewick (Artist)*
    (London, 1871), vol. 2, pp. 169–70

18 *Autobiography*, p. 49

19 ibid., pp. 49–50

20 ibid., p. 111

21 ibid., p. 114

22 ibid., p. 116

23 *Diary*, vol. 2, pp. 196–7

24 ibid., pp. 325–6

25 *Autobiography*, p. 79

26 ibid., p. 92

27 ibid., p. 280

28 *Correspondence and Table-Talk*, Sir George Beaumont to
    Haydon, 1 July 1815, vol. 1, pp. 288–9

29 ibid., p. 340

30 Sir George Beaumont to William Wordsworth, 24 October 1803, from Gill, Stephen, *William Wordsworth: A life* (Oxford, 1989), p. 219

31 ibid.

32 De Selincourt, E. (ed.), *The Letters of William and Dorothy Wordsworth: The Middle Years*, vol. 2, p. 100. William Wordsworth to Lady Beaumont, undated letter probably enclosed in Dorothy Wordsworth's letter to Lady Beaumont, 22 or 23 December 1806

33 Sutherland, Douglas, *The Yellow Earl* (London, 1965), p. 14

34 Gore, John (ed.), *Creevey's Life and Times* (London, 1934), p. 245

35 *Letters of John Keats*, to Tom Keats, 25–27 June 1818, p. 104

36 'Confessions of a Drunkard', first published in the *Philanthropist*, 1813; reprinted as an Elia essay, *London Magazine*, 1822

37 De Quincey, Thomas, *North British Review*, November 1848, in a review of Talfourd's biography of Lamb

38 Priestley, J. B. (ed.), *Tom Moore's Diary: A Selection* (Cambridge, 1925), pp. 49–50

39 Morley, Edith J. (ed.), *The Correspondence of Henry Crabb Robinson with the Wordsworth Circle* (London, 1927), vol. 2, pp. 125–6

40 Coburn, Kathleen (ed.), *The Letters of Sara Hutchinson* (London, 1954), p. 111

41 *Letters of Charles Lamb*, to Mr and Mrs Clarkson, August/September 1810, vol. 1, p. 301

42 Talfourd, Thomas Noon, *The Final Memorials of Charles Lamb* (London, 1848), pp. 321–2

43 For information about Mary Lamb's illness I am indebted to Mary Blanchard Balle's 'Mary Lamb: Her Mental Health Issues', *Charles Lamb Bulletin*, January 1996, new series 93, pp. 3–11

44 Weinreb, Ben and Hibbert, Christopher (eds), *The London Encyclopaedia* (London, 1983), p. 62

45 *Letters of Charles Lamb*, to Maria Fryer, 14 February 1834, vol. 2, pp. 336–7

46 ibid., to Wordsworth, 22 February 1834, vol. 2, p. 338

47 *Letters of John Keats*, to George and Tom Keats, 5 January 1818, pp. 45–6

48 *Autobiography*, p. 319

49 *Correspondence and Table-Talk*, vol. 1, p. 110

50 Wordsworth, William, 'I wandered lonely as a Cloud'. Gill, Stephen (ed.), William Wordsworth (Oxford, 1984), p. 304

Epilogue

1 *Correspondence and Table-Talk*, vol. 2, p. 55

2 George, Eric, *The Life and Death of Benjamin Robert Haydon 1786–1846* (London, 1948), p. 294

3 Haydon is misquoting *King Lear*: '. . . He hates him / That would upon the rack of this tough world / Stretch him out longer (V, 3, 311–13)

4 *Diary*, vol. 2, p. 177

5 *Diary*, vol. 2, p. 463

6 *Autobiography*, pp. 352–3

7 *Diary*, vol. 2, p. 198

8 *Autobiography*, p. 603

9 1817: Haydon's memory misled him.

10 *Correspondence and Table-Talk*, vol. 2, pp. 54–5

Select Bibliography

The following are books to which I have chiefly turned. I have also consulted a number of other nineteenth-century books, documents, journals and periodicals.

Ainger, Alfred, *Charles Lamb*, Macmillan, London, 1909

Auden, W.H. and Mayer, Elizabeth (eds and trans.), *J. W. Goethe: Italian Journey 1786–1788*, Penguin Books, London, 1970

Bailey, James Blake, *The Diary of a Resurrectionist 1811–1812, to Which are Added an Account of the Resurrection Men in London and a Short History of the Passing of the Anatomy Act*, London, 1896

Balle, Mary Blanchard, 'Mary Lamb: Her Mental Health Issues', *Charles Lamb Bulletin*, January 1996, new series, 93

Bate, Walter Jackson, *John Keats*, Hogarth Press, London, 1992

Besterman, Theodore, *Voltaire*, Longman, London, 1969

Black, Maggie and Le Faye, Deirdre, *The Jane Austen Cookbook*, British Museum, London, 1995

Blythe, Ronald (ed.), *William Hazlitt: Selected Writings*, Penguin Books, London, 1982

Bovill, E.W., *The Golden Trade of the Moors*, Oxford University Press, London, 1958

Bovill, E.W., *The Niger Explored*, Oxford University Press, London, 1968

Brown, David Blayney, Woof, Robert and Hebron, Stephen, *Benjamin Robert Haydon 1786–1846: Painter and Writer, Friend of Wordsworth and Keats*, Wordsworth Trust, Grasmere, 1996

Brown, Eluned (ed.), *The London Theatre 1811–1866: Selections from the Diary of Henry Crabb Robinson*, Society for Theatre Research, London, 1966

Burton, Mary E. (ed.), *The Letters of Mary Wordsworth 1800–1855*, Oxford University Press, London, 1958

Butler, Marilyn, *Romantics, Rebels and Reactionaries: English Literature and Its Background 1760–1830*, Oxford University Press, 1981

Butter, P.H. (ed.), *William Blake: Selected Poems*, J. M. Dent, London, 1982

Byatt, A.S., *Unruly Times: Wordsworth and Coleridge in Their Time*, Hogarth Press, London, 1989

Cave, Kathryn (ed.), *The Diary of Joseph Farington*, vols 15 and 16, Yale University Press, New Haven, Conn., 1984

Cecil, David, *A Portrait of Charles Lamb*, Constable, London, 1983

Christiansen, Rupert, *Romantic Affinities: Portraits from an Age 1780–1830*, The Bodley Head, London, 1988

Clarke, Charles and Mary Cowden, *Recollections of Writers* (1878), ed. Robert Gittings, Centaur Press, London, 1969

Coburn, Kathleen (ed.), *The Letters of Sara Hutchinson*, Routledge and Kegan Paul, London, 1954

Cook, B.F., *The Elgin Marbles*, British Museum, London, 1997

Cook, Elizabeth (ed.), *John Keats*, Oxford University Press, 1990

Cooper, Bransby Blake, *The Life of Sir Astley Cooper, Bart., Interspersed with Sketches from His Note-Books of Distinguished Contemporary Characters*, 2 vols, London, 1843

Cummings, Frederick, 'Benjamin Robert Haydon and His School', *Journal of the Warburg & Courtauld Institutes*, vol. 26, 1963

Cunningham, Allan, *The Life of Sir David Wilkie; with His Journals, Tours, and Critical Remarks on Works of Art; and a Selection from His Correspondence*, 3 vols, John Murray, London, 1843

Dawkins, Richard, *Unweaving the Rainbow: Science, Delusion and the Appetite for Wonder*, Allen Lane, Harmondsworth, 1998

Dawson, Warren R. (ed.), *The Banks Letters: A Calendar of the Manuscript Correspondence of Sir Joseph Banks*, British Museum, London, 1958

De Quincey, Thomas, *Selections Grave and Gay from the Writings of Thomas De Quincey*, Edinburgh, 1854

De Selincourt, Ernest (ed.), *The Letters of William and Dorothy Wordsworth: The Middle Years*, 2 vols, Oxford University Press, London, 1937

Fleming, Fergus, *Barrow's Boys*, Granta, London, 1998

Fox, Celina (ed.), *London World City: 1800–1840*, Museum of London, 1992

Fraser, Flora, *The Unruly Queen: The Life of Queen Caroline*, Macmillan, London, 1966

George, Eric, *The Life and Death of Benjamin Robert Haydon 1786–1846*, Oxford University Press, London, 1948

Gill, Stephen, *William Wordsworth: A Life*, Oxford University Press, 1990

Gittings, Robert, *John Keats*, Heinemann, London, 1968

Gittings, Robert (ed.), *The Letters of John Keats*, Oxford University Press, London, 1970

Greaves, Margaret, *Regency Patron: Sir George Beaumont*, Methuen, London, 1966

Gross, John, *The Rise and Fall of the Man of Letters: Aspects of English Literary Life since 1800*, Weidenfeld and Nicolson, London, 1969

Hallett, Robin, *Records of the African Association 1788–1831*, Thomas Nelson, London, 1964

Hamilton, James, *Turner: A Life*, Hodder and Stoughton, London, 1997

Hamilton, James, *Turner and the Scientists*, Tate Gallery, London, 1998

Haydon, Frederic Wordsworth (ed. with a memoir), *Benjamin Robert Haydon: Correspondence and Table-Talk*, 2 vols, Chatto and Windus, London, 1876

Hayter, Alethea, *A Sultry Month: Scenes of London Literary Life in 1846*, Faber, London, 1965

Hewlett, Dorothy, *A Life of John Keats*, Hurst and Blackett, London, 1949

Hibbert, Christopher, *Africa Explored: Europeans in the Dark Continent 1769–1889*, Allen Lane, London, 1982

Hill, Alan (ed.), *A Selection of the Letters of William Wordsworth*, Oxford University Press, 1984

Holmes, Richard, *Shelley: The Pursuit*, Penguin Books, London, 1974

Housman, Laurence, *Cornered Poets: A Book of Dramatic Dialogues*, Jonathan Cape, London, 1929

Howard, C. (ed.), *West African Explorers*, Oxford University Press, London, 1951

Howe, P. (ed.), *William Hazlitt: Collected Works*, 21 vols, J.M. Dent, London, 1930–34

Hunt, Leigh, *Autobiography*, Smith, Elder, London, 1860

Hutchinson, Thomas and De Selincourt, Ernest (eds), *Wordsworth: Poetical Works*, Oxford University Press, London, 1969

Jackson, Peter, *George Scharf's London*, John Murray, London, 1987

Johnson, Paul, *The Birth of the Modern: World Society 1815–1830*, Weidenfeld and Nicolson, London, 1991

Johnston, Kenneth R., *The Hidden Wordsworth: Poet. Lover. Rebel. Spy*, Norton, New York, 1998

Jolliffe, John (ed.), *Neglected Genius: The Diaries of Benjamin Robert Haydon 1808–1846*, Hutchinson, London, 1990

Jones, Stanley, *Hazlitt: A Life, from Winterslow to Frith Street*, Oxford University Press, 1991

Joseph, M.K. (ed.), *Mary Shelley: Frankenstein or The Modern Prometheus*, Oxford University Press, London, 1969

Keynes, Geoffrey, *Selected Essays of William Hazlitt 1778–1830*, Nonesuch Press and Random House, London, 1944

Knight, David, *Humphry Davy: Science and Power*, Cambridge University Press, 1992

Lamb, Charles, *The Essays of Elia*, Edward Moxon, London, 1840

Lamb, H.H., *Climate, History and the Modern World*, Methuen, London, 1982

Landseer, Thomas (ed.), *Life and Lettersof William Bewick (Artist)*, 2 vols, Hurst and Blackett, London, 1871

Lloyd, Christopher, *Mr Barrow of the Admiralty: A Life of Sir John Barrow 1764–1848*, Collins, London, 1970

Lloyd, Christopher, *The Search for the Niger*, Collins, London, 1973

Lucas, E.V., *The Life of Charles Lamb*, London, 1907

Lyon, G.F., *A Narrative of Travels in Northern Africa, in the Years 1818, 19 and 20*, John Murray, London, 1821

Moore, Thomas, *The Fudge Family in Paris*, London, 1818

Moorman, Mary, *William Wordsworth: A Biography, The Later Years 1803–1850*, Oxford University Press, London, 1965

Morley, Edith J. (ed.), *Henry Crabb Robinson on Books and Their Writers*, vol. 1, J.M. Dent, London, 1938

Morley, Edith J. (ed.), *The Correspondence of Henry Crabb Robinson with the Wordsworth Circle*, 2 vols, Oxford University Press, London, 1927

Morpurgo, J.E., *Charles Lamb and Elia*, Carcanet, London, 1993

Motion, Andrew, *Keats*, Faber, London, 1997

Murray, Venetia, *High Society: A Social History of the Regency Period 1788–1830*, Viking, Harmondsworth, 1998

Nicolson, Harold, *The Congress of Vienna: A Study in Allied Unity 1812–1822*, Constable, London, 1946

O'Brian, Patrick, *Joseph Banks: A Life*, Harvill Press, London, 1997

O'Leary, Patrick, *Regency Editor: Life of John Scott*, Aberdeen University Press, 1983

O'London, John, *London Stories*, London, 1911–12

Owen, Felicity and Brown, David, *Collector of Genius: A Life of Sir George Beaumont*, John Wiley, London, 1988

Owen, Hugh, *The Lowther Family*, Phillimore, Chichester, 1990

Paston, George, *B. R. Haydon and His Friends*, James Nisbet, London, 1905

Patmore, P.G. [Emily Morse Symonds], *My Friends and Acquaintances*, Saunders and Otley, London, 1854

Pope, Willard Bissell (ed.), *The Diary of Benjamin Robert Haydon*, vols 1 and 2, Harvard University Press, Cambridge, Mass., 1960

Prance, Claude A., *Companion to Charles Lamb: A Guide to People and Places 1760–1847*, Mansell, London, 1983

Priestley, J.B. (ed.), *Tom Moore's Diary: A Selection*, Cambridge University Press, 1925

Raymond, John (ed.), *The Reminiscences and Recollections of Captain Gronow, being Anecdotes of the Camp, Court, Clubs and Society 1810–1860*, Bodley Head, London, 1964

Rhys, Ernest (ed.), *The Letters of Charles Lamb*, 2 vols, London, 1926

Rollins, Hyder E. (ed.), *The Keats Circle: Letters and Papers 1816–1878*, 2 vols, Harvard University Press, Cambridge, Mass., 1948

Sadler, Thomas (ed.), *Diary, Reminiscences and Correspondence of Henry Crabb Robinson*, London, 1869

St Clair, William, *Lord Elgin and the Marbles*, Oxford University Press, 1998

Schlee, Ann, *Laing*, Macmillan, London, 1987

Scott, John, *A Visit to Paris 1814* and *Paris Revisited in 1815*, Longman Hurst, London, 1816, 1817 respectively

Sharp, William, *The Life and Letters of Joseph Severn*, London, 1892

Simmons, Jack (ed.), *Letters from England by Robert Southey*, Cresset Press, London, 1951

Simond, Louis, *Journal of a Tour and Residence in Great Britain during the Years 1810 and 1811*, 2 vols, Edinburgh, 1817

Southey, Robert, *Letters from England by Don Manuel Alvarez Espriella*, 3 vols, London, 1807

Summerson, John, *Georgian London*, Pleiades Books, London, 1946

Sutherland, Douglas, *The Yellow Earl*, Cassell, London, 1965

Tancock, Leonard (ed.), *Voltaire: Letters on England* (1734), Penguin Books, London, 1980

Taylor, Tom, *The Autobiography and Journals of Benjamin Robert Haydon 1808–1846*, London, 1853; ed. with an introduction by Malcolm Elwin, Peter Davies, London, 1950

Tomalin, Claire, *Mrs Jordan's Profession*, Viking, Harmondsworth, 1994

Treneer, A., *The Mercurial Chemist: A Life of Sir Humphry Davy*, Methuen, London, 1963

Weinreb, Ben and Hibbert, Christopher (eds), *The London Encyclopaedia*, Macmillan, London, 1983

White, Michael, *Isaac Newton: The Last Sorcerer*, Fourth Estate, London, 1998

Woof, Pamela (ed.), *Dorothy Wordsworth: The Grasmere Journals*, Oxford University Press, 1991

Woof, Robert, *The Wordsworth Circle*, Wordsworth Trust, Grasmere, 1979

Woof, Robert and Hebron, Stephen, *John Keats*, Wordsworth Trust, Grasmere, 1995

Wordsworth, Jonathan, Jaye, Michael C. and Woof, Robert, *William Wordsworth and the Age of English Romanticism*, Wordsworth Trust, Grasmere, 1987

Wright, David (ed.), *Thomas De Quincey: Recollections of the Lakes and the Lake Poets*, Penguin Books, Harmondsworth, 1988

Index

Page numbers in *italic* indicate illustrations and captions; the abbreviation BRH signifies Benjamin Robert Haydon